EARLY C

Advisory ......

Genishi, Alice Sterling Honig, Elizabeth Jones, Gwen Morgan,
David Weikart

TEACHING AND LEARNING IN A DIVERSE WORLD

Multicultural Education for Young Children

PATRICIA G. RAMSEY

TEACHERS COLLEGE PRESS

Teachers College, Columbia University
New York and London

Published by Teachers College Press, 1234 Amsterdam Avenue, New York, N.Y. 10027

Library of Congress Cataloging in Publication Data

Ramsey, Patricia.

   Teaching and learning in a diverse world.

   (Early childhood education series)
   Bibliography: p.
   Includes index.
   1. Intercultural education—Study and teaching—United States. 2. Teaching—United States. I. Title. II. Series.
LC1099.3.R36 1987   370.19'6   86-14560

ISBN 0-8077-2828-4 (pbk.)

Manufactured in the United States of America

98 97 96 95 94 93   5 6 7 8

In memory of my mother,
Elinor Jameson Ramsey

Contents

Preface

It was well after I had finished college that I realized that my education had been segregated into two different tracks. On the one hand, I had attended "good" public schools and an expensive private college and had been taught the wit and wisdom of Western civilization. On the other hand, I had always wanted to understand other ways of life. Why did some people go to temple and others to different churches? What was it like to live in the urban low-income housing projects? How did people live in other parts of the world? These questions were sharpened as I became aware of the economic injustices that separated people, and I began to seek out some answers for myself. I worked in a barrio in Tegucigalpa, Honduras; I joined VISTA and worked in a Mexican-American community in Sacramento, California; I taught in a daycare center that served a black neighborhood in San Francisco. In each setting I was the learner. As day after day I confronted my stereotypes, my naiveté, and the narrowness of my perspective, I became increasingly frustrated that my formal schooling had left me so poorly prepared for living outside of the confines of the white middle class. Rather than expanding my knowledge beyond my immediate experience, my school experiences had instead reinforced a narrow and Anglo-American perspective. It was my "other teachers"—who included farmworkers, cannery workers, children, parents, community workers, priests, and neighbors—who helped me to "unlearn" some of my misconceptions and to broaden my range of understanding.

My interest in teaching grew from a desire to try to merge these two tracks of learning. I am convinced that education can do more than simply reproduce the status quo. Teachers are in a unique and powerful position to have an impact on the way that children think. My own work with children, my involvement with teacher education, and, most recently, the writing of this book have all been oriented toward effecting this synthesis in education.

The focus and style of this book reflect my belief that teachers are, above all, active learners and creative problem solvers. As a teacher educator, I have been disappointed in the kinds of books that are available for preservice and in-service teachers. Activity books, in which lesson plans are presented in detail, are useful but often offer cookbook approaches that do not help teachers think about why they might do a certain activity and how it fits into the larger goals for their specific children. At the other extreme are child development texts and books on curriculum theory. The first offers invaluable insights into the development of children, while the latter clarifies the philosophical underpinnings of different teaching approaches, but rarely does either provide specific guidance for applying theories and research in actual classrooms. Few of the available texts encourage teachers to integrate their knowledge of child development, curriculum design, and the needs of their specific children to develop their own creative applications.

To offer such a synthesis, this book includes several sections on child development theory and research and some examples of how teachers might apply this information in their classrooms. It provides general goals and a model for incorporating a multicultural perspective in all phases and areas of teaching. In order to engage readers actively in this process, this book includes questions that encourage them to reflect on their own experiences, the specific social contexts of their teaching, and their current practices. The questions and examples are designed to help readers to see and generate new possibilities for their teaching and for the children in their classrooms.

Teachers at all levels can benefit from this process. Students who are entering the field can use this text as an opportunity to think about their own school experiences, as well as the practices that they observe during their student teaching, and to challenge and expand their ideas about education as they begin their teaching careers. The book offers more experienced teachers a chance to reflect on past and current practices and to look at the complex relationships between their teaching and the immediate and broader social values. It may provide new perspectives on their teaching and stimulate interest in broadening the social base of their curriculum. The book offers administrators a chance to think about both the immediate and larger social and economic contexts of their programs and ways of responding more effectively to the needs and possibilities of working with children in a diverse and changing social environment.

I express to all readers my hope that this book will challenge assumptions, assist in "unlearning" misperceptions, stimulate discussion, and encourage creative responses to the challenges and joys of teaching and learning in a diverse world.

Acknowledgments

I am grateful to many colleagues and friends in Tegucigalpa, Honduras; Sacramento and San Francisco, California; and Boston and Cambridge, Massachusetts, for teaching me the importance and pleasures of learning from a multicultural perspective. Hundreds of children and dozens of teachers have helped me to understand the complexities of trying to make this kind of teaching work. I am deeply appreciative of their willingness to share their experiences with me. Many students at the University of Massachusetts, Indiana University, and Wheelock College tried out the ideas in this book and provided invaluable feedback and suggestions. The teaching staff at Gorse Child Study Center at Mount Holyoke College has been a recent source of inspiration. Their interest and creativity have contributed to the continuing development of these ideas.

The guidance and teaching I received as a doctoral student at the University of Massachusetts provided the theoretical framework for this work. George Forman introduced me to the work of Jean Piaget and inspired my quest to understand how children think about their social environment. Carolyn Edwards helped me to understand the role of culture in the development of social expectations and behaviors and guided my investigation into the research on social development and children's understanding of their social environment. Sam Bowles helped me to articulate more clearly the relationships between education and the social and economic systems. Bob Suzuki introduced me to the concept of multicultural education and gave me a framework for combining my interests in teaching and social change. Grace Craig, Alfred Karlson, Beaty Blaine, Bobbe Navon, David Day, and Ernie Washington all provided support and suggestions at many points during my graduate career. My fellow graduate students, Joan Lester, Fleet Hill, and David Fernie, contributed many insights and helpful comments about this work in its early stages.

My former colleagues at Wheelock College were generous in the time they spent reading and commenting on early drafts of the manuscript. I particularly thank Mieko Kamii, Sherri Oden, Diane Levin, Ilse Mattick, Joan Bergstrom, Fran Wacksler, and Mary Iatrides.

Most recently, I have received many helpful suggestions from Sonia Nieto at the University of Massachusetts, Leslie Williams at Teachers College in New York, Edwina Battle Vold at Indiana University in Pennsylvania, and Jonas Rosenthal at Colby College in Maine.

Finally, the encouragement, patience, and support of my husband, Fred Moseley, gave me the confidence and opportunity to start this project and to persist in finishing it.

TEACHING AND LEARNING IN A DIVERSE WORLD

Multicultural Education for Young Children

1 A Multicultural Perspective in Education

"I'm gonna kick all those black people out of the workplace!" Four-year-old David clenched his fists as he spoke. "They can't be there," he exclaimed, "They're bad!"

I probed gently, trying to preserve this moment of raw emotion so that I could peer into it and try to see the imagery behind the vehemence. My questions only elicited reaffirmations and exasperation. There were no reasons, only certainty. "I'll punch and kick them if they go there!"

Later in the interview, David was selecting friends from photographs of classmates. Two of his designated playmates were African American. When I casually observed that "some friends are white and some are black," he emphatically disagreed. "Oh no! Michelle is brown!"

In his reactions, David expressed explicitly the convictions and contradictions that often characterize both adult and children's responses to racial differences. He spoke as a child who is exposed to adult attitudes about "those people," yet plays with their children. He is on a psychological boundary between the penetration of adult prejudice and his immediate experience with his classmates.

His use of the term *workplace* suggests that he is simply parroting adult comments; he probably has only a vague idea of what it means. However, his vehemence implies that he is not simply repeating—he is also feeling the intent of the words with the full force of his four-year-old anger and aggression. Furthermore, in his elaborations about how he would punch and kick people, he is constructing new images about his actions vis-à-vis black people.

David's comments are not surprising or unique, but they do remind us that, despite legal and educational efforts to diminish racial discrimination, the cycle of prejudicial thinking is still strong and easily takes root in the minds and feelings of young children.

1

The intransigence of prejudice and discrimination has frustrated the efforts of many social scientists, teachers, and community leaders in this country for the past several decades. There have been some gains in civil rights, but our society's responses to national and international economic conditions have shown how shallow that progress has been, as intergroup tensions have emerged over jobs, housing, government funding, and social policy.

Ironically, these economic pressures are also forcing people to come into contact with many different groups. Changes in employment patterns have caused many domestic migrations that have brought workers to new regions of the country. Worldwide economic problems and political unrest have stimulated the arrival of immigrants and refugees to this country in greater numbers than ever before (Maeroff, 1983). The resentment and, in come cases, the violence that have greeted domestic and foreign newcomers attest to the level of distrust and threat that people feel. Thus, at a time when demographic changes require increased flexibility and mutual tolerance, feelings of alienation and suspicion are rising (Cordes, 1984). David's comments explicitly reflect the protectionism that many groups feel in the face of economic threat.

Current national policy is shifting away from efforts to equalize opportunity and resources among all members of the society. Instead, entrepreneurship, making money, and consumerism are the icons of the time. As the gap between rich and poor gets wider, it becomes easier for the affluent to forget or ignore the inequalities that continue to exist.

While schools and educators cannot change the economic incentives and constraints that are the root of many of these problems, they can provide an alternative to the cycle of withdrawal, suspicion, and discrimination. This book is written to help teachers incorporate into all areas of their work with young children a more realistic view of the world, a respect for diversity, and a sense of shared humanity.

FOCUS OF A MULTICULTURAL PERSPECTIVE

This book focuses on (1) young children's understanding of differences, (2) children's interpersonal and intergroup relationships, and (3) related teaching practices. It is written primarily for current and future teachers of children aged three to eight, the period when children's early perceptions of differences develop into more crystallized attitudes. Many of the issues are common to all levels of education, however, and the suggested pedagogical guidelines and activities can be adapted for both younger and older children.

Commonly labeled *multicultural education*, the perspective described here is broader than the name implies. First, it encompasses many dimensions of human differences besides culture: race, occupation, socioeconomic status, age, gender, sexual orientation, and various physical traits and needs. Second, it is relevant to all children, even those who live in markedly homogeneous settings. Third, it extends beyond the boundaries of this country to beliefs and attitudes about people all over the world. Traditionally, multicultural education and international or global education have been seen as distinct pedagogical areas. In terms of the general intent and content, however, the two areas complement one another and can be viewed as part of the same perspective (Cortés, 1983). For simplicity's sake, the term *multicultural education* will be used in this book, even though it refers to a way of thinking that is more complex and inclusive than the term implies.

GOALS OF A MULTICULTURAL PERSPECTIVE

The broad goals of teaching from a multicultural perspective are as follows:

1. *To help children develop positive gender, racial, cultural, class, and individual identities and to recognize and accept their membership in many different groups.* The cross-group antagonisms that were discussed earlier often reflect negative feelings about one's own group or internal conflicts about group allegiances. As young children are forming their early identities, they need to learn how to define themselves within a context of diversity.

2. *To enable children to see themselves as part of the larger society; to identify, empathize, and relate with individuals from other groups.* In order to interrupt the cycle of resentment and protectionism that David's comments illustrate so well, children need to have early exposure to the idea that they share many characteristics with other groups of people. The reduction of cross-group antagonisms also requires the ability to see other points of view, to use highly developed communication skills, and to be flexible in social expectations and behaviors.

3. *To foster respect and appreciation for the diverse ways in which other people live.* Cross-group suspicion often rests on erroneous and fear-

provoking assumptions about the habits, lifestyles, and attitudes of unfamiliar people. These concerns are evident when residents worry about other groups "invading" their neighborhoods. In their earliest explorations of domestic and occupational roles, children can learn to accept a broad range of lifestyles.

4. *To encourage in young children's earliest social relationships an openness and interest in others, a willingness to include others, and a desire to cooperate.* Positive group identities and more understanding of many ways of life may reduce children's avoidance of differences, but their motivation for reaching out to other groups rests on the enjoyment that they derive from social interactions and interpersonal relationships. As they develop their earliest social patterns, they can acquire the interests and skills that will help them enjoy a broad range of social experiences.

5. *To promote the development of a realistic awareness of contemporary society, a sense of social responsibility, and an active concern that extend beyond one's immediate family or group.* One source of cross-group alienation and antagonism is the unrealistic expectation of individual success that is widely promulgated in this country. The resulting disillusionment often leads people to "blame the victim," to look for scapegoats, and to feel personally inadequate. If children learn about society from a more objective perspective and see how all people are affected by the same forces, they may feel more akin to and emphathic toward others' misfortunes and less constrained by narrow self-interest.

6. *To empower children to become autonomous and critical analysts and activists in their social environment.* Economic hardships and unrealistic expectations often generate feelings of personal defeat and inefficacy. By encouraging children to trust their perceptions and judgments and to question and challenge common social assumptions, schools may help children gain and maintain a confidence in their power and potential, despite the prevailing discrimination that they observe and experience.

7. *To support the development of educational and social skills that are needed for children to become full participants in the larger society in ways that are most appropriate to individual styles, cultural orientations, and linguistic backgrounds.* In order to be more effective in fulfilling the charge to create and provide equal opportunities for all children, ed-

ucational content and practices must respect and reflect children's unique backgrounds.

8. *To promote effective and reciprocal relationships between schools and families.* Schools do not always live up to their potential as unifying and equalizing forces among disparate groups. The same cross-group tensions and patterns of discrimination and alienation found in a community or society often are reflected and perpetuated in school-family interactions. By establishing more flexible and collaborative relationships with the community, schools will be in a position to play a more proactive role in social change.

Obviously, these goals can have no direct effect on the larger social and economic problems that exacerbate and, in some cases, create intergroup tensions. However, they can influence the ways that new generations interpret and participate in social relationships. For instance, David is learning that the economic frustrations of his parents and their friends are the fault of people who are in an even less advantageous position. This preoccupation blinds people to the larger economic and social forces that are responsible; it also generates intergroup suspicion and antagonism and precludes any unified action for change. If David is encouraged to express and examine his feelings and is given experiences that challenge his assumptions, he may be more resistant to the rejecting comments that he hears. At the very least, he can experience a sense of community with other groups that may alleviate some of the immediate feelings of intergroup threat and suspicion; at best, he may learn to be a proactive force in the creation of a more equitable and just society.

The majority of early childhood programs are racially, culturally, and socioeconomically homogeneous, and teachers often question the appropriateness of multicultural education in these settings. A basic premise of this book is that the goals of multicultural education are most relevant to children who are growing up without the opportunity to have contacts with people different from themselves. In a sense, their classroom experiences have to compensate for their social isolation. Teachers in these settings frequently are perplexed about how to make the diversity of our society and the world seem real to their children. Although this book is written to be used by all teachers, a special effort has been made to address continuously the question, "How can I teach from a multicultural perspective in a homogeneous classroom?"

PROCESS OF TEACHING FROM A MULTICULTURAL PERSPECTIVE

Multicultural education is not a set curriculum, but a perspective that is reflected in all decisions about every phase and aspect of teaching. It is a lens through which teachers can scrutinize their options and choices in order to clarify what social information they are conveying overtly and covertly to their students. In a sense, it is a series of questions to induce educators to challenge and expand the goals and values that underlie their curriculum designs, materials, and activities. This perspective infuses educational decisions and practices at all stages and is an expansive way of thinking that enables teachers to see new potential in both familiar and novel activities and events.

This perspective is relevant to all curriculum areas and to all children. Some fields may, on the surface, seem very distant from these concerns, but all teaching occurs in a sociocultural context and all materials and practices reflect social values. For example, math activities are usually considered to be noncultural, but teachers often illustrate certain principles by using examples that carry very clear social messages, such as the virtues of buying, selling, getting the most, making something the biggest, and owning private property. When planning math activities teachers might want to consider the impact of these kinds of illustrations on children whose families have very little money and no private property. Are they unwittingly contributing to children's feelings of alienation from school? On the other hand, children from affluent families may construe these examples as reinforcement for the idea that everyone has lots of resources, further obscuring the reality that inequality exists. As teachers consider these questions, they can think of ways of explaining quantitative relationships with examples that present other social values and experiences, such as equality, collaboration, donating, and sharing.

Besides the social values conveyed in problems and examples, teachers also can consider what groups of people are represented by the instructional materials. Using objects related to different cultures and lifestyles for counting and sorting activities is one way in which diversity can be incorporated into math activities for young children. Preschoolers also enjoy counting in different languages and singing songs with a variety of rhythms. In the primary grades, children can learn about the various ways that people measure and record numerical relationships by using different kinds of calendars, time keeping mechanisms, and numerals. Both younger and older children can be introduced to basic geometric concepts by examing and comparing designs used in the art work of different groups.

Because social skills and autonomy are goals of this perspective, teachers should evaluate the structure of an activity according to whether or not it fosters children's skills in these areas. Math activities can be done in collaborative groups that give children a change to practice skills in cooperating and problem solving. Teachers also can help children expand their relationships by forming groups of children who do not usually select each other. By learning to consult their peers instead of relying on teacher direction, children will begin to develop skills and confidence in working autonomously.

In addition to the subject areas, this process can be applied to all curriculum themes, even those that may seem rather removed from cultural, racial, and socioeconomic diversity. For example, a multicultural approach to learning about pets could include the following activities and topics:

Caring for pets; social responsibility
Cooperative care of a classroom pet
Similarities among all pets
Diversity of pets
Learning about pets belonging to people in the classroom
Friendships between people and pets, despite differences
Names of animals in other languages
Pets in other places
Communicating with pets
Animals communicating with each other
Protecting the rights of pets
Different ways that animals feed, clean, and care for their young
Working to change conditions that are harmful to animals

These are only a few of the myriad possibilities, but they serve to show how teachers can use a multicultural approach in all decisions related to curriculum and teaching practice.

As mentioned previously, a multicultural perspective encompasses all human differences, not just cultural ones. In order to provide a sharper focus and more depth, I have chosen in this book to discuss research and curriculum primarily related to children's understanding of race, culture, and socioeconomic status. This selection does not imply that the areas of gender, age, sexual orientation, and physical abilities and needs are less important. Teachers are encouraged to apply the developmental information and suggestions given here to other areas of human difference.

The following chapters will elaborate on the general goals and process of a multicultural perspective by providing concrete examples of how it can be incorporated into all aspects of young children's educational experience. In order for these efforts to be successful, they must be developmentally appropriate for children. Chapter 2 provides an overview of the relevant research in children's understanding and attitudes regarding differences. The need for teachers to be very clear about their own biases and the social context in which they work is introduced in chapter 3 and is stressed throughout the book. The subsequent chapters describe specific ways that teachers can build on children's early perceptions and concepts in all curriculum areas. As they engage in this process, teachers will also increase their level of understanding and see new possibilities. In short, multicultural education is an opportunity for both children and teachers to learn and grow in their understanding of diversity.

2 Is Multicultural Education Appropriate for Young Children?

DEVELOPMENTAL CONSIDERATIONS

Teachers often describe their difficulties in trying to explain to children the concepts related to cultural, economic, and racial differences. Sometimes they feel that their attempts exaggerate intergroup differences rather than promote positive relationships. Other times they wonder if children are even interested in these issues.

Early in my teaching career I had the experience of taking a group of 3- and 4-year-old children to a Japanese doll exhibit in San Francisco as part of the school's observance of Japanese Children's Day. On the way, our bus was briefly delayed because of road work. Upon our return to school, I asked the children what they remembered about the trip. Eagerly I awaited the responses that would show insightful connections between their dolls at home and school and the ones at the exhibit. I even dared to hope that they would express some sense of identification with Japanese children.

To my dismay, everyone talked with great enthusiasm about the road construction that we had passed. They eloquently described the machinery and the workers. No one spontaneously mentioned the doll exhibit. When I asked about it, the children answered somewhat listlessly and soon lost interest. Still positive that somewhere in their minds there lurked some great revelations about cultural similarities and differences, I gave each of them a piece of paper and had them draw what they remembered from the trip. As I should have expected, they all made pictures of the road work. When I specifically asked them to draw a picture of the doll exhibit, two children drew pictures of their own dolls at home, a few others drew family members, and the remainder refused to draw anything.

Many teachers have this kind of experience as they try to find ways of incorporating cultural information in the classroom. This anecdote illustrates some of the most common problems. First of all, the doll exhibit did not allow any immediate involvement on the part of the children. They could not touch, move, or feel the dolls, only look at them. It is likely that the children did not even categorize the objects they saw as dolls. Not only did they look different from what they knew as dolls, but the format of the exhibition contradicted the one thing most associated with dolls—active play. Second, while we had some other activities related to Japanese Children's Day, such as kites and fish prints, there were no discernible connections between these experiences and the doll exhibit. Since the term *Japanese* was not a meaningful concept to the children, it did not provide a meaningful association or context for the doll exhibit.

When conveying information about other cultures, it is easy to rely on the kinds of information traditionally presented in schools: facts, artifacts, maps, and stories about famous people. Abstract categories such as "Japanese" and "Israeli," which do not have any intrinsic meaning for children, are often introduced and used to categorize and describe people, foods, music, and art. All too often, multicultural education becomes a series of fact-focused lessons that are inappropriate for the children's stage of development.

There is clear evidence, however, that children notice human differences at a very early age and that these distinctions become part of the earliest constructions of their social world. Not only do they see differences, but their ideas about them begin to reflect the prevailing adult attitudes at an early age. Furthermore, as they engage in their early peer interactions, they begin to form their general social orientations and beliefs about what people are like. Early childhood educators have the opportunity to expand, challenge, and influence children's social perceptions. To design meaningful and effective ways of accomplishing this goal, teachers need to understand how children think about human differences.

Preoperational Thought

Most children in early childhood programs (ages three through eight) are cognitively at the stage of preoperational thought. During this stage, children live in a concrete and static world. Abstract speculations, causal relationships, and events outside of their immediate realm of experience are not meaningful. Children can enjoy exploring tools, foods, and clothing of many different groups but are unlikely to understand the relationship between traditional and contemporary lifestyles or to comprehend the impact of geography.

One teacher introduced her kindergarteners to the idea that people in other countries speak different languages by teaching them songs and a few words in different languages. Later she overheard two children arguing about whether or not the children who lived in the next town spoke the same language that they did. While the children enjoyed experimenting with new words and were beginning to grasp the idea that a relationship between locality and languages existed, the specific nature of that relationship eluded them. The children also may have heard people in their own family or community speaking other languages and then fused the concepts of town and nationality.

Children at this stage of cognitive development tend to organize information in broad and concrete categories. Frequently they notice visually salient features rather than more functional ones. For example, children may organize a group of objects by color, even though functionally some are tools, some are vehicles, and some are food. They would be very unlikely to sort objects by national origin, since terms and concepts such as *French* and *Cambodian* would have no meaning for them. Children's groupings are also usually rigid and dichotomous; that is, they see extremes rather than gradations. If they decide that two groups are different, then they have a hard time seeing ways in which the groups might be similar.

Young children also focus on single attributes rather than multiple ones. For instance, they may group peers by gender or race, but not by both. They also cannot think in terms of class inclusion, for example, that all the people in a set of photographs are children and that some are white, some are black and that some are boys and some are girls. In short, they can only see one attribute at a time. Like adults, children remember dramatic information; unlike adults, they cannot balance this information with other facts. Thus, a single conflict with a particular child may relegate that child to the category of "kids I don't like," although there may have been more positive than negative interactions with that child. As children begin to learn about social distinctions, they frequently overgeneralize and focus on one attribute at the expense of others.

At the preoperational stage of thought, children cannot perform certain mental operations, so that they are often confused by misleading perceptual clues. The classic example is their inability to conserve the volume of liquids when identical quantities are placed in containers of different proportions. Because they cannot mentally perform or reverse the pouring that has occurred, they assume that there is more liquid in the tall, thin container than there is in the short, wide one. In a similar way, children are also confused by superficial discrepancies in certain human characteristics. For example, young children often assume that a haircut or change of dress indicates a change in gender. Racial and cultural cues are likewise seen as changeable.

Social Cognition

Cross-group understanding and respect require an ability to see others' perspectives and to interpret their actions within their own context. This capacity is referred to as *social cognition* and is the study of how children and adults construct their understanding and expectations of how individuals and groups know, feel, and behave. This area of research has explored the ways in which children's construction of the social world parallels the development of their understanding of the physical world.

Children at the preoperational stage of development are egocentric in their interpretation of events and information. For example, when shown a photograph of a mother comforting a child, these children may begin to talk about a recent incident when they themselves were comforted, rather than focus on the attributes or situation of the mother and child in the picture. This egocentrism, while it limits the child's ability to see information objectively or from multiple points of view, does facilitate a kind of self-referenced empathy toward other people. Teachers and parents often report that children of two and three will attempt to comfort a peer with their own favorite dolls or blankets because they assume that the crying child will find them as comforting as they themselves do.

Findings of research in this area corroborate these observations. John Flavell and his collaborators (1968) have analyzed how the ability to "take the roles of others" develops and have subsequently designed several measures that are adaptations of Piaget's "mountain task," in which children try to visualize the same scene from different perspectives. They include assessments of children's ability to determine accurately another person's visual, emotional, and informational point of view. While this area of research has focused on children's understanding of individuals rather than groups, it provides some clues about children's potential to understand cross-group experiences. The findings suggest that children most quickly learn to identify emotional states of others from facial expressions and situational information (Borke, 1971). The early appearance of empathy, which has been observed in infants (Sagi & Hoffman, 1976), and children's memories of their own intense emotional experiences may facilitate this development.

Thus, while children at the preoperational stage cannot conceptualize another's point of view, they can respond to another's emotional experience. This early capacity is a good potential "handle" for teachers to use in helping children see their similarities with unfamiliar people. For example, young children cannot explain how Americans might appear to Mexican observers, but they are able to identify the emotional expressions of Mexican children and empathize with them in scenes or stories portraying situations that they themselves have experienced.

There is no conclusive evidence as to whether or not there are parallel stages of development between social and physical knowledge; however, recent studies have suggested that children's understanding of the social world may develop earlier (Gelman & Spelke, 1981). While social knowledge is more complex and certainly less predictable than physical knowledge, the emotional investment that children have in social interactions, the continuous feedback that they receive from people, and their ability to empathize with others' feelings may enable them to understand other people and social causality before they grasp equivalent concepts about the physical world (Hoffman, 1981). Ross (1981) found that the younger children (ages five to seven) more frequently interpreted events situationally, whereas their older counterparts (nine to eleven) saw them dispositionally. For example, the younger group assumed that the boy was running away from the dog because it was fierce; the older children said that the boy was timid and scared. Thus, while young children cannot understand abstract social concepts, they can accurately predict human responses to meaningful situations. They cannot grasp the causes and concept of emigration, but they are capable of describing how people might feel when they leave their friends and families. This ability to empathize, to project oneself into another's situation, is one way that children can reach beyond their immediate situations and establish emotional bonds with strangers.

This emotional arousal, however, can also distort perceptions of others. Dramatic information often becomes overly associated with the child's image of a particular person (Kosslyn & Kagan, 1981). While this phenomenon is true of people at all ages, children are less able to suppress the emotionally laden information in order to see other and perhaps more relevant information about a person. In my interviews with children I have been struck with how often they describe in great detail the "bad behavior" of their classmates. When I asked teachers about the accuracy of these accounts, they were sure that the children were exaggerating. Children will recall the exciting, "hot" cognition, even if the event was occasional, is long past, and is atypical of the person. One white kindergartener told me that "black kids are always bad and have to go to the office." Here dramatic classroom events have superseded the other information that this child may have about her African American peers. Thus, while emotional arousal may enable children to feel empathy and identification with other people, it may also distort the image that a child retains. Children's interpretations of new information about people should be carefully monitored to insure that they are not overgeneralizing dramatic or exotic information.

Young children are continuously learning more about how people react and feel, as they engage in numerous social interactions. Because of their investment in others and interest in their own emotional experiences, they rather early develop the capacity to empathize and to predict others' feelings. These abilities and interests enable them to identify with people who may look, speak, dress, and act in unfamiliar ways. Although children readily absorb prevailing social attitudes and stereotypes that create intergroup distance, their empathic interest in other people enables them to bridge the gap between themselves and strangers.

These characteristics should be viewed somewhat flexibly. As we work with children from the ages of three through eight, we find a great deal of variation in children's level of thinking. Still, the general characteristics of preoperational thought should be kept in mind as teachers hear and interpret children's comments and plan curriculum.

Process of Development

Children continuously organize their perceptions and experiences of the social and physical worlds into cognitive structures. While the way this construction occurs is far from understood, it is generally viewed as an active process in which children both assimilate information into their existing categories and previous knowledge and adapt their previous categories to accommodate information that contradicts them. These dual functions of assimilation and accommodation cause the change and growth in children's thinking that constitutes cognitive development.

Piaget and Inhelder (1968) maintain that cognitive development cannot be accelerated, although it can be enriched by extending the children's thinking into new areas. Experiencing dilemmas and unexpected responses in both the social world (Edwards, 1983) and physical world (Forman & Hill, 1983) stimulates children to articulate their expectations and to realize that they may not apply in all cases. This "disequilibrium" or momentary confusion leads children to puzzle about events and to create new cognitive structures.

If it is to be effective, multicultural education must be conceptualized and designed in ways that recognize the developmental capabilities and needs of young children and also involve them in the active process of constructing knowledge. These ideas carry us far from the fact-oriented geography and history lessons that are often implemented as multicultural education.

The following sections will review research on children's interpretations of specific social distinctions. The discussion will draw on selected studies that have been done over the past five decades. Teachers' and parents' observations of children's responses to differences also provide a rich source of information. In addition, findings from my own work in this area will be included. I have interviewed and observed several groups of children (ages three through six) from different socioeconomic, ethnic, and regional groups. My observations have focused on children's same- and cross-race contacts. Using photographs, I have asked children to categorize, describe, and select as friends cross- and same-race classmates and unfamiliar children. Also using photographs, I have interviewed children about their ideas related to social-class differences.

YOUNG CHILDREN'S RESPONSES TO RACIAL DIFFERENCES

The term *race* is used here to identify groups that share discernible physical characteristics that have been conventionally defined as racial differences. This concept is controversial, as it is unclear whether *race* is a biological or social distinction. Generally referring to differences in skin color, hair type, and facial structure, three racial groups have traditionally been identified: Negroid, Caucasoid, and Mongoloid, or, in more common terms, black, white, and yellow or African, European, and Asian.

The application of this distinction has been characterized by many biases and inconsistencies. In some states a person is designated as black if she or he has as little as one thirty-second black ancestry or even "any known black ancestry," regardless of the person's appearance or self-identification. The very notion of dividing human beings into three distinct "races" suggests that all people are not "equally human"; and these divisions have been used to justify slavery, colonization, and other forms of exploitation. Despite civil rights gains over the past few decades, racial distinctions are still used to characterize certain derogatory personality and physical traits and to justify discriminatory practices.

Related to the ambiguous nature of the concept of race is the difficulty in finding terms to refer to different racial groups. Color labels— black, brown, red, yellow, and white—are the most succinct, but do not accurately describe the physical appearance of individuals from different groups. Because they distinguish groups on the basis of one physical dimension, they objectify the groups and convey a sense of polarization. Furthermore, color labels have become associated with evaluative and stereotyped images. Current usage favors terms that refer to the continent of origin, such as African American, European American, and Asian American. Although these terms are more precise and are not imbued with evaluative connotations, they preclude many groups whose immigration history may not fit these categories. These labels are also inadequate to describe people native to this country. While clearly "Indian" is a misnomer, is "Native American" an accurate description of people whose residence here long predated the arrival of the explorer Americus Vespucius? In short, the terms for different groups reflect the confusion that characterizes efforts to make distinctions among people. In this book, I have used primarily labels that refer to the continent of origin, but also have used color terms when the former seemed inaccurate or too cumbersome. As social values and the relationships among groups change, labels and descriptions will continue to evolve, and it is likely that the terms used in this book will become obsolete. Readers are encouraged to continue to be sensitive to what messages are implied by specific terms and to modify their language to reflect the changing identities and relationships.

The issue of race has become further complicated with the increasing numbers of "racially mixed" children and the arrival of immigrants from varied "racial backgrounds." Teachers often find it difficult to determine "race of child" or find that the official designation of race is at variance with the one that the child and/or family uses. The following discussion on "racial differences" is written not in support of the validity of such a concept, but in recognition that these distinctions are conventionally and widely used and often become part of children's earliest social categories.

Most U.S. research in this area has focused on children's views about the differences between African Americans and European Americans. Thus we know little about children's perceptions of people who came from other places, such as Asia, the Middle East, and Latin

America. Moreover, the studies done in this country reflect racially related perceptions, experiences, and concerns that are unique to the last fifty years of this society.

The many aspects of young children's responses to racial differences that have been studied illustrate the complexity of their views. Cognitive, affective, social, and behavioral dimensions all interact in the construction of social perceptions and attitudes. In order to articulate this process more fully, this discussion is divided into six sections: perceptual awareness, evaluative concepts, racial identification, racial preferences, behavior toward other races, and knowledge of racial differences. When considering ways of incorporating racially related content into the curriculum, it is useful to know which of these processes are involved and how they interact for a particular group of children.

Perceptual Awareness of Racial Differences

Children appear to notice racial cues during infancy (Katz, 1976). Infants have been observed to notice differences between individual people (Thurman & Lewis, 1979). A parent recently reported that when her three-month-old white infant first met his African American babysitter, he had a startled reaction that was not evident when he saw strangers of his own race. By age three to four, most children have a rudimentary concept of race (Katz, 1976) and are quite accurate in the application of the socially conventional racial labels of *black* and *white* to pictures, dolls, and people. It is not known exactly when children first observe racial cues, but it is presumed to be early in the child's life.

There is some variation in the onset of this awareness that appears to relate to a child's contact with people from different racial groups (Katz, 1976; Ramsey, 1983). Furthermore, initial misperceptions often precede a clear sense about what constitutes these differences. In my interviews, one European American three-year-old who had had very little contact with African Americans looked at a picture of a smiling black child and said, "His teeth are different." Then he looked again and said with some hesitation, "No. His skin is different." Children of the same age from more racially mixed neighborhoods, however, very readily categorized photographs of children by race.

Despite these variations, it has been shown in numerous studies (e.g., Clark & Clark, 1947; Goodman, 1952; Porter, 1971) that young children by the age of three or four can easily identify, match, and label people by racial group. Since children at the preoperational stage tend to focus on one attribute at a time, it is likely that, when they are observing racial differences, they may not notice other characteristics of a particular individual. There is evidence that race has some influence on children's ability to distinguish individuals. Katz (1973) found that children more readily distinguished shade variations among individuals of their own racial group than those of others. In another study, Christie (1982) found that Chinese American children frequently were unable to identify photographs of their African and European American classmates, but readily named photographs of their Chinese American classmates. When looking at photographs of Asian American children, European American subjects frequently misidentified the gender of the children in the photographs (Ramsey, 1985).

Although adults often sheepishly admit that they have trouble distinguishing individuals from cross-racial groups, young children, who can only focus on one characteristic at a time, may be particularly distracted by racial differences. Teachers may be tempted to avoid drawing children's attention to racial differences in hopes of keeping them "color blind." Since children will become aware of skin color differences at some point, however, a better strategy is to acclimate them to the existence of differences and help them learn to distinguish within group variations.

Given that all children are potentially aware of racial distinctions, the next question is what characteristics they use to make these determinations. In my interviews with children, they most frequently mentioned skin color as the differentiating factor. They did not seem to be aware of facial features. In fact, a picture of a child with Caucasian features and dark skin was almost always labeled "black." In a racially mixed community, photographs of Asian American children were usually referred to as "white" by African American, European American, and Asian American children alike. Hair was frequently mentioned by the children, but it usually was described in terms of length, color, and adornments and often used to differentiate between individuals within the same racial group as well as between racial groups, so it was not exclusively a racial descriptor.

Children are capable of distinguishing different skin colors and perhaps other facial features, but how often do they choose to make these distinctions? Relative salience of race seems to be associated with children's experiences and their minority versus majority status in their particular communities. In my research (Ramsey, 1983), I found that European American preschoolers in a predominantly white community more frequently categorized peers by nonracial physical traits than by racial ones. However, African American children in the same community always grouped the black children together. In a racially mixed urban neighborhood, racial categories were more commonly used by all the children. Another study (Doke & Risley, 1972) found gender to be a more prominent category than race in a racially homogeneous group of children.

The immediate situation also may exert an influence. In my interviews (Ramsey, 1983), the question, "How are you different from this person?" was asked when children were looking at a photograph of a racially different child. More comments about race were elicited by this task than by questions that did not specifically mention differences. In another study (Katz & Seavey, 1973), children more frequently grouped pictures by race when they were "introduced" with racial labels. In contrast, when children were given more open-ended tasks and questions—such as, "Tell me about this person"—they rarely mentioned race (Ramsey, 1983; Rotheram & Phinney, 1983). Another factor that may be relevant is the race of the person administering the task. Although efforts to determine the effects of this variable with young children have been inconclusive (Brand, Ruiz, & Padilla, 1974), it is a factor that should be considered when assessing children's awareness of racial differences.

Thus, race is a category that children use, but the readiness to use it may depend on their previous social contact, the kinds of distinctions that they are asked to make, and the immediate social situation. Since young children have a hard time coordinating multiple attributes, the salience of one characteristic may obviate others. Children may appear "color blind" because race is not significant in that particular situation; however, low prominence should not be confused with lack of awareness. David's comments about "blacks in the workplace," discussed at the beginning of this book, illustrate how salience can vary between situations. Race was prominent to the exclusion of other characteristics when he was talking about "black people" in general and more incidental and even denied when discussing cross-racial friends. Older children and adults might say, "Well, I really don't like Anglos, but John is different, he's nice." Children at the preoperational stage cannot coordinate that shift in salience between the two conditions.

When teachers are wondering to what extent race is an important category for a particular group of children, they may want to consider the frequency with which children are in situations where they may observe the differences. Another factor is the importance of these distinctions to the parents and other significant adults in that community. Furthermore, varied questions and activities will have a differential effect on the immediate salience of race in children's perceptions. All these variables should be considered when planning curriculum. For instance, in a community where race is a prominent yet divisive issue, activities and photographs that emphasize similarities may be most appropriate. In contrast, teachers in monoracial communities may want to "introduce" children to the range of human physical characteristics and encourage them to express their curiosity and possible fears.

Evaluative Concepts

Evaluative concepts, if they are part of a child's environment, are likely to be incorporated into very rudimentary racial awareness (Katz, 1976). During the preschool and early elementary years, children continue to differentiate and elaborate their concept of race (Katz, 1976). Prevailing social attitudes and realities become associated increasingly with observed physical differences. Goodman (1952), in her well-known book, quotes a four-year-old African American child who is playing with black and white dolls. "The people that are white, they can go up. The people that are brown, they have to go down" (p. 45). David's comments, quoted earlier, attest to the readiness with which children incorporate adult attitudes into their perceptions of people. It is not clear to what extent young children understand these sentiments, but they do appear to be associated with feelings and, in time, with friendship choice. Because young children tend to think in absolute terms, even casually disparaging comments or jokes may be interpreted as social truths. When children make evaluative comments related to racial differences, it is an opportunity to explore with them what meaning they attach to these comments and racial differences in general.

Some evaluative comments do not explicitly refer to social information but still reflect prevailing attitudes. In my study (Ramsey, 1983), both African American and European American children frequently made disparaging remarks about the colors black and brown. In one study (Stabler, Johnson, & Jordan, 1971), where children had to decide if positive and negative comments were coming from a white or black box, negative statements were consistently associated with the black box. Some researchers (e.g., Williams & Morland, 1976) assert that this aversion stems from an innate fear and dislike of the darkness. It could be argued, however, that these feelings are perhaps initially stimulated and certainly maintained by the prevalent avoidance of dark colors and the negative connotations of terms referring to darkness, such as blackball, blacklist, and black lie. This contrasts with the positive connotations of terms related to lighter colors, such as *pure white* and *white lie*. These associations do appear to be malleable. In one study (Williams & Edwards, 1969), positive reinforcement was successfully used to weaken the "good-white" and "bad-black" associations that children initially expressed.

As one looks at environments and materials designed for children, it is evident that bright colors are used almost exclusively and dark colors avoided. Teachers may want to analyze the ways that they use colors in their classrooms to see to what extent they may be reinforcing the disparagement or avoidance of dark colors.

Racial Identification

The effects of the evaluative content of race have been evident in studies of racial (black/white) identification. In many early studies (e.g., Clark & Clark, 1947; Radke & Trager, 1950; Morland, 1962), European American children never expressed a wish to be black, but African American children frequently appeared either to wish that they were white or to believe that they actually were. Goodman, who wrote at about the same time (1952), offered a poignant example. She quoted an African American child in a predominantly white nursery school assuring her friends, "This morning I scrubbed and scrubbed and it came almost white" (p. 56).

More recent studies (e.g., Cross, 1981) have pointed out that these tasks and observations measure reference-group identity, not personal identity, and that these findings do not mean that African American children have poor individual self-esteem or personal identities. In fact, these critics have suggested that this misidentification may be an attempt to resolve the contradiction between feeling personally valued, yet disparaged because of group membership. As Porter (1971) said, "The [black] child cannot learn his racial membership without being involved in a larger pattern of conflicts and emotions which are part of his growing knowledge of what society thinks of his race" (p. 112).

Studies that have been done since the civil rights movement suggest that the more positive images of African Americans that have been promoted by the black community and in some media productions have had a positive effect. African American children today are more likely to identify themselves as such than they were some years ago (Cross, 1981; Farrell & Olson, 1982). In my research (Ramsey, 1983), they readily identified themselves as black or brown, but some adamantly pointed out that they were not as dark as some of their peers. Thus it would appear that there is still some feeling of "lighter is better." This attitude is not limited to African American children. In his autobiography, Hispanic author Richard Rodriguez (1981) described his efforts as a child to "shave off" his dark skin with his father's razor. Given the prevailing attitudes about darker colors in this society, it is not surprising that children learn to dislike their darker pigmentation.

Children's self-portrayals should be interpreted in the context of the many conflicts and mixed messages that children may be experiencing in terms of their personal value and their group-referenced identities. One clear incongruity is that the more positive images of African Americans in the media are often contradicted by the economic discrimination that still prevails. Young children, who cannot coordinate more than one context, may find it confusing that their group identities are validated in the classroom yet negatively characterized in the outside world. As we strive to foster positive group identifications, we need to help children make the distinction between the intrinsic worth of their group and the deleterious effects of discrimination.

Racial Preferences

Many studies have focused on the role of race in children's preferences for unfamiliar peers. They have ranged from having children choose "friends" from a multiracial group of puppets, dolls, or photographs to having children select either a white or black doll or picture in response to certain evaluative comments. In earlier studies (e.g., Asher & Allen, 1969), both African American and European American children fairly consistently associated the white stimulus objects with positive characteristics and desired social interaction. As with the studies of racial identification, recent studies have shown a more mixed picture. While some findings indicate that the white preference is still dominant (Rohrer, 1977), others suggest that both African Americans and European Americans show a same-race preference (e.g., Farrell & Olson, 1982) and that whites are more accepting of blacks now than they were earlier (Jarrett, 1981).

Children's choices of classmates also have been analyzed to see what patterns of same-race preference occur in racially mixed classrooms. In my interviews with children (Ramsey, 1982, 1983) I found that, among children aged three through six, gender was a stronger determinant of friendship choice than was race. In a longitudinal study of children during their elementary years (Asher, Singleton, & Taylor, 1982), it was likewise found that gender was the strongest predictor of friendship choice. However, race, while secondary to gender, did seem to exert an influence on the intensity of the relationships. When children were asked to nominate their "best friends," they usually chose same-race (as well as same-gender) children. When asked simply to sort their classmates according to those with whom they liked to play/work and those with whom they did not, there was less evidence of same-race preference (Asher et al., 1982).

There is some evidence of a link between intergroup and interpersonal orientations. In a recent study of children in an all-white community (Ramsey, 1986a), subjects who responded negatively to their classmates were more likely to react negatively to cross-racial strangers than were their peers who expressed more positive feelings about their classmates.

Young children's playmate preferences reflect very concrete experiences in shared and enjoyed activities (Ramsey, 1985). In my interviews, children often supported their friendship nominations with references to very specific events that had occurred that day. Since children quickly learn that gender is a more reliable predictor of who will engage in preferred activities than is race, it is not surprising that same-gender preferences are most common.* However, since racial difference does appear to play a secondary role and may limit the range of peer involvement, teachers should monitor children's friendship choices and listen for any racially related assumptions about friendship.

Behavior Toward Other Races

How do children behave toward their same-race and cross-racial peers? It is interesting to note that there have been few studies on children's actual behavior toward other races. Further investigation of contacts would be very useful in revealing how race does or does not influence children's social decision making and the quality of their cross-racial and same-race contacts. The observations and insights of early childhood educators would contribute a great deal to the understanding of this aspect of cross-racial relationships.

There is no consistent relationship between attitudes expressed by preschoolers in an interview and their actual choice of friends (Porter, 1971). As one would expect of children at the preoperational stage, the immediacy of a classmate's activity or possession is more important than abstract ideas about race or perceptions about physical characteristics. Many preschool teachers feel that there is relatively little divi-

---

*While this book will not be specifically addressing gender-related stereotypes, teachers may want to use some of the strategies discussed later to challenge these gender preferences.

sion by race in their classes; however, there is some evidence of a tendency for preschoolers to play with their own racial groups (McCandless & Hoyt, 1961).

During the early elementary years, there appears to be increasing racial cleavage in children's informal contacts, as seen on the playground, at lunch tables, and so forth. Some early studies (Criswell, 1937; Radke, Sutherland, & Rosenberg, 1950) found more racial segregation by this age. As children absorb more of the prevailing social attitudes and are cognitively less tied to the immediate situation, they may no longer keep the experiential and attitudinal realms separate. Furthermore, as the concepts of "us" versus "them" are established and intergroup differences become accentuated (Katz, 1976, 1982), in-group preferences become stronger and are applied more consistently to social decisions. In addition, due to the segregated nature of most neighborhoods, children are likely to have more out-of-school contact and therefore familiarity with same-race peers. By late elementary years, their ideas and feelings related to racial differences have crystallized (Katz, 1976). Studies of interracial middle schools and senior high schools (Patchen, 1982; Schofield, 1981) show how vehemently and explicitly peers discourage intergroup contact and how cross-group perceptions have hardened, as has the conviction that cross-group relationships are impossible.

In racially mixed classrooms, teachers have the opportunity to monitor the effects of social attitudes on children's friendship choices. They can challenge these effects in a variety of ways and help children maintain as broad a social base as possible. In monoracial classrooms, it is harder for teachers to assess how children would actually react in a multiracial environment; however, through simulations and other vicarious experiences, children can be encouraged to think and talk hypothetically about their reactions.

Knowledge of Racial Differences

As children are experiencing these perceptions, social contacts, and social norms, what is happening cognitively? What ideas, concepts, and questions do they have? One obviously related cognitive process is categorization. Over thirty years ago, Allport (1954) described prejudice as "overcategorization" in which people assume that people in the same category will behave, look, feel, think (and so forth) the same. Generally these assumptions are impervious to new information that is contradictory. As discussed previously in this chapter, young children often make similar assumptions because they cannot focus on multiple attributes. While it is important that this stage of thought not be interpreted as revealing early signs of prejudice, children's tendencies to overgeneralize can be disturbing. For example, a white mother recently reported that her son had a fight with one of two African American children in his school. Afterward, he repeatedly declared, "I don't like brown people! They always fight!"

While they try to understand the differences between groups, children often exaggerate the intergroup differences and minimize the intragroup ones (Katz, 1976, 1982; Tajfel, 1973), and this makes it more difficult for children to identify with individuals from another group. They are also unable to separate their expectations of a group as a whole from their experiences with individuals. One time we had an Algonquin woman visit our classroom of three-year-olds. She had long braids and wore some Native American jewelry, but the children did not recognize her as an indigenous person. The children happily heard her stories and sang with her, until she told them that she was an "Indian," whereupon several children shrieked with fright and refused to stay in the group. Here an immediate association of pleasurable experience was overwhelmed by the children's preconceived notions of "Indians."

Children's knowledge about the nature of racial differences has been studied by looking at the questions that they ask about them (Derman-Sparks, Higa, & Sparks, 1980). It was found that the preschoolers asked very concrete questions about difference in skin color, including its causes and permanence. Six- and seven-year-olds speculated about more complicated situations, such as how to define the race of children of mixed marriages. They also more explicitly questioned the social aspects of racial differences, such as the negative and unequal treatment of some groups in the media.

Children's understanding of the origins of racial differences appears to be parallel with their grasp of physical phenomena such as causality and conservation (Clark, Hocevar, & Dembo, 1980; Ramsey, 1986c). At the earliest stage, children attribute the differences to the actions of the supernatural or a powerful other ("God made her that way"). At the next level, children explain differences with arbitrary causality ("I went to sleep and woke up black"). At the third level, children give inaccurate physical explanations ("He was born in Africa"). As children approach the concrete operational stage, they are able to see that "some people are born that way."

Children probably do not understand that race is an irrevocable characteristic until they have acquired gender permanence (Katz, 1976). The gradations in skin color may make the racial distinction more confusing (as indeed it is) than the more clearly defined genital distinction. For young children, skin color difference seems to be confused with color transformations that most children either observe or experience, such as suntanning, painting, and dyeing. In my interviews with children (Ramsey, 1982), most of the four- and five-year-olds believed that everyone was inherently white and that brown people had been painted, sunburned, or dirtied. Only one child, an African American, had another notion: "If those white kids had left their skin on, they would be black and shiny like me!" To everyone else, African American and European American alike, black people were flawed or at least changed white people.

Before children see that racial differences are permanent, they go through different phases of denying its permanence. In an activity in which preschool and kindergarten children were washing black and white dolls, there was a clear progression from the three-year-olds, who were sure that the black dolls would become light; to the fours, who thought there would be a change and were puzzled when one failed to happen; to the fives, who were positive that the black doll would not change (Ramsey, 1986b).

Knowledge about children's assumptions and questions vis-à-vis racial differences is useful for incorporating racially related content into classroom activities. While teachers cannot accelerate children's readiness for understanding of concepts such as racial permanence or the rather complex explanations for why skin colors do differ, they can challenge some of the derogatory assumptions that arise from misperceptions. For example, young children are not going to understand the function of melanin, but they can learn through observation that it is not dirt or paint that causes darker pigmentation.

Children's responses to racial differences are complex and often contradictory. Despite the great number of studies that have been done, many questions remain unanswered. In particular, very few studies have looked at perceptions of and about children other than blacks and whites. However, early childhood teachers can generally assume that children by the age of three and possibly even younger are aware of skin color differences and can label and differentiate accordingly. Moreover, they may have a harder time recognizing individuals from races different from their own. It is likely that they will show some same-race preference, particularly when meeting unfamiliar people and, at the early elementary stage, when naming their "best friends." All children may express a dislike of dark colors; some may associate this aversion with darker skin tones. Children's racial concepts will probably be characterized by overgeneralizations, erroneous associations, and some confusion about the source and permanence of racial differences.

Some aspects of children's responses to racial differences appear to be related more to children's previous experience and the prevailing attitudes in the community than to cognitive development. Teachers may want to explore these questions with the children to see what is true for their particular group. First, how prominent is race in children's perceptions of others? Do children already have evaluative connotations related to racial differences? While it is likely that white children will identify themselves as such, a teacher might want to see how her black children identify themselves, as there has been a history of misidentification. Finally, teachers in an interracial classroom will want to observe the children's interactions and grouping behaviors to see if there are patterns of same-race preference in children's playmate choices.

The changes in preference patterns and group identification choices between studies done before and after the civil rights movement are promising. They suggest that, despite its seeming intransigence, the cycle of racial prejudice can be mitigated through education. Specific strategies will be discussed in later chapters, but here one point must be emphasized: We have to let go of the myth that "children are color-blind" and untouched by prevailing social attitudes. As study after study has shown, children's awareness, identification, preferences, and assumptions do reflect the attitudes of the adult world. Because of their level of cognitive development, their attitudes may be even more contradictory, global, and rigid than those of most adults. Therefore, it is crucial that teachers help children to articulate their ideas about race, in order to find effective ways of challenging their misperceptions and expanding their understanding.

YOUNG CHILDREN'S RESPONSES TO CULTURAL DIFFERENCES

The terms *culture* and *subculture** can be defined as the overt and covert expectations of particular social groups. *Culture* usually refers to

---

*For some time, I personally resisted using the term *subculture*, as the prefix *sub* often implies an inferior status (e.g., *sub*normal). After many discussions with my sociologist colleagues, I am convinced that it is the appropriate sociological term. It is used here to describe component entities of a larger whole (as in *sub*divisions), not ones of lesser worth or status.

one's national group (such as the American culture); *subculture* refers
to distinct groups within a society that are delineated by such factors
as national origin, gender, religion, occupation, region, generation, and
age. In this country, most people belong to several subcultural groups.
For instance, a person might identify herself as a "child of the sixties,"
a woman, a Jew, a teacher, a parent, and a Texan. The relative influence of each subcultural influence depends on past and current contacts and formative experiences of a particular person. Also, the extent
to which someone identifies with a particular group may change during her lifetime. Young adults often ruefully admit that child rearing
has brought them close to their parents' way of life, which they had
previously rejected. The relationship between the larger society and a
particular subculture also has an effect on how people identify themselves. People frequently mention how, as children during a period
when groups were trying to assimilate, they were ashamed of their
family's immigrant background; but as adults in a more pluralistically
oriented society, they would like to regain a sense of their "roots." With
all these factors and the interrelationships among them, simply knowing a person's national origin does not constitute a full understanding
of her or his cultural identity.

This discussion will focus primarily on ethnic groups, defined as
people who share a national origin and who, due to their recent arrival, discrimination practiced by the larger society, or their own choice,
remain an identifiable group within the larger cultural environment.

The relationship between the national society and a subgroup is
complex and varied. One must consider the history of the relationship, the distribution of power, and the immediate situation and status of the particular members in question. For instance, while
Cambodian refugees share many common experiences in terms of the
context and timing of their arrival, the ones who settled in the Mid-
west may have very different experiences from those who are living in
California.

Cultural and subcultural expectations influence all aspects of behavior. Outsiders most frequently notice concrete manifestations such
as language, food, clothing, art, music, and crafts. However, one's cultural context also shades more subtle dynamics such as social interactional style and role expectations. These kinds of differences can create
a great deal of cross-cultural misunderstanding and tension if they are
not recognized. A classic example of this dynamic is the proximity at
which people converse. Hall (1959) describes a scene where an American businessman is backing into a corner to avoid the close contact
sought by his Arab colleague. Many subtle social behaviors, such as

pace of conversation, use of words or nonverbal gestures, entry behaviors, and acceptable levels of conflict, are all influenced by our cultural backgrounds (Hall, 1977).

These covert differences can create misunderstanding between teachers and children. When one party's responses do not conform to the other's cultural norms, misinterpretation of cues may lead to misjudgments and failed communication. Downcast eyes are a sign of respect in some cultures, but evidence of evasiveness in others. Reluctance to bring attention to oneself is considered a positive form of group alliance in some social settings, but in others it is interpreted as underachievement or laziness. At one school there was an Iranian child who had been trained not to cry or complain if he was hurt. After the teachers realized that they sometimes failed to notice when this child was in need, they learned to watch for more subtle signs of distress. A recent videotape of a skilled American psychometrist assessing the English language vocabulary of a Vietnamese child provided another example. While the tester's approach was warm, respectful, and creative, her pace was too fast and it appeared that she was overwhelming the child with words. As teachers learn about the social norms, styles, and expectations of the families with whom they work, they will be able to communicate with them more effectively.

Despite its profound influence on the development of social expectations, very few studies have looked at children's understanding of culture. From what we know of children's thinking, the fact that *culture* is an abstract concept means that young children do not consciously recognize it as a category. Being egocentric, they cannot see their behavior or group membership from an outsider's point of view. Furthermore, because they do not use class inclusion as a way of organizing information, they are unable to grasp the relationship between society and subcultures. Piaget (1951) found that children under six could not conceptualize the relationships between town, state, and country. They adamantly denied that a person could be both a Genevan and a Swiss. Lambert and Klineberg (1967) found that, even at six, children only had a vague sense of what different nations were. In short, while they can describe, label, and identify the more visible differences among racial groups, children cannot articulate their reactions to different cultures. Thus, we do not have the broad and differentiated body of research in this area that we have in children's racial awareness; most of the information is derived from behavioral observations rather than from children's answers to specific questions.

At the same time, there is evidence that children do absorb various influences from their culture that shape their expectations of the world at an early age (Longstreet, 1978). In their earliest representational thought, children develop certain expectations through imitating adults. A teacher of two-year-olds told me recently that she heard a great outburst in the housekeeping corner one day. When she arrived at the scene, she discovered an Israeli girl pushing a play milk bottle from the table that was set for "dinner." Her American playmate kept putting the milk bottle back on the table. While it would have been futile to try to explain kosher laws to the American child, or, in fact, to the Israeli child, it appeared that the rule of not serving milk with meat had been internalized by the Israeli child, and the expectation that milk accompanies dinner had been established for the American child.

Children of three and four do not understand countries and cultures, but they do notice and remember concrete differences, especially when they emerge in a familiar realm such as food and clothing. When three- and four-year-old African American and European American children see pictures of Asian American children, they sometimes label the children as "Chinese" and then talk about Chinese food and shoes and "those stick things."

Preschoolers also have developed certain role expectations. For example, in a recent parent conference, a Thai mother expressed her distress about the behavior of the American children who visited her child. In the discussion, it became evident that, according to her cultural expectations, she should not set limits with other people's children. The American children, who were more accustomed to being reprimanded by other parents, were probably confused, as their misbehavior apparently was going unnoticed. They, in turn, kept testing the limits to see what the rules were.

By the time they are five and six, children are able to compare their expectations with actual events. In other words, they notice and often disparage behaviors and artifacts that violate their own cultural expectations. A teacher told me how one of her first graders became the target of much teasing when he came to school wearing lederhosen that his German grandparents had sent to him. In a kindergarten, the coconut oil that a child from India had on his hair earned him the name of "garbage head."

During the elementary years, children also begin to associate certain types of social behavior with members of different ethnic groups. In a study of ethnically mixed third through sixth graders who watched videotapes of African American and Hispanic American child actors role playing different social situations (e.g., needing to borrow an eraser), there was a positive relationship between age and a tendency for all of the groups to become increasingly definite and unanimous in their descriptions of what they thought the specific actors would do in each situation (Rotheram & Phinney, 1985).

A sense of cultural relativity—the ability to see conventions as unique to a particular culture, rather than as universal—does not develop until children are eight or nine (Carter & Patterson, 1982). However, Carter and Patterson also found that the youngest subjects (kindergarteners) were more tolerant of different social conventions than were their eight- and nine-year-old counterparts. Thus, while young children cannot decenter from their own point of view in order to see their way of doing things as simply one of many possibilities, teachers can use their greater receptiveness to introduce them to a variety of cultural conventions. Later, when they can understand cultural relativity, they will have more content and experience to support those insights.

Young children do not see membership in a particular group as permanent. In one study, Aboud (1986) found that when children dressed in Eskimo clothing, they assumed that they then became Eskimos. As with racial permanence, children are easily misled by superficial changes in attire or appearance.

Another way in which national origin affects interactions is the tendency of children who speak the same language to cluster together, particularly at the beginning of the year. When I was interviewing preschoolers in multilingual classrooms, no one ever mentioned language differences when they were describing their classmates. Functionally, however, these same children did respond to language differences. Not only did they choose playmates who spoke their language, but they frequently compensated for the lack of a shared language in other contacts by using gestures. In another study, Doyle (1982) found that, while children were aware of language differences and frequently selected friends who shared their tongue, they did not tend to categorize their peers by language. Children are also attuned to accents. In a classroom of four-year-olds, one child spoke with a German accent whenever he addressed a German classmate who spoke English with an accent. He did not appear to be mocking her but simply trying to speak in a way that she would understand.

By the age of five, children are more consciously aware of language differences and can understand the plight of someone who is linguistically isolated. In kindergartens and primary classrooms, bilingual children frequently translate for their monolingual teachers and peers.

Cultural and subcultural backgrounds influence behavior, interactional styles, and social expectations of children at an early age, yet young children are not able to understand this category nor even identify their own culture. However, they do notice the unfamiliar and may avoid or reject people when their expectations are violated. Frequency of contact with teachers and peers and the outcomes of these interactions are also influenced by cultural differences. Teachers need to be aware of different cultural styles, yet not make sweeping generalizations about families based on their ethnic identification. Knowledge of these variations will guide efforts to develop more effective learning environments and teaching practices. In monocultural environments as well as multicultural ones, teachers can counteract children's tendency to reject the unfamiliar by incorporating activities and materials that represent a variety of cultural experiences.

YOUNG CHILDREN'S RESPONSES TO SOCIOECONOMIC DIFFERENCES

Another less concretely visible social distinction is the socioeconomic status (SES) differential that exists among families in this country. This disparity includes not only absolute income but also educational background, occupational prestige, place of residence, lifestyle, and relative autonomy and power. While particular criteria for designating SES have been developed for research purposes, different communities and regions may vary in their income levels and definitions of prestige. Thus, when talking about SES, it is necessary to consider both national and local definitions. For instance, in some communities, children may feel deprived if their families do not have a swimming pool; in others, the addition of a porch to a mobile home may be a sign of affluence.

In this country, wealth is not always completely visible; it is kept in banks, bonds, and stocks, all of which are well outside the child's interactional and conceptual realms. Even if they could see wealth, children at the preoperational stage cannot understand the causal relationships between money and the standard of living. When asked about why some people do not have as much money as others, young, middle-class children in typical preoperational egocentrism will often respond with, "Well, why don't they ask their mothers for more money?"

Young children assume that money comes from the concrete transactions with which they are familiar. Preschool children believe that their parents "get money from the store" or "go to the bank for money" (Ramsey, 1986d). They see their parents receiving money in change from shopkeepers or from tellers or machines at banks and conclude that these are the sources of their parents' money. Hans Furth (1980) found that seven- and eight-year-olds still assumed that the change that their parents received in stores was the primary source of the family income. Likewise they believed that their lunch money paid the teachers' salaries and maintained the schools.

Although they cannot grasp economic relationships, children who have been exposed to other kinds of information or economic hardships may have a somewhat broader understanding of the economy. In a recent study (Luce, 1982), children as young as five years old associated poverty with the lack of jobs.

Despite their lack of understanding of the nature or source of socioeconomic status, children still experience its subtle influence on their perceptions of self and others. Having parents with flexible work schedules (more common with white-collar jobs) who can come to school more often is one way that the occupational backgrounds are covertly "felt." Children's discussions of trips, presents, and possessions all make the SES differences apparent, even if not explicitly recognized or remotely understood. In their studies of children's perceptions of their peers, Livesley and Bromley (1973) found that children from five to seven frequently remarked about the possessions that their classmates owned. It is not surprising that children who are growing up in a society where personal worth is often measured by property should in turn describe their peers within this frame of reference. Several studies on children's understanding of economic differences (Leahy, 1981, 1983; Naimark, 1983; Naimark & Shaver, 1982) appear to show that not only do children begin to differentiate according to wealth at an early age, but they also associate evaluative concepts with status. In the Naimark studies, children by the age of seven were able to sort pictures of people into five different levels, from very rich to very poor. They also assumed that rich people were more likeable than poor people. Even preschoolers can differentiate rich from poor (on a two-point scale), and they assume that rich people are happier than poor people (Ramsey, 1986d). It is an interesting point that both the preschoolers and the early-elementary children predicted that the rich would help the poor (Naimark & Shaver, 1982; Ramsey, 1986d).

A prevailing assumption in this country is that individuals are to blame for their economic misfortune. American emphasis on individualism leads to a tendency to interpret events dispositionally instead of situationally (Ross, 1981). For instance, people will often criticize food-stamp recipients for being "just too lazy to go to a supermarket where the food is cheaper." They view the frequenting of small neighborhood stores as a reflection of the characters and personalities of the

shoppers instead of a choice made in the context of transportation difficulties, the intimidation of going into an unfamiliar neighborhood,
special ingredients needed for certain ethnic foods, or the need for bilingual clerks. Children appear to incorporate these assumptions into
their perceptions of economic differences. A teacher who recently interviewed first graders about why some people had more money than
others found that many of the children assumed that poor people were
lazy and bad.

Children also learn about the relationship between race and eco-
nomics at an early age. A study done some time ago on children's perceptions of the social roles of African and European Americans (Radke
& Trager, 1950) found that white preschool and kindergarten children
consistently matched the shabby clothes, menial jobs, and poor housing to the black dolls. While the African American subjects did not
consistently make this match, they did connect their race with poverty more frequently than the white children linked their race with
poverty.

Economic status is internalized into children's aspirations at an early
age. DeLone (1979) describes the process as the development of a tacit
theory of social reality. He interviewed a number of elementary-school
children from different economic groups and found that children with
comparable IQ scores but different SES backgrounds had very disparate perceptions of the world of work and the relationship of school to
their futures. For example, a middle-class child said that she worked
hard in school in order to get into a good college. Her lower-income
counterpart said that he worked hard in school in order to get out. In
his book, *Black Children, White Dreams,* Cottle (1974) quotes an African
American child as saying, "Rich folks like you are lawyers and poor
folks like me go into the army" (p. 136). While younger children cannot describe their futures as explicitly, they are daily experiencing the
effects of privilege or discrimination by watching their parents interact
or not interact with the work world. In subtle ways their images and
expectations are being formed.

Racial difference is also associated with dispositional or situational
interpretations of economic misfortune. In the Luce study (1982), poor
white people were assumed to have lost their money through a mis-
hap such as being robbed or having a fire in their house. Poor blacks
and Native Americans were assumed to have lost their money through
their own criminal acts.

Socioeconomic status, although not explicitly understood by young
children, is part of their early self-image, perceptions of others, aspi-

rations, motivation, and evaluations. By learning how children think and feel about their relative status and that of others, and their own future prospects, teachers can design activities that challenge evaluative assumptions and the tendency to blame the victims and admire the beneficiaries of the economic system.

SOURCES OF PREJUDICE

Teachers and parents frequently ask why children develop stereotypes and negative characterizations of other groups of people. Often they express dismay that, even with efforts to raise children to be respectful of human differences, intergroup antagonisms seem to be inexorably re-created with each generation.

While there are no clear causes, there are some theories and speculations. One theory that has been substantiated by considerable research links prejudice with authoritarian personalities (Adorno, Frenkel-Brunswik, Levinson, & Sanford, 1950). According to this conceptualization, children who are raised in authoritarian and rigid households develop little tolerance for ambiguity, differences, and change (Harris, Gough, & Martin, 1950). The hostility and frustration resulting from strict and punitive child-rearing practices are often displaced onto disadvantaged groups such as ethnic minorities (Berkowitz, 1959). Much of the research based on these theories has been criticized because the comparison between child-rearing practices and personality types has often been confounded by SES differences that might be related to the variations in attitudes. Furthermore, this theory does not explain why so many people who are well adjusted in other areas express and act on prejudiced feelings.

While personality differences and child-rearing experiences might account for some extreme forms of prejudice, all children seem to acquire some evaluative concepts as they construct their earliest impressions of what constitutes the social environment. As evident in the review of research in this chapter, children readily form associations, make assumptions, and create categories in their early efforts to make sense of their observations of human differences and behavior. Furthermore, during this process, they are typically only exposed to one point of view, so that their evaluations are virtually unchallenged and thus become certainties (Tajfel, 1973).

An important factor that relates to attitude development is the avoidance of cognitive dissonance, which is the confusion that arises when we encounter conflicting information. Adults have been ob-

served to avoid the dissonance that accompanies the exposure to contradictory information by selectively attending to only certain facts or
by disregarding material that does not fit their preconceived ideas
(Sherwood, Barron, & Fitch, 1974). Because of their level of cognitive
development, young children cannot process a lot of discrepant information and tend to see information in absolute rather than relative
terms. People are seen as "bad" or "nice" but not as being both. In a
study of gender stereotypes, Mapley (1983) found that when children
were presented with information that violated their expectations of
gender roles, they were less likely to remember it than they were information that was congruent with their stereotypes (e.g., several children insisted on calling a male nurse "Dr. Brown"). Thus, if children
are exposed to evaluative information about other groups, they are apt
to incorporate it into their perceptions in an unquestioning and over-
generalized way. Interestingly, they may not act on it because, as described earlier, they do not necessarily connect their expressed beliefs
with their immediate social choices. However, even if acquired only
by rote association, these evaluative feelings begin to influence expectations and interpretations of new information.

Where do children learn these evaluative notions? One obvious
source is the attitudes of the parents. Somewhat surprisingly, the
studies of the relationships between children's and parents' attitudes
have not shown conclusively that this is true (e.g., Bird, Monachesi, &
Burdick, 1952; Radke-Yarrow, Trager, & Miller, 1952). Problems of accurately assessing parents' points of view, in particular when their
conscious attitudes and unconscious feelings are in conflict, have made
it difficult to draw conclusions from studies of this dynamic. However,
observations and children's comments sometimes reveal very explicit
parental instructions about avoiding certain groups. One Chinese
American preschooler said, when she saw a photograph of an African
American child, "My mommy says, 'Look at those bad people!'"
(Christie, 1982, p. 62). Older children interviewed by Coles (1977) reported how their parents had tried to discourage their feelings of concern or affection for other groups of people and efforts of teachers to
counteract the feeling of prejudice. As one twelve-year-old put it, "They
[his parents] think the Indians aren't the same as white people, and we
should stay away from them, just like they stay away from us. The
teachers have a different opinion; they like the Indians" (p. 193).

Another source is the implicit or unconscious display of attitudes
by parents and other significant adults, which may account for the discrepancy between children's and parents' attitudes found by Bird et al.

(1952) and by Radke-Yarrow et al. (1952). Parents may try to instill acceptance and respect into their children's world view, yet act in fearful and intolerant ways. In my work with teachers and college students, we frequently discuss early memories of racial, class, and cultural differences. People often recall subtle signs of fear and avoidance, such as locking car doors in certain neighborhoods, their parents' tension and nervousness around particular people, and patronizing statements that diminished a particular group (e.g., "It's not their fault, they just do not know any better"). Young children cannot analyze their parents' actions, but they do recognize and resonate to the fear and tension they see in adults. These uncomfortable feelings begin to be associated with certain people and become part of children's early awareness.

The de facto segregation that typifies most families' social lives also gives an implicit message about who is acceptable and not acceptable. Most churches, clubs, and service organizations tend to be homogeneous; hence, despite efforts to teach them to be tolerant, children are learning another message by example. At the very least, they are not learning to be at ease and to communicate effectively with a variety of people.

Classmates, older siblings, and other children in the neighborhood are sources of negative stereotypes and myths. Young children learn through imitation. In one study (Christie, 1982) the following dialogue was recorded while a group of children were looking at photographs of different groups of people. "I don't like black people!" said one child. Another child who had expressed no negative feelings toward African Americans during an individual interview immediately said, "I don't like them either!" One kindergarten teacher told me how one child started a whole scapegoating incident which ended up involving several children aligned against a child from India, whom the initial child saw as "black." These negative statements are contagious, as they provide momentary reassurance of one's own value and group membership. As children get older, ethnic jokes become a popular means of cementing in-group relationships.

Schools also contribute to the development of discriminatory attitudes. While textbooks and other materials have become more representative of racial, cultural, and class diversity, grouping practices in elementary schools often re-create these divisions. The tacit message is that "some people are not as equal as others." While ability grouping does not occur in most preschools, these programs nonetheless are often segregated because of their location, fees, and selective accessibility. Moreover, school staffing patterns often reflect the larger social discrimination, with European American administrators and senior teachers and African American or Hispanic American aides and janitors.

Finally, the effect of the media cannot be ignored. Children are exposed to an enormous amount of print, pictures, and television, all of which present images that influence children's perceptions of their social environment. In the past decade, there have been efforts to improve the range of representation. Still, many groups, especially those of Asian, Hispanic, and Middle Eastern descent, are not represented in the media and so, by omission, are relegated to obscurity. Blacks now are portrayed more often, but they are cast disproportionally in self-effacing comedic roles. The successful, white, middle-class, and economically secure nuclear family is still vastly overrepresented. Even the most tired old stereotypes tenaciously persist in the media. Recently a student teacher spent a month working with her kindergarteners on different aspects of Native American lifestyles. In order to see how well they were able to apply the material she had presented, she asked her students what "Indians" did. Although the children had obviously learned a great deal, she listened in dismay as several of them recounted a recent "Mighty Mouse" cartoon where Mighty Mouse had rescued the "good mice" from the "bad Indian cats."

We are all bombarded with images in stores, on billboards, on television, and in books and magazines. Advertisements that are carefully designed to capture everyone's attention and memory are geared to the affluent, young white population. In contrast, when people of color and poor people are seen on the news, it is usually related to hunger, poverty, a crime, or a disaster.

In a study done some time ago, Radke and Sutherland (1949) found that children by the ages of seven and eight had formed very strong opinions about African Americans and Jewish Americans but were unable to articulate the source of these ideas. Children are constantly constructing their understanding of the social environment, and much more learning occurs unconsciously. As stated in the beginning of this section, there are no clear reasons why children develop prejudice, but it is almost inevitable that they will. In this country, as in most others, stereotypes and perjorative attitudes covertly and overtly permeate all of their experiences, even in the most tolerant environments. For young children, who tend to think in global and absolute terms, stereotypes and evaluative statements are particularly easy to grasp. Counteracting these social and maturational forces requires a critical examination and challenge of the assumptions underlying all teaching practices.

In terms of the goals of a multicultural perspective, children between the ages of three and eight are developing their group-referenced identities, early perceptions of human differences, and interpersonal skills. Likewise they are experiencing, although not necessarily at a conceptual level, some of the realities of the larger society. At this stage, children are also establishing early patterns of learning, so that the match between their home and school environments and the quality of communication between the two are particularly relevant. As children develop their learning and social patterns and a greater awareness of the larger social environment, teachers can be instrumental in facilitating their adjustment to and appreciation of the diversity of values, expectations, and styles.

3 Where to Begin

The crucial first step for teaching from a multicultural perspective is to examine and analyze teachers' values and perspectives, intergroup relationships in the community, parental attitudes, and children's awareness and social patterns. Without this information, multicultural education is simply an overlay of curriculum unrelated to the unique needs and resources of the particular children and teachers in each classroom.

The following sections will discuss ways that each of these factors might influence teachers' approaches to multicultural education. Each section includes a list of questions or activities that may be used to assess specific needs and potentials of each classroom and community.

TEACHERS' KNOWLEDGE AND ATTITUDES

In multicultural education, as in every aspect of education, the teacher is the critical variable. It is the teacher who makes the goals of accepting, respecting, and appreciating oneself and others an honest and authentic dynamic in the classroom (Proshansky, 1966). With the curriculum, the teacher provides opportunities for children to expand their understanding of the social world. As a person, the teacher provides a model and the inspiration for children to adopt a pluralistic point of view.

This role requires constant self-scrutiny because teachers, like everyone else in this society, have grown up with their own share of biases and prejudices. It is very painful for anybody to admit that they have prejudiced feelings, and this is particularly true for teachers, who often are motivated by their idealistic desires to create a more fair and responsive world for children. In my workshops with teachers and education students, I have been struck by how readily participants claim that they have no prejudices. Yet, as we talk, they begin to realize that they do have points of view and biases that shape their perceptions of other people.

Prejudice is both more prevalent and more subtle than we sometimes realize. People often assume that it only occurs in the context of racial relationships, whereas many feel bias on the basis of class, gender, political perspective, and lifestyle. In some cases, white teachers may extend themselves to establish relationships with their African American children's families, yet feel intolerant of their conservative white families. Prejudice clearly is associated with explicit and dramatic racism, such as we see in the statements and actions of the Ku Klux Klan; yet it also is present when we disparage another person's taste in dress, food, or music or when we dismiss children as "unlikable" because they have a different cultural style of interaction or a background of neglect that makes it hard for us to relate to them. Sometimes our stereotypes and antipathies emerge through humor. People who are very cautious about what they say about other groups will often tell or at least enjoy ethnic jokes. Moreover, prejudice does not consist only of negative stereotypes. A Chinese American friend of mine talks ruefully about how hard it was as a child to have teachers always expect her to be well behaved and smart because she was Chinese.

We all approach social interactions with some expectations and preformed ideas about what people will be like. These assumptions shape our perceptions and responses, which in turn influence the actions of the person or people with whom we are in contact. The extent to which expectations change behavior was dramatically illustrated by the Rosenthal and Jacobson study (1968) in which children who had been described to their teachers as "likely to have a growth spurt" made significantly more progress than their peers who had equal potential. In another well-known study, Rist (1970) found that a kindergarten teacher made ability placements, after eight days of school, that precisely matched the socioeconomic hierarchy of the children. Two years later in the second grade most of these children were in the same relative position in the classroom stratification. Many studies (e.g., Coates, 1972; Simpson & Erickson, 1983) have demonstrated the overt and covert ways that teachers' responses vary according to race and gender of students. These behaviors include offering supportive versus critical attention, giving eye contact, and making nonverbal gestures. In many cases, teachers may not be aware of their differential reactions but are simply operating from their subconscious assumptions.

Teachers in white middle-class communities may not encounter as many cultural variations among the children, but how they respond to all children's differences will have an impact on how children come to view differences. It is easy for teachers in these settings to feel that issues related to multicultural education do not apply in their classrooms. When I have raised this question among teachers in homogeneous settings, I have often been assured that "we do not need to know about multicultural education because we don't have any ethnic groups in our school." In many ways, multicultural education is *most* critical in these settings. It is these children who are at risk for growing up ignorant of the diverse nature of the society in which they live, not the children growing up in ethnically mixed neighborhoods. Teachers who are not challenged by the immediate situation to consider these issues must expand their thinking to consider the whole society, in all its diversity, as the social context for their children.

Many teachers may feel reluctant to approach these issues, regardless of the ethnic and class composition of their classroom. Because taboos are associated with race, culture, and class, many of us were taught to not "see" these distinctions, but to see only individuals. As teachers, we often dismiss these differences by describing children as "just kids, the same the world over." Sometimes as proof of their "color blindness," teachers will say, "I can't remember how many black or Chicano children I have in my classroom." Unfortunately, it is virtually impossible to grow up in this country (and probably in most countries) without absorbing some of the prevalent racial, cultural, and economic stereotypes and attitudes. Rather than suppressing these perceptions and related feelings, teachers need to recognize and analyze their biases. A veneer of tolerance makes it difficult to confront our true feelings. For example, during the busing crisis in Boston, many liberals, from the sanctuary of their suburban neighborhoods and schools, assailed the violence and racism of the lower-income city dwellers. Rather than examine their motivations for staying away, they criticized the racism of the people who could not leave.

Another problem with the "color blind" approach is that it ignores the effects of the social environment. To assume that a child who has been raised in an affluent suburb is the same as a child who has lived in an urban ghetto is to distort reality. True, everyone has the same basic physical attributes, emotional capacities, and stages of development. However, the course and content of development are strongly influenced by experiences that depend largely on the environment. To understand children more fully, teachers must be able to see beyond the credo of "I love all children" to a grasp of each child's specific adaptation to the demands, lifestyle, and priorities of her or his particular social environment. In homogeneous classrooms, this understanding can be conveyed through the ways that teachers introduce material about other ways of life.

One thing that makes it hard for us to recognize our biases is that most people assume that everyone else shares their view of the world. It is difficult to see what we don't know and therefore hard to differentiate our own perspective. We base our judgments on our own accumulated experiences and often forget that they reflect our unique perspective, not universal truths. Thus, when parents insist that their children not be allowed to go outside during the cold weather, our first reaction is to assume that they are wrong, not that they are behaving in a way that is consistent with their experience and beliefs.

We must recognize not only that there is much that we do not know, but also that there are things we will probably never know. I remember as a VISTA volunteer in the late 1960s fancying that my two years of living as an "Anglo minority" in a Mexican American community and existing on a subsistence allowance would enable me to understand their experiences. It is true that I had a glimpse of some of the effects of discrimination and poverty, but the privilege, support systems, and resources of my middle-class European American background were never more than a phone call away. Nor could I ever know firsthand what it was like to grow up knowing poverty and discrimination.

These caveats are not written to discourage teachers from trying to learn all that they can, but rather to recommend approaching the experiences of other groups as learners and to maintain a stance of respect for the integrity of other ways of life and a sense of humility for the limits of our own understanding. Each of us has a perspective on the world that is a unique reflection of our own experiences; we may often have to accept preferences and opinions of others that we cannot understand.

As with children, teachers benefit from working with people from diverse backgrounds. When hiring staff, selecting student teachers, and recruiting volunteers, all efforts should be made to attract people from different backgrounds.

Exploring Our Own Backgrounds and Reactions to Differences

To begin to understand the roles that race, culture, and class play in perceptions of the world, it is helpful to explore experiences and reactions in a safe and supportive environment. These discussions most often occur in staff meetings and teacher-education classes. The hierarchy and the evaluation inherent in both situations can make it difficult for people to disclose their feelings. The person conducting the sessions should consistently reassure participants and demonstrate to them that personal disclosure will not affect their evaluation or job status. By revealing their own assumptions and biases, instructors and directors (i.e., the people with power) help to create a "safe" environment. As an alternative, some teachers have formed support groups in which they help each other confront and challenge their prejudices. Sometimes outside consultants can help to reduce these constraining effects. To insure that there is enough time for people to overcome their reticence, discussions should be continued throughout the year.

To engage participants in actively examining their attitudes, workshop leaders might want to try some experiential methods. Simulations often trigger people's realization about the limits of their own perspectives. One such activity is a commercially available game called "Ba Fa, Ba Fa,"* in which participants are divided into "societies," each of which learns a contrasting fictional "culture." After being orientated to their respective cultures, members of each group try to enter the other culture. As they confront unfamiliar and inexplicable rules and expectations, participants often experience feelings of frustration and isolation. In the debriefing sessions following the simulation, it becomes clear that in this brief exercise people have begun to see some of the ways that their own perspectives can make it difficult to accept others'. Participants frequently make comments such as, "Now I can see what it must feel like for a child from another culture to enter my classroom." People are also shocked to discover that after only about five minutes of orientation to a particular culture they feel intolerant toward the "other" culture.

There are several ways to heighten awareness of the uniqueness and diversity of each person's lifestyle and experience. Sometimes I have assigned a journal activity in which participants record all of their activities during a week as though they were being observed by an anthropologist from another country. This perspective often helps people to begin to see their own "everyday" activities as reflections of a particular cultural and social background. This awareness can be further enhanced if participants have an opportunity to see films or read books that portray other lifestyles.

Exploring and sharing our own backgrounds is another way to heighten awareness of how our lifestyles and attitudes reflect our backgrounds. I have often had students interview a relative (usually a grandparent, if they have one) about some aspect of their family history. In reading their reports, I have been moved by the richness and power of their stories and the fact that the interview itself had opened

---

*Invented by R. G. Shirts, "Ba Fa, Ba Fa" is available from Similie II, P.O. Box 910, Del Mar, CA 92014.

up some channels of communication, often for the first time. A popular activity that is both fun and illuminating is to have everyone describe his or her own cultural background to the group. Asking people bring in an object that has some significance to their lives can sharpen and enliven these discussions. Ethnic dinners, where everyone brings a dish that has some significance in their families, is also a good context for comparing backgrounds and early experiences.

These activities enable people to see the uniqueness of their own histories, the range of personal experiences within their peer group, and the ways in which these experiences have influenced their thinking. The actual discussion process can be used to compare and contrast people's social styles, as participants observe each other's use of verbal and nonverbal ways of communicating. Teachers and students who do not identify with a particular ethnic group may initially resist these kinds of activities and feel that they are "just plain Americans" and have nothing to contribute. However, when they begin to think of stories, traditions, foods, and objects that are significant in their families, they inevitably discover that they too have a rich and unique background.

Learning about other cultural and subcultural groups through traveling, conversation, and reading is another way to see one's own background in a broader perspective. Anyone who has visited different countries, unfamiliar regions of the United States, or even new neighborhoods usually returns full of excitement and many new perceptions. A couple of teachers said recently that the part of multicultural education that they liked the best was the stimulation of learning about different cultures. As people experience different ways of life, their ideas about all aspects of life, from social values to food preparation, are expanded.

The Development of Attitudes Toward Others

As a way of focusing on the sources and development of attitudes, participants can describe and compare their early memories of racial, cultural, and class differences. By reflecting on their early impressions and memories of adult reactions to other groups of people, teachers can gain some insight into the kinds of perceptions children might have. Furthermore, these explorations help people to articulate the sources of some of their own biases and fears. During one discussion, a participant abruptly said that she could feel herself "becoming prejudiced" as a result of some recent street crimes in her neighborhood. This disclosure stimulated a very open discussion about how fear and dramatic events can affect our perceptions about a whole group of people. Participants can use these sessions to consider many biases that they may have related to religion, sexual preference, and political values, as well as ones about racial, cultural, and class differences. They can look at how specific factors such as events, media representation, and isolation have contributed to the development of their own pre-conceptions and assumptions.

To move beyond their embarrassment or guilt, people need to see prejudicial feelings not as personal failings, but as results of growing up in an environment in which such views are constantly reinforced. Further discussion of prejudice and discrimination can focus on ways in which these dynamics serve certain interests in this society.

In order to have these kinds of discussions, it is absolutely crucial to provide a mutually honest and supportive environment for this process. As soon as even one participant feels a need to prove that she is "not prejudiced," then it will be hard for others to be open about their feelings. The person who is leading the experience must be very clear in establishing the ground rules and in protecting people when they are taking risks.

Since fear is a strong element in the development and maintenance of prejudice, confronting it and dispelling it are further goals for teachers. There may be certain neighborhoods that have a "bad" reputation that people are avoiding. Visiting these neighborhoods in small groups and shopping and eating in restaurants there may reduce some of the anxiety that people feel. Inviting people from that community to come and talk about their experiences of growing up and their hopes for their children will challenge stereotypical images.

Questions to Ask Teachers

The following questions are written in the first person, with the idea that people can ask themselves these questions as they think about their own personal and professional lives. However, they can also be used by group discussion leaders to stimulate thinking and conversation about these issues.

1. What are my own racial, cultural, class, language, and linguistic backgrounds? How do I identify myself?
2. What are three traditions, objects, or foods that symbolize my family to me? Why are they important? What values and/or history do they represent?
3. How do my values and expectations reflect those of my family?

4. What are my earliest memories of human differences? What did I notice? What did I think and feel about it at the time? Was I afraid? Curious? Attracted? Did I ask any adults about the difference? If not, why not? If I did, what was the response?
5. When was the most recent time I felt afraid or even a little uneasy about a person or group of people? Exactly what features of their appearance, dress, or actions made me feel uneasy? Were my reactions reality based, or was I reacting to stereotypes of people who look like that? [Try to ask yourself this series of questions each time you have an aversive reaction to a stranger. It is a way of uncovering and challenging many unnecessary fears of others.]
6. When have I felt that I was the target of discrimination? What was the reason for it (gender, occupation, size, sexual orientation, ethnicity, age and so forth)? How did I react? Feel? What did I do? Wish I had done? What kind of support would have been helpful in this situation?
7. [Ask yourself these questions when making educational decisions about children.] What is the basis of my decision? What actual behaviors, needs, and skills have I observed in forming this opinion? Are there any physical characteristics, mannerisms, or cultural styles that may have exerted a positive or negative influence on my perceptions of this child?

KNOWLEDGE OF THE COMMUNITY

In order to respond effectively to the particular needs, concerns, and interests of each group of children and their families, teachers need to see the community as the context of their work and to study it systematically. This analysis should include not only which racial, cultural, and SES groups are represented in the community but also the media representation of these occupational and ethnic groups. For example, doctors, executives, and police are frequently featured on television; whereas hospital maintenance workers, assembly-line workers, and street cleaners are rarely portrayed and certainly not in heroic roles.

Knowledge of current controversies about or among different groups is a necessary context for understanding and interpreting children's comments and actions. Local newspapers and radio shows, community meetings, and conversations with store owners and community leaders as well as with parents are good sources of local news. An African American teacher told me recently that a European American boy in her first-grade class had invited her to his Halloween party, then suddenly had retracted the invitation, explaining, "We don't let you people come into our neighborhood." Because the teacher knew the community, she was aware that this child lived in a white neighborhood where increasing numbers of black families were moving in. The child's retraction reflected the feelings of fear and territoriality that he had heard adults express. With this background information, the teacher was able to put the child's comments into a meaningful context and to help him see the contradiction between what he had heard others say and his affection for his African American teacher and classmates. Had she not known about the tension in that community, she might have interpreted the child's comments as being more personally antagonistic.

Knowledge about children's previous intergroup contact is also relevant. Studies of interracial behavior in desegregated high schools (Patchen, 1982; Schofield, 1981) have shown some evidence that children who live in racially mixed communities are less fearful of their cross-racial peers than those who live in homogeneous neighborhoods. If children have had no interracial contact, their questions and concerns about racial differences are likely to be quite different from those of children raised in a more mixed community.

Teachers and administrators can use the following questions to assess the extent of their knowledge about the local community and to define areas that need to be studied further. Teachers who have lived in the community for a long time can use this exercise as an opportunity to clarify, challenge, and change some of their assumptions. These questions can be given to new teachers or student teachers, to help them become oriented to the community and begin to make some local contacts. Teachers also can use this exploration as a way to gather materials, to plan field trips, and to become acquainted with potential classroom visitors.

1. What racial, cultural, and linguistic groups are represented in your class? How many children are there in each group?
2. How are these racial, cultural, and linguistic groups regarded by the immediate community and the larger society? Are they over- or underrepresented in the media? Are they positively or negatively stereotyped? Are members of these groups generally portrayed in inferior or superior roles?
3. What are some important holidays, foods, and traditions for each of the groups represented? How well can you speak the languages spoken by the children in your class? Are there any staff people who speak the represented languages?

4. What are the socioeconomic backgrounds of the children in your class? What are the occupations of their parents? How are these occupations generally regarded and portrayed by the larger society? What positive and negative stereotypes are prevalent? To what extent are they over- or underrepresented?

5. How much contact have the children had with people from other racial, cultural, and SES groups? What were the circumstances and length of that contact? What groups have the older children studied in school? To what extent has that information been retained? Forgotten? Distorted?

6. What are the prevailing attitudes in the school, immediate community, and the larger social environment about intergroup relationships? What recent events or transitions have influenced these relationships?

7. How do specific families interact with the community? How much power do they have in the community? What have been their experiences with community services, such as police, welfare workers, and the schools? What informal support systems exist among family members, neighbors, co-workers, and so forth?

KNOWLEDGE OF PARENT ATTITUDES

In addition to gaining an overall picture of the community responses to differences, it is also helpful to know how specific parents feel. Issues of race, culture, and class are emotionally charged and often stimulate strong feelings. Being able to predict how parents might react to different activities and information can help the teacher select an approach that will maximize parental acceptance of a multicultural focus in the classroom. Moreover, since parents do convey their feelings to their children, knowledge of their attitudes is useful in interpreting and responding to children's comments.

It is difficult to measure adult attitudes accurately, as most have learned to sound reasonably tolerant. Rather than giving parents a questionnaire or directly asking them about their feelings, teachers may learn more by informally approaching the issue.

In private schools and centers, where parents apply to send their children, the initial interview with parents might include some questions about families and peers with whom the child had contact. Public school teachers can include these inquiries in the initial parent-teacher conference. In my experience, these questions, if asked in a neutral and nonjudgmental manner, often elicit parents' feelings about the racial, class, and cultural composition and changes in their neighborhoods. By listening receptively, teachers can learn a great deal about the parents' view of their immediate community, the larger social environment, and specific groups of people. Also, the more teachers know about the community, the better able they will be to ask appropriate questions and understand the parents' responses.

At the initial parent meeting or open house, teachers can display photographs, books, clothing, and artifacts that represent the diversity of human experience. The presence of these materials might stimulate some approving or disapproving reactions that may provide some insight into parental reactions to a multicultural focus in the classroom. They also may elicit questions and discussions that reflect the extent of parents' interest and knowledge about different groups. By seeing that diversity is valued in the curriculum, some parents may be encouraged to share some things from their own backgrounds.

If the school has children from diverse backgrounds, observations of how the parents interact with each other at school functions will give some information about the relative ease or tension that parents feel about intergroup contact. Do the parents divide themselves into homogeneous groups? If so, how rigidly are these groups maintained? Do certain groups seem to have more power than others? Are there some parents who seem willing to make intergroup contacts?

If there are families who have recently immigrated to this country, it is important to understand the extent to which they want their children to be assimilated into the American society. Often their wishes depend on the reason for immigration, their future plans, and their status in this country. In one class that I visited, there were many children who had recently arrived from other countries. Some of the families were here temporarily as graduate students and planned to return to middle- and upper-class lives in their home countries in two or three years. These families wanted their children to retain their native language and identity. In contrast, there were refugee families who had left their homes under adverse circumstances and planned to live here permanently. While they also wanted their children to retain some of their homeland's traditions, they were most concerned that their children learn the skills needed to be successful in this country. Furthermore, these families were adjusting to a new country in the context of coping with the pain of loss and concern for relatives who were left behind.

Families of similar cultural backgrounds may disagree about the extent to which they want their children to be assimilated or exposed to other cultural information. Other experiences may influence their priorities. For example, in a study of the attitudes of a group of Lakota parents about multicultural education, the findings suggested that parents who had spent significant time living off the reservation were more receptive to a multicultural focus in the schools than parents who had stayed on the reservation (Swisher, 1982).

Continuing contact with parents during conferences, on the phone, and during arrival and departure times will enable teachers to monitor parental reactions to activities that reflect a multicultural perspective. Depending on parents' responses, teachers may decide to discuss a multicultural perspective more formally or they may want to start a group in which parents can talk about their community, intergroup relationships, or their feelings about how their group is or is not represented in the media. (Chapter 9 will discuss ways to respond to specific issues that parents raise.) As with every other aspect of parent-teacher relationships, teachers' abilities to listen openly and respectfully will elicit helpful insights about how best to respond to the unique needs, background, and interests of each child.

The following questions are examples of ways that teachers might approach the topic of diversity with parents during an initial interview or conference. Questions should be phrased and introduced in ways that seem most appropriate for each parent. These questions are not designed simply to elicit the specific information requested, but rather to encourage parents to share their perceptions about the community and the ways that the family interacts with it.

1. What other children has your child had contact with? Do they live in your immediate neighborhood?
2. Has your child had the opportunity to know people from other backgrounds? What languages has your child heard or spoken? How has your child responded to these differences?
3. Have you lived here for a long time? Where were you from before that? How is this community different from your previous home?

KNOWLEDGE OF CHILDREN'S RESPONSES TO RACIAL, CULTURAL, AND CLASS DIFFERENCES

In order to design curriculum that is appropriate to the specific children in each class, it is necessary to have some idea about how they respond to racial, cultural, and class differences. Chapter 2 described the general range and trends of young children's thinking and feelings about these distinctions, but each group of children arrives with its unique composition, experiences, and outlooks. In particular, teachers will want to ask, how do the children identify themselves? What attributes do they notice? What associations do they make regarding these human differences? What evaluative concepts do they link with various characteristics? What role do differences play in their social decision making? Cognitively, how readily do children categorize, see causal relationships, and coordinate two disparate pieces of information?

Learning this information can be difficult, as young children do not readily express their ideas about differences and intergroup preferences and behavior. By asking questions and listening carefully to children's conversations and spontaneous comments, a teacher can learn about some of their assumptions about the social environment. For example, one teacher was alerted to her white children's negative views of black people when she heard one child insist that "only the white dolls wear the pretty dresses." Upon further observation she noticed that the black and white dolls were always placed in separate beds and that the black dolls were much more likely to be called the "bad baby" than were the white dolls.

Many times, however, children do not say or do anything that provides an occasion for these observations and questions. To elicit children's ideas, teachers might try some of the following activities, which are all adapted from methods used in research in this area. These activities can be implemented as part of the curriculum. Although they require an initial acquisition of photographs and dolls, these materials can be used repeatedly. The primary task for teachers is to stimulate and monitor children's responses and later briefly record them.

1. Present the children with photographs of people who represent a wide range of cultural, racial, and income groups. Tell the children to "put the ones together that go together," to see what criteria they use in grouping people.
2. Use the same photographs in language arts activities, asking the children to tell stories about different people. They also can be asked to describe all the things that they notice about a person in the photograph.
3. Provide children with opportunities to play with puppets and dolls that represent diverse groups. Teachers may be able to learn about children's expectations and assumptions about social roles by observing the roles that children assign to the different dolls and puppets and the interactions that occur among them.
4. Using photographs or dolls, obtain general measures of identity and

preference by asking children questions such as, "Who is the one that looks like you?" "Who would you like to be?" "Which dolls (or puppets) would you like to have as friends?"

5. While it is harder to portray different levels of affluence, photographs of people in clothing, houses, and cars that imply various levels of wealth can be used to elicit children's reactions in terms of identity, preference, and assumptions as to the reasons for economic disparity.

6. To get a sense of children's assumptions about intergroup relationships, ask them to react to arrangements of dolls or puppets showing different compositions by race, gender, age, and socioeconomic group. Also, ask them to group photographs, dolls, or puppets "who might be friends with each other."

7. Display photographs of people engaging in familiar activities but in unfamiliar ways (e.g., eating with chopsticks, carrying water on their heads, and wearing sarongs), noting how the children react to manifestations of different cultures. Do they immediately reject the people as being "silly" or "yukky," or do they appear curious and interested in knowing more?

8. Observe reactions to linguistic diversity by looking at children's responses to their classmates who speak languages with which they are not familiar. Of particular interest is how children with a first language other than English feel about speaking their language in the classroom. Do they deny that they speak Thai or Hebrew, or are they willing to teach other children some words from that language? If all the children in the class are English speaking, then records with songs and stories from different languages can be used to start discussions about the fact that people speak different languages. Listen to children's reactions. Do they assume that people who speak a different language cannot talk? Do they want to learn the words in the other language?

9. Carefully monitor children's responses to activities designed to heighten their awareness of human diversity, as their reactions will provide insights into the kinds of information children notice and the ways that they interpret it.

KNOWLEDGE OF SOCIAL SKILLS AND GROUPING PATTERNS

The final area of assessment is the social skills and grouping patterns in the class. Multicultural education is inextricably bound with children's social orientation. As mentioned previously, there is some evi-

dence that specifically links negative responses to classmates with a tendency to reject cross-racial strangers. Skills that are necessary for positive interpersonal relationships are integral to the development of positive intergroup attitudes and behaviors. These processes include the ability to understand and accept other points of view, a sense of social responsibility, and a willingness to initiate and maintain interactions and to broaden the range of one's contacts.

Young children are beginning to develop these skills and may vary considerably in their social competencies. By observing this area of children's development, teachers can see which children may need more encouragement and which ones might serve as good models. They also can observe the types and relative flexibility of children's grouping patterns. Specific ways of fostering and expanding children's interpersonal skills will be addressed in chapter 7.

Observations and discussions of children's social behavior are often problem oriented because negative social behaviors such as aggression are conspicuous and disruptive. Teachers will often comment on the number of fights they saw but will focus less frequently on positive social behaviors. As part of a multicultural perspective, peer interactions should be observed for the following indicators of the positive development of social competencies and intergroup relationships.

1. *Ability to take another person's point of view.* Do children express interest in other persons' emotional states, ideas, or visual perspectives? How accurately do they identify others' feelings? When observing films or actual events that involve emotionally laden responses, how empathic are their responses? Do they recognize and enjoy their similarities and differences with others?

2. *Level of social responsibility.* Which children go to help another child in need? Respond to a peer's distress? Take responsibility for getting the group together? Redistribute materials in order to effect a fair allocation? In short, to what extent is the well-being of others a salient factor in children's responses to their social world? Are children willing to set their immediate needs aside to assist or comfort another child?

3. *Inclusionary versus exclusionary behavior.* Since the need or desire to exclude others limits the range of peer contacts and promotes the tendency to find excuses to reject others, it is contradictory to the goals of multicultural education. Teachers can observe the ways in which children initiate, maintain, and end their social contacts, to see to what extent they are exclusionary or inclusionary. Do children rely on the "common enemy" (excluding a third person) to

maintain their contacts? How do groups respond to "outside" children's entry bids? Are specific areas or materials associated with either type of behavior? What factors appear to influence whether they include or exclude particular children? Are they drawn by possessions, types of activities, or specific individuals? How do they respond to overtures by less familiar children? What reasons do they give for rejecting certain peers?

4. *Grouping patterns of children.* In addition to observations of the processes by which children engage and disengage themselves from social contacts, records of the composition of children's groups will provide some indication of children's same- and cross-group preferences. Do the children divide themselves by gender, race, language, class, or culture? How rigid or fluid are these groups? What happens when activities are structured so that children are forced to interact with peers other than their customary playmates?

USING ASSESSMENTS TO PLAN ACTIVITIES

The reader may be feeling that the whole year might be spent trying to obtain all of this information, with no chance to implement it in the curriculum. These assessments should be viewed as a continuing and integral part of the teaching process. As activities designed to increase awareness and respect for diversity are implemented, the responses of teachers, children, and parents will provide information that will be useful for planning subsequent activities.

The crucial aspect of both the initial and continuing assessments of children's, parents', and teachers' ideas and attitudes is that they occur in an accepting and genuinely responsive environment. As mentioned in the section on teacher attitudes, admissions or expressions of intolerance should not provoke preaching or criticism, but rather questions to help clarify feelings and challenge assumptions. On a recent radio talk show, a caller declared, "You cannot trust the Russians!" After the host asked him a few questions about what he was basing his conclusions on, the caller became much more conciliatory in his tone and seemed to be questioning his assumptions. While there is only a limited amount of questioning that can occur in a one-minute interaction on the radio, teachers have the advantage of more prolonged contact with colleagues, parents, and children. As they learn about the assumptions, misconceptions, and aversions that exist, they can find ways of helping people both recognize and question them.

The following examples may help to clarify how the assessments help in planning activities.

- In staff meetings at one school, it has become clear that many of the teachers have negative feelings about the families who are on welfare, because they do not appear to care if they work or not. Arrangements could be made to have each teacher visit with a welfare family, interview a welfare-rights activist, and listen to the experiences of unemployed workers. If no release time is available for these activities, then teachers can be encouraged to ask their welfare parents (nonjudgmentally) about their efforts to find work and what impediments they have found in that process. A social worker or welfare-rights activist could be invited to attend a staff meeting or training session. Staff members would not be told that they are wrong, but rather would be provided with experiences and support to help them examine the assumptions that they have. With more immediate and personal knowledge of the ennervating effects of poverty and joblessness, teachers may begin to question their earlier generalizations about their welfare parents.

- A school is located in a community that is in transition. In conversations with the parents, teachers learn that the parents are angry about the fact that many Vietnamese families are moving into their neighborhood. When planning an evening for the parents, the teachers might want to arrange to have a Vietnamese nurse come and talk about children's health. This experience would allow the parents, at a neutral location, to meet a Vietnamese person as an individual in a helping role. Teachers do not directly confront or criticize parents for their feelings, but simply provide an experience that may cause some reevaluation of assumptions.

- In discussions with rural European American children who have had no contact with African American people, teachers discover that the children assume that people with darker skin are covered with paint that can be washed off at any time. Teachers can encourage the children to wash the black baby dolls and observe carefully to see what happens to the color. Also, children can compare their different skin tones and freckles and see if anyone's skin changes color with washing.

- Recall for a moment David's comments, quoted at the beginning of the first chapter, regarding black people in the workplace. Teachers can use such occasions to display photographs of African American and European American people working together and to read stories about interracial teams of workers. Since it is likely that David and his classmates do not have a clear idea of what a "workplace" is, a trip to a racially integrated worksite might challenge many misconceptions about work and working relationships. David and his African American friend Michelle might be assigned a project to work on together, so that they are part of an interracial team. Children also benefit from seeing teachers from diverse ethnic and SES backgrounds working cooperatively. David would not be reprimanded for his comments but instead would be given experiences that challenge his assumptions.

- A teacher in rural Maine reported that the one Vietnamese child in her school is officially listed as Hispanic on the school records. When she showed photographs of African American children to her kindergarteners, they referred to them as Chinese. In this school, both teachers and children need to learn more about the different groups that live in this country and throughout the world. Photographs, books, and dolls of other races and cultures might be used to provide this experience vicariously. To provide a meaningful context for children to think about racial differences, teachers could have the children in the class compare their physical similarities and differences.

- A kindergarten boy from India is being teased and called "garbage head" by his classmates, who notice the smell of the coconut oil on his hair. The teacher plans a series of activities in which she has the children compare the coconut oil with a variety of shampoos, creme rinses, hairsprays, and setting lotions. After many discussions about all the different things that people put on their hair, the children are able to see the coconut oil as simply one of an array of hair products. They also recognize that everyone's hair has some smell.

- In the analysis of family occupations in a particular class, teachers discover that there are many children of migrant farm workers. When they search for some appropriate children's books, they find that most farm stories convey the bucolic bliss of the white male farm owner with his cows, chickens, and pie-making wife. To combat such a limited view, they could work with the families of their students to collect or take photographs of people at work and home. Then, using family stories or ones the children invent, teachers and children could make some books that reflect the lives of the children in the class.

• In a teacher's observations of children's social interactions, there is little evidence of children helping each other. Whenever a child needs assistance, she or he turns to the teacher. In response to this information, teachers could institute a system where children are expected to go to each other for help before they ask a teacher. Younger children can help each other dress to go outside or push peers on the swings. Elementary-school children can provide peer assistance on various assignments and projects. Teachers may want to arrange some helping activities across age groups. Four-year-olds are usually eager to help still younger children; third graders are excellent tutors for kindergarteners.

In conclusion, this emphasis on analysis is intended to insure that efforts to incorporate a multicultural perspective are meaningful and appropriate to the specific children, families, and community in each setting. Knowledge of what children are thinking and feeling will provide guidelines for both curriculum and classroom organization. Awareness of the community and parents' views will enable teachers to respond to children in their immediate social context. Self-scrutiny is crucial in assuring that we as teachers provide genuine and clear models of positive intergroup attitudes and behavior.

4 Representing Diversity in the Physical Setting

The selection of equipment, materials, and displays is critical in the implementation of a multicultural perspective. Because young children rely on concrete experiences for their learning, the concept of diversity is most effectively conveyed through direct interactions with various materials. As mentioned before, children at the preoperational stage cannot grasp the concepts of cultural and socioeconomic differences in the abstract. However, their expectations about the social environment can be challenged and broadened through experiences on a personal and concrete level. The physical setting can be used to foster the following four goals:

1. Positive racial, cultural, and class identity
2. Empathy and identification with individuals from other groups
3. Respect and appreciation of other ways of life
4. Realistic awareness of the larger social environment

Before reading this chapter, look around your classroom and make a list of the different racial, cultural, and socioeconomic groups that are represented in the props, materials, displays, and books, and think about the following questions:

1. What groups are overrepresented?
2. What groups are underrepresented?
3. What are the prevailing images of different groups?
4. What occupations are displayed in the dress-up corner? In the pictures on the walls? In the block area?
5. To what extent is the lifestyle of the children in the class reflected?

Compare your answers to these questions with your findings from the racial, cultural, and class analyses described in chapter 3.

The choice of which racial, cultural, class, or occupational groups to represent in the physical environment depends on the specific goals for a particular group of children. According to your analysis (chapter 3), are the groups in your classroom over- or underrepresented in the media? In cases where children's groups are underrepresented, the classroom should be a place where, in contrast to the media, they see their own lives reflected, validated, and supported. Remember also that children whose lifestyles more closely match the white middle-class "norm" may have unrealistic ideas about the universality of their way of life. In these cases, the focus should be on extending their knowledge with materials that illustrate the diversity of human attributes and lifestyles.

This chapter will offer guidelines for selecting materials and equipment that will help teachers to create a positive multicultural environment. Materials will include

1. Props, instruments, tools, and other items that have the potential to broaden children's cultural experience through their active play
2. Photographs and books that represent human diversity
3. Toys, decorations, and other articles in colors that counteract prevailing negative associations with darker skin colors

This chapter will focus primarily on criteria and issues related to selecting specific materials and setting up the physical environment. Chapters 5 through 8 will provide more details about how these materials might be used in the curriculum. This chapter is designed to help teachers reflect on their multicultural goals as they engage in the initial stages of ordering and arranging equipment and materials. If a classroom is already fully equipped, these guidelines can be used when purchasing replacement materials and making changes in the existing physical environment. This chapter offers students some ways of analyzing the ways in which diversity is recognized and expressed in classrooms where they are observing or student teaching.

PROPS, TOOLS, AND MATERIALS FOR ACTIVE PLAY

Young children do not organize their information by country and ethnic group; however, they can enjoy and use materials, tools, and props that reflect different cultural experiences. Through this process they learn at a concrete level that there are many ways of doing such familiar routines as cooking, eating, caring for babies, and transporting materials. These varied experiences challenge the assumptions of socially correct absolutes that underlie many negative judgments of unfamiliar people and customs.

In order to engage children actively, there needs to be a balance of familiarity and novelty. Children use props and materials to reenact their own experiences. If confronted by a completely unfamiliar scene or tool, they may simply ignore it. If the unfamiliar is woven into familiar activities, however, children can blend the known and unknown in their play.

In the following discussion, it is assumed that classrooms will have areas and/or activity periods in which children can engage in sociodramatic play, block play, art, music, and science. In some primary classrooms, there are no designated areas for these activities, but the following ideas can be implemented by integrating the suggestions into role-playing, art, construction, and music activities. Many of the materials and props can be made available for children to explore on their own, even if there is not a specifically designated area.

Sociodramatic Play

DOMESTIC THEMES

Children spend a great deal of time enacting various scenes related to food preparation, child rearing, and interactions with the community, such as shopping and recreational activities. When setting up the housekeeping corner, where many of these activities occur, it is important to consider the assumptions that are often implicit in the equipment commonly found in this area. Standard middle-class furnishing of stoves, sinks, and refrigerators reflect the usual image of American kitchens. While these appliances are familiar to most children in this country, they do not represent universal domestic arrangements. Teachers can elicit problem-solving and challenge children's assumptions by having them experiment with other ways of doing familiar routines. The substitution of some standard equipment with alternative props and illustrative photographs may encourage children to enact other ways of cooking, cleaning, and storing food. In one classroom, the teacher removed the stove and the children constructed different kinds of stoves with blocks. Their activities led to a discussion of the different ways that they had seen people use fire to cook food, such as barbecues and campfires. Photographs of a variety of cooking stoves from all over the world enriched their experiments. Older children who are less likely to have a housekeeping area in their classroom can be challenged to design models of alternative cooking areas.

In addition to providing alternative kitchen equipment, teachers may also want to have children experience "living" in structures that differ from the four straight walls of our "carpentered" world. A variety of homes can be constructed in different sizes and shapes and with all kinds of materials (such as cloth and boxes) to give the children the "feel" of living in various kinds of houses. As they move in and out of these quarters, their ideas about boundaries, relative sizes, and topographical relationships will be reexamined and challenged. Pictures of different kinds of living spaces such as mobile homes, tents, apartment houses, and houseboats can be used to challenge children's assumptions that everyone lives in the same kind of dwelling. If there is no house area in the classroom, these structures could be made outside or as scaled-down models inside.

Different utensils for cooking and eating can be introduced, to extend children's ideas of these two familiar routines. Nowadays it is relatively easy to find inexpensive cooking utensils from a variety of cultures, and children can use these in actual cooking projects under teacher guidance and in enacted cooking scenes in the housekeeping area. Different utensils and postures for eating are also of interest to children. After a student teacher introduced her kindergarteners to chopsticks, they became a favorite item and the children incorporated them into many subsequent activities, including an enactment of "McDonald's Restaurant." Here the children were combining the familiar and unfamiliar in a way that was meaningful to them. Food props, too, can be expended beyond the usual Cheerios and Saltines boxes by including containers of foods from different groups. Even in rural areas, supermarkets carry canned and packaged goods from many cultures. Teachers can introduce some of them for snacks and then place the containers in the housekeeping area.

Children also enact domestic themes by dressing up in different adult roles. In many classrooms, available clothing is usually representative of middle-class American women and is therefore limited by gender, culture, and class. Showing photographs of people dressed in different ways and supplying materials that are more flexible than the usual clothes may inspire the children to experiment with different ways of dressing. For example, long pieces of material can be used to make a variety of clothing from head wraps to saris. Using photographs and books, teachers can emphasize the practical reasons for different kinds of clothing so that the children do not assume the difference in dress merely reflects exotic "costumes." In their daily lives, children experience the need to dress for varied weather conditions and different kinds of activities. Helping children see some of the analogous uses of clothing in other people's lives encourages them to experiment with different kinds of clothing within a practical context. For example, they can experiment with the many ways one can wear a sarong and see how its versatility makes it a useful garment for many activities from sleeping to working in the fields.

Caring for children is also a common "housekeeping" theme, with the usual props of dolls, high chairs, cribs, and carriages. Diverse ways of caretaking can be illustrated with photographs and enacted with materials such as swaddling clothes, cradle boards, carrying slings, hammocks, and sleeping mats. The idea that there are many different family constellations and child-rearing patterns can be shown with photographs of fathers, grandparents, siblings, and teachers caring for children, as well as mothers. Puppet and doll families can likewise represent this diversity.

Parents are sometimes willing to lend the school clothing, tools, and utensils that represent their own lives. In one school an Indian parent showed the children how to wrap a sari and left a sturdy one for the children to use. The bright colors and the flowing style made this garment extremely attractive to all the children. If materials are too fragile to subject to the rigors of an early childhood classroom, parents may be able to help teachers make sturdy replicas of various objects. Alternatively, photographs of families using certain materials in their homes also expand children's ideas and may inspire some inventiveness on their own parts.

Dolls and puppets provide a way for children to experience different racial groups vicariously. They are the only way that children in monoracial settings have to interact cross-racially. Most current early childhood settings have, as a matter of course, both black and white dolls and puppets, but there often is not a true representation of the range of skin, eye, and hair colors that exist. White dolls often represent the prototype of the blue-eyed blonde Caucasian; black dolls frequently have Caucasian features and uniform shades of brown skin and hair; Asian features are rarely represented. This incomplete representation helps to create a verbal and conceptual polarity between "black" and "white." To challenge this notion, classrooms should have dolls and puppets with a variety of skin tones, facial structures, and hair and eye color.

WORK ROLES

Children often enact work roles that they have either seen in their own lives or watched on television. As mentioned previously, some occupations are overrepresented on the media, while others are generally ignored. As part of understanding the context in which they are teaching, teachers should have a fairly clear idea about how the occupations of their children's parents are portrayed in the media. If the children in a particular class all assume that adults are executives, doctors, or teachers, then photographs, clothing, and tools can be used to introduce the idea that many people do more physical work. A lot of jobs that are often considered "menial" by our society, such as trash collecting and street cleaning, can be incorporated into the chores around the room, to emphasize how important these jobs are to all of us.

Because they are fascinated by tools and machinery, children are often very drawn to construction, road work, and factories. Teachers can use this attraction to foster respect for these workers. Factory work can be simulated by setting up small assembly lines for various projects, such as making the peanut-butter-and-jelly sandwiches for the class picnic. When I have done this project with children, it has posed some interesting dilemmas for them about "which sandwich is mine," which of course touches on a central economic reality that workers do not own the products that they make. While young children are not going to understand these issues for many years, these activities begin to expand their awareness of the nature of work.

Parents can often provide props for the work roles that are common to their particular community. Usually the clothing is sturdy and can easily withstand the hard use it gets in an early-childhood classroom. In a school on the coast of Maine, there were so'westers and heavy boots that parents had donated. The children enacted the fishing expeditions that were a way of life for many people in that community.

BLOCK PLAY

Blocks are another medium with which children represent and enact their images of the work and domestic worlds. Children often become very involved in building structures that replicate those that they see in their daily lives or on television. Teachers can encourage children to try building less familiar structures by displaying photographs of a variety of structures such as hogans, pagodas, mobile homes, and lighthouses and by providing different materials including cloth, paper cups, twigs, pipe cleaners, egg cartons, straw, and stones.

Transportation is another favorite theme in the block area. Children build roads, airports, and rocket ships and invent many ways of moving people and cargo. Most children in this country are very car oriented and, when asked how people would travel without cars, are genuinely perplexed. Teachers can help to broaden this rather narrow conception of "how the world moves" by providing photographs that show different means of transportation, from rickshaws to supertrains. The cars and trucks could be removed for a while, to encourage the children to find other ways of moving things, using animals, people, wind, or water.

Blocks also provide an opportunity for children to represent their images of their neighborhood. While young children cannot abstract their experience enough to make models or maps, they can remember and describe different stores, parks, and homes in their neighborhood. One preschool teacher put photographs of different local buildings on some of the blocks and found that the children enjoyed "going to" familiar places in their block play. In this case the children lived in a poor urban neighborhood that did not match the images of neighborhoods found in most children's books. This activity fostered children's familiarity with and appreciation of their own neighborhood.

In primary-school classrooms where there may not be a block area, children can use other materials to construct models of different dwellings, neighborhoods, and transportation systems. As with the blocks, photographs and other stimulus materials can be used to expand children's ideas.

TELEVISION PLAY

Children often enact characters and situations that they see on television. In particular, they like to play the adventurous and aggressive roles of superheroes and mechanical wizards. A discussion of the reasons why children are so attracted to these roles and the relationship between television viewing and play is beyond the scope of this book. However, incorporating intriguing new experiences and stimulus materials as suggested in this chapter may help to broaden children's interests beyond the excitement generated by television shows.

Arts

Music and art are other areas where the physical setting can be used to expand children's perceptions about other people. As in other curriculum areas, the combination of photographs of people using a variety of art media or musical instruments and access to the actual materials or equipment will challenge children's assumptions about particular materials and provide them with the opportunity and stimulation for exploring other ways of creating new visual or musical effects.

Many art projects replicate crafts that are found in different cultures, so that finding pictures of artisans from diverse groups is relatively easy. Activities such as weaving, dyeing material, printing, making masks, painting, working with clay, and making jewelry are part of both contemporary and traditional life in many cultures. When purchasing art supplies for the year and "scrounging" for materials, teachers may want to keep in mind trying to have a range of tools and materials that go beyond the usual early childhood fare. In one preschool classroom, teachers posted photographs of people from all over the world wearing jewelry. As the children attempted to replicate the artifacts that they saw in the pictures, they experimented with new ways of using the materials. Because several photographs showed men wearing jewelry, the boys were more willing to wear their products than they had been in previous jewelry-making projects.

Musical instruments and records should be selected with an eye toward exposing the children to a variety of musical styles. Folk music is particularly appropriate for young children, as it is often rhythmic and easy to dance to. Folk songs often tell stories that are appealing to young children. Work songs are also relevant to children's interests and complement efforts to introduce children to a wide variety of occupations. It is probably not feasible to acquire authentic musical instruments from many cultures, as they tend to be very expensive; however, creative scrounging and improvisation can go a long way. In one classroom, some children who were fascinated by the sounds of a Barbados steel drum band diligently "played" inverted saucepans and coffee cans. Drums and shakers are found in most cultures and can be easily constructed by children and teachers. Photographs of different people playing instruments, singing, and dancing can illustrate the universality of music and diversity of its expression. Records such as those produced by Ella Jenkins and Folkways not only offer a variety of music from many traditions but also include background material about the songs so that teachers can introduce them in a more meaningful context.

Science

Many early childhood science activities focus on parts of the human body and their functions. Pictures and models used to illustrate these concepts should be carefully selected or designed to represent a range of skin colors and facial features. A second area of science is the natural environment. Pictures illustrating human responses to various natural phenomena (e.g., "We wear boots when it rains") frequently reflect a limited range of possibilities. Illustrations and materials related to the observation of and reactions to natural phenomena should reflect a wide variety. This area will be discussed in greater detail in chapter 6.

This discussion is a brief overview of the ways in which props, tools, and materials that children use in their active play support the goals of validating children's own home experiences and extending their interest in and appreciation of how other people live, in a very concrete and personalized way. There is an infinite number of ways to incorporate the diversity of cultural experiences into the setting. The examples described here are only a few of the many possibilities, but I hope that they will help teachers see some of the potential within their own classrooms and communities.

PHOTOGRAPHS

Photographs have been recommended at several points in this book as a way of visually representing diversity. Because they are such a central part of the implementation of a multicultural perspective, this section will discuss some guidelines for their selection and use.

First, why should one use photographs instead of drawings or paintings? It is difficult to portray the range of human variety and the depth of human feelings in drawings. Some painters such as Rembrandt have captured the subtleties of human characteristics and feelings, but most artists who illustrate educational materials are not of that caliber. Although some illustrations are done with sensitivity, drawn pictures often look stereotyped and shallow. Children's responses to photographs and drawn pictures have not been systematically compared, but Christie (1982) found that in one class the children made fewer negative cross-racial comments when looking at photographs of cross-racial children than they did when looking at drawings of them. With the photographs, children were more likely to talk about facial expressions and individual traits. This finding is not surprising, as photographs show actual individuals with unique and yet identifiable expressions, rather than impersonal and generalized representations. As discussed in chapter 2, children have more trouble discerning individual differences among cross-racial groups than among same-race groups. Photographs of persons from many backgrounds provide opportunities for children to observe and compare facial expressions and individual characteristics in people who may initially look "all the same" to them.

As mentioned previously, which groups are represented in the photographs will be determined in part by the analyses of the classroom discussed in chapter 3. In a class where there are many different groups represented, displaying family photographs of the children in the class might help the children focus on their similarities as well as their differences. For more homogeneous groups, particularly middle-class European Americans, photographs representing less familiar lifestyles are more appropriate. If several of the children are fearful about a particular group (such as the children in my class who were scared by our "Indian" guest), then photographs of members of that particular group engaged in familiar activities such as going to school, playing games, eating, and caring for children might cause children to question some of their assumptions about that group.

Ideally, a collection of photographs will consist of a wide range of individuals who represent many varieties of skin color, hair texture, facial features, dress, and adornment. They would be shown in identifiable situations and expressing many different emotions. With these photographs, children could observe that people look and dress differently but have the same feelings and do some of the same things that their families do.

When selecting photographs, it is helpful to have several people review them before they are displayed. If at all possible, members of the groups that are being portrayed can be asked to assess the authenticity and representativeness of the pictures. Contemporary images of groups should be emphasized more than traditional ones, so that children do not confuse cultural, racial, and economic differences with historical ones. Thus, publications such as *National Geographic*, which tends to focus on the more dramatically different images of people, should be used with care. Photographs in contemporary news magazines and publications for children—such as *Ebony, Ebony Junior, China Pictorial,* and *National Geographic World*—are good sources for photographs of current life in different ethnic and national groups.

Representing the range of income levels is particularly difficult. Almost all magazine photographs show the lifestyle of the affluent and powerful, as advertisements are designed to appeal to the wealthy and upwardly mobile. Lower-income groups are usually featured only in stories and photographs about misfortune or disaster, which then portray their subjects as miserable and desperate. However, series such as Steichen's *Family of Man*, UNICEF's *Family of Children*, Reich's *Children and Their Fathers* and *Children and Their Mothers*, and Raynor's *This Is My Father and Me* present a wide racial, cultural, and economic range of human experience. Where feasible, teachers might take their own photographs, and parents and community people may be able to contribute relevant photographic materials.

Photographs of families are useful for many purposes. First, they can be used to talk about how families are all different and yet have similar emotional bonds. Second, since children often assume that darker skin colors are the result of painting or overexposure to the sun, pictures of parents and children showing the similarity of skin color and features will help children reexamine this assumption. Finally, photographs showing people expressing identifiable emotions are relevant to young children who are learning to identify others' feelings and reactions.

To be a part of children's visual field, photographs should be hung at the children's eye level and be large enough to be seen and interpreted easily. In order to avoid having them simply blend in with the wall, they should be changed often. As a frequent visitor to the classrooms, I am dismayed when I see the same pictures remain on the walls month after month. Not only do they often become torn and dingy, but they lose their potential to interest and instruct children. A few well-placed, authentic photographs that are frequently changed and are used as a focus for discussion will have more impact than walls full of aged clutter. Often wall displays are considered incidental to the curriculum, which is developed around children's active involvement and interpersonal relationships. When teaching from a multicultural perspective, however, photographs are a central feature of the classroom setting and curriculum. They are particularly crucial in monocultural and monoracial settings, as they can compensate, in small measure, for the lack of contact with other cultural, class, and racial groups.

BOOKS

Stories introduce children to unfamiliar people in a personalized and appealing fashion. By involving the children with characters and situations that they can identify with, books increase children's appreciation of other ways of life and help them see unfamiliar people as individuals.

It is not easy, however, to represent the complexities of various cultures, common human issues, and appealing characters in a fifteen-to-twenty-page children's book. Many authors who have tried to portray a broad range of human experiences have been criticized for presenting stereotypical or unrealistic portraits. Some authors work so hard to present a political or social statement that the stories sound dogmatic and lose their appeal to young children. No one book is ideal, and, in fact, no single author has managed to address all the issues satisfactorily. Teachers will need to select books that together present a comprehensive perspective of this country and the world.

When selecting books, staff people should consider the points raised in "Ten Quick Ways to Analyze Children's Books for Racism and Sexism," written by the Council on Interracial Books for Children (1974). They provide an effective way of screening books for obvious stereotypes and the reinforcement of the traditional power relationships based on race, culture, class, and gender. This checklist can be used in classes, workshops, and staff meetings to heighten teachers' and parents' awareness of stereotypes that are prevalent and to critique the books currently being used in the classroom. An abbreviated version of this checklist is shown in Figure 4.1.

Materials published by the Council on Interracial Books for Children, including the reviews of children's books that appear in the Council's *Bulletin*, are helpful in identifying some of the more subtle kinds of stereotyping that might not be evident by simply using the "Ten Quick Ways. . ." checklist or the guidelines in Figure 4.1. The *Bulletin*'s reviews are written by members of the group portrayed in specific books and offer particularly helpful insights. In her new book, Sims (1983) also discusses criteria for assessing the authenticity in books written about various groups.

When they begin taking a critical look at children's books, some teachers despair of ever finding nonbiased materials. Here the question of balance is important. It may be necessary to use materials that are less than perfect, but knowing their limitations enables teachers to use them in a more realistic context. For instance, Ezra Jack Keats's books, which were some of the earliest children's stories about black urban life, have been criticized for the bleak and rather frightening images of the city that they portray (e.g., *Apt. 3*, written in 1971), but children respond with empathy and interest to the characters and story lines. Teachers who want to continue using the Keats books should make sure they also have photographs and other stories that present more positive images of black urban life.

As with props and materials, books also should provide a balance

Figure 4.1: Checklist for Racism and Sexism in Children's Books

1. **Check the illustrations.**

   Look for stereotypes. Watch for oversimplified generalizations about particular groups and/or any images that have derogatory implications.

   Who's doing what? Are people of color and women of all races in subservient roles?

2. **Check the story line.**

   Standard for success. Do people of color have to adopt European American standards or "understand" European Americans or exhibit extraordinary skills in order to be successful or accepted?

   Resolution of problems. Are people of color considered the problem? Are problems presented as simply "personal" rather than related to the larger society? Are problems resolved by white benevolence?

   Role of women. Are achievements of women and girls related only to their looks or relationships?

3. **Look at lifestyles.**

   If people of color are depicted as "different," are negative values implied? Are stories about certain groups placed only in ghettos, barrios, or migrant camps?

4. **Weigh the relationships between people.**

   Are whites in power? Who is subservient? Are certain family relationships assumed to be associated with particular groups?

5. **Note the heroes and heroines.**

   When heroes and heroines are people of color, must they avoid conflict with whites and middle-class values? Do people of color always end up helping whites?

6. **Consider the effects on a child's self-image.**

   Are norms established that limit the child's aspirations and self-esteem? Does the book counteract some of the negative, stereotypical images of particular groups?

7. **Consider the author's and illustrator's background.**

   If they are not members of the group that they are depicting, what qualifies them to deal with this subject?

8. **Check out the author's perspective.**

   What cultural, social, and economic perspectives does the book embody?

9. **Watch for loaded words.**

   Are there words with derogatory overtones and connotations, such as "savage," "primitive," "wily," and the like?

10. **Look at the copyright date.**

    In the early 1960s, many books depicted people of color from a white point of view. Some of the more recent books have more authentic points of view.

Adapted from "Ten Quick Ways to Analyze Children's Books for Racism and Sexism," *Council on Interracial Books for Children Bulletin,* 1974, 5 (3), 1–6.

between novelty and familiarity. Series such as the *Face to Face* books (Crowell-Collier) and *Children of the World* books (Macmillan) show the daily lives of children in various regions of this country and in other countries, who look, speak, and dress in many ways. Yet their activities—such as going to school, playing with friends, doing household chores, and spending time with their families—are familiar to young children. Children in primary grades enjoy books that present more detailed biographical material as well as descriptions and photographs. A particularly good example of this kind of book is Yee and Kokin's *Got Me a Story to Tell*, in which five children representing different ethnic groups tell about their experiences of living in this country. Since several of the children have recently arrived here, it is also a good book for stimulating children's thinking about the impact of immigration on children and their families.

In contrast, some books present groups in ways that dramatize events or traditions but do not make the characters seem very real to their young readers. The books in the *Indian Traditions* series (Voluntad Publishers), which portrays legends of the North, Central, and South American native people, are examples of this kind of book. These books are useful because they present the many cultures of native people in an attractive and differentiated way, but because there is no character development the children do not empathize with the people in the story. Teachers, however, can make the stories more personal by asking children to consider how some of the characters might have felt at various points in the stories. They also can be used to expand children's ideas about the ways that some people live or lived. For example, *The Chasqui* by Franco, which portrays the running messengers used by the ancient Incas, could be used to stimulate children's thinking about all the ways that people try to communicate and what life would be like if we did not have telephones. As discussed earlier, children tend to retain dramatic events and exotic information more than they recall more mundane information. Exciting stories should be balanced with ones about everyday life so that children do not end up with a distorted view of how people live. Thus books such as the *Indian Traditions* series might be used in conjunction with stories that portray native people in a more personal way, such as Perrine's *Nannabah's Friend* or Miles's *Annie and the Old One*.

Besides critiquing and selecting with care the books that include explicit information about diverse cultures, teachers also may want to review critically books that, at first glance, appear to be "culture free." Here I am referring to books about animals, machines, or people who do not appear to have any explicit cultural context. All books, regardless of their content, embody a perspective about the social environment. For example, while most of its protagonists are animals, *The Story of Babar* (de Brunhoff) extols the virtues of a European, middle-class lifestyle and disparages the animals and people who have remained in the jungle. The plot of Silverstein's *The Giving Tree*, ostensibly a story about the relationship between people and nature, glorifies the privilege of a boy/man to own and exploit his private property in any way that he wishes. Not only does the story reinforce the idea that everyone has property, but it also perpetuates the assumption that boys/men are the takers and exploiters, and that nature, depicted as a woman, is the willing and passive giver. Another theme in children's stories that reflects the idea that everyone has wealth and privilege is the frequency with which the story's central problem is solved by the purchase or acquisition of a new possession. Not only does this support a materialistic view of life, but it also invalidates the experience of many children for whom lack of money precludes that solution.

Books often portray a limited view of the kinds of work that people do. As mentioned previously, most work does not fall into the romanticized vision of doctors and fire fighters. Gross and Woodruff (1979) have compiled a bibliography of books related to work that is a useful resource. To broaden the collection of books related to work, teachers may need to make their own books based on the life and work of local people.

Another dilemma that teachers often face is the contradiction between the values that they want to impart in the classroom and the values expressed in particular books. One Puerto Rican folktale, *Perez y Martina*, which is published in a bilingual series, shows appealing animal characters and is a good way for children to see how different words can have the same meaning. However, many teachers feel uncomfortable using this story because the characters enact very stereotyped gender roles. Teachers might be able to counteract the stereotypes by adding episodes that present the characters in less stereotyped ways. They also might use the book to have children talk about the other ways that men and women might relate to each other. In order to develop a representative collection of children's books, teachers will probably end up including some volumes that pose this dilemma. Again, if this book is balanced by others that show nontraditional male and female roles, then its inclusion would be consistent with the goals of a multicultural perspective.

Books that are about certain groups but not written by members of that group pose a similar dilemma. Sims (1983) questions whether authors who are not members of a particular ethnic group can authentically write about it. Her point is valid; there is an authenticity in Eloise Greenfield's and Lucille Clifton's stories about African American children and families that is not evident in books written by outsiders. At the same time, eliminating all volumes written by nonmembers would drastically reduce the number of books one could use to portray diverse lifestyles. Careful scrutiny and preferably some review by a member of the group portrayed will help teachers decide which of the books in this category present the most balanced and accurate images of various groups.

Another dimension is the balance between realism and idealism. Books for young children usually have happy endings and have been criticized for minimizing or trivializing the depth of pain that people experience. At the same time, there is a need to shield children from feeling complete despair. (This issue has been discussed in great detail by people studying and designing curriculum around the threat of nuclear war.) One book that has raised this issue for teachers is Nolan's *My Daddy Don't Go to Work*, a story about an African American family coping with the recent unemployment of the father. An initial question that people raise is, Does the book reinforce the stereotype of unemployed black males? At the same time, the unemployment rate is highest among these men, so one could argue that this book represents reality. In our discussions about this book, teachers and I have talked about the necessity of using stories about working African American men and unemployed European Americans, to balance the images portrayed.

The next question that has been raised about this book is, Does it present too rosy a picture about unemployment? In the book, the family is clearly under some stress, but the father can do special things for his daughter because he is home all day, and the family seems to be able to manage on the mother's paycheck. The only real crisis is when the father is trying to decide whether to go to another city to find work. The family's love and affection convince him to stay. How well does this image match the increased family tensions and domestic violence that often accompany unemployment? How does a child, whose unemployed parent is depressed and spends the days watching TV, feel when she or he sees this fictitious father using the days to play with his daughter? At the same time, this book does offer a picture of hope and resilience as the family finds ways of compensating for the loss of income and esteem that accompanies joblessness. When they are selecting and using books, teachers should be aware of the extent to which stories reflect reality as the children perceive it. Where gaps exist, teachers should think about how to use a particular book in a way to bridge them.

One teacher used *My Daddy Don't Go to Work* in her kindergarten/ first-grade class in a high-unemployment area. After reading the story, she commented that sometimes parents got really mad when they did not have a job; then she asked the children what their experiences had been. A few children quoted some of their parents' resentful comments about their jobs and other workers. The teacher felt that, because she had balanced the image presented in the book, she had elicited a wider range of responses than she would have without this additional comment.

Books offer an excellent way to introduce the idea of different languages to young children. There are increasing numbers of books that are written in the language of the protagonists, as well as in English translation. A particularly good example is Paek's *Aekyung's Dream*, which is about a Korean girl who moves to this country and finds the transition difficult. It touches on the problems of trying to function with an unfamiliar language and the effects of discrimination. Because the book is written in Korean as well as English, it provides children with a concrete example of a different language. As children who are unfamiliar with Korean look at the writing and perhaps try to decipher it, they experience in a very direct way some of the confusion that is felt by the heroine of the story.

In brief, books are a very effective and powerful way to validate children's unique lifestyles and to expand their awareness beyond their immediate experiences. In selecting books, however, teachers need to review them closely to eliminate ones that promote prevalent and negative stereotypes of particular people or intergroup relationships. At a more subtle level, they should be scrutinized for class biases and the assumption of privileges that are not shared by all people. Finally, the balance between novelty and familiarity and between realism and idealism needs to be considered. Because no single book or author can truly represent the cultural, racial, and occupational diversity of this country and the world, books should be selected and reviewed with the idea of developing a collection that, as a whole, provides a balanced representation of diverse physical characteristics and lifestyles, levels of affluence, and social values.

USE OF COLORS

Before reading any further in this section, make a list of the colors used in the decoration of your classroom or other setting. Think of the toys, the walls, the furniture, the partitions, and so forth. Now think about

your art supply closet at the end of the year or session, and make a list
of the colors of leftover paint and paper.

Unless your setting is very unusual, it is likely that most of the
colors used in the classroom decor, excluding natural wood floors,
walls, and trim, are generally light and bright. Moreover, the colors
left over in the art supplies are probably the browns and the blacks.
Think for a moment about the implicit message that underlies this distribution of color usage: a preference for the lighter colors and an
avoidance of the darker ones.

As you may recall from chapter 2, several children (both white and
black) explained their antipathy toward darker skin colors as a dislike
of black or brown in general. While some psychologists claim that hu-
mans inherently favor lighter colors over darker ones, it is undeniable
that, from the time children are born in this country, they are taught
to prefer light colors. With the exception of teddy bears, almost all toys
for young children are brightly colored. Children's clothes and room
decorations are also in bright shades. In a book called *Let's Find Out
about Color* (Campbell), brown is included peripherally and black is not
mentioned. Children's experiences of brown and black are likely to be
limited to fecal matter, dirt, and the nighttime.

As children learn to speak, they absorb the well-documented connotative values of *black* and *white* in our language. In their fledgling
efforts at art, children are apt to hear more praise for their "pretty blue
picture that looks like the sky" than for "all those black squiggles, I
can't see anything." The brown color that usually results from mixing
several colors is frequently regarded as a "mess" by adult appraisers.
One teacher vetoed a child's request that the play-dough be colored
black by saying, "It would look ugly, and no one would want to play
with it." Generally, these adult reactions are not deliberately racist, but
rather the result of many years of associating light colors with positive
values and dark ones with negative ones.

As teachers, we cannot erase the pervasive attitudes regarding color
that children are exposed to from birth, but we can try to challenge
them by using dark colors in decorating the classroom and encouraging the children to explore and appreciate the browns and blacks by
providing materials in those colors. While children may initially complain about the black water in the water table or the brown play-dough,
these are opportunities for teachers to help children express their negative reactions and then to challenge them with counterexamples. For
instance, children might assume that the brown play-dough will have
an unpleasant smell. Teachers can encourage children to smell it and
see that it smells just like any other play-dough. Adding different spices

and extracts to it may further dispel the association between dark colors and unpleasant odors. One preschool teacher and her class mixed colors of paint for several weeks. As the culminating event, the children put all the colors together and came up with many shades of brown. In contrast to the negative associations that are often made, here the color brown was seen as the most exciting color because it included all of the others.

The polarization of black and white is another concept that teachers can challenge with art materials. Children can be encouraged to mix these two colors in different proportions so that they can see darker and lighter as two equally valued ends of a continuum, rather than as mutually exclusive opposites. Providing different shades of brown is another way of helping children see skin color gradations in a more realistic and less polemic way.

Painting and printing materials can be designed and used to challenge the common assumption that all people are initially white and that they are painted, dyed, or suntanned to become brown. Instead of always having white paper and cloth that are painted or dyed with darker colors, teachers might also provide dark materials that are lightened with white chalk, paint, or crayons. While these experiences do not directly challenge children's assumptions about darker skin, they do show that things do not inevitably change from light to dark.

Books such as Adoff's *Black Is Brown Is Tan*, Giovanni's *Spinning a Soft Black Song*, and Bond's *Brown Is a Beautiful Color* can also be used to counteract children's negative associations with dark colors and their assumptions of black/white polarity.

CHECKLIST FOR THE PHYSICAL SETTING

At the beginning of the year and at a few points during the year, you might take stock of the extent to which the physical environment is potentially stimulating or inhibiting children's understanding of diversity by reviewing the following questions.

1. What groups are represented by the pictures and photographs currently displayed in the classroom? How does the distribution fit with the goals that you have set for your classroom?
2. How authentic are these displays? Do they represent real individuals or more stereotyped images?
3. What racial groups are represented in the doll collection? Do they

represent a more differentiated range of racial groups than simply black and white dolls?

4. What cultural traditions are represented in the equipment in the housekeeping area? How are children enacting food preparation? Child-rearing practices? What clothing are they wearing?

5. What kinds of structures are the children making in the block area? What lifestyles are they representing? What are they using as stimulus materials?

6. What kinds of work roles are the children enacting? What props are available for them to use?

7. What ethnic, racial, occupational, regional, linguistic, and socioeconomic groups are represented in the books in the classroom? How balanced is the collection as a whole in terms of familiarity versus novelty and realism versus idealism?

8. What colors are used in classroom displays? In art projects? For which colors do children usually express a preference?

The physical features of early-childhood settings can be used to help children experience diversity of culture, race, and class in concrete ways. By creating an immediate multicultural environment, schools can compensate in a small way for the segregation that prevails in most communities and regions. With photographs, books, tools, props, clothing, and art materials that represent diversity, children can react to differences, ask their questions, and test their assumptions.

5 Experiencing Diversity Through Holidays

Holiday celebrations combine many activities that children enjoy, such as cooking, eating, singing, dancing, and making decorations and costumes. Because of their appeal to both children and teachers, holidays have often been a focal point of curriculum. In many schools you can tell the time of the year by the display of valentines, Christmas trees, pumpkins, or depictions of George Washington chopping down a cherry tree.

Holidays, like the physical environment, provide occasions for children to experience cultural diversity in a variety of concrete, immediate ways. It is not surprising that one of the earliest implementations of multicultural education was the incorporation of holidays from many different cultures. Nowadays, cultural distinctions are often blurred when comparing daily life, due to the international similarities of contemporary dress, housing, and transportation. Holidays, however, with their traditional ceremonies, foods, and dress, offer more tangible ways of distinguishing one group from another. Specific dates also make it easy to plan the observance of a particular holiday, in contrast to achieving the more amorphous goal of "implementing a multicultural perspective." Thus, holidays offer a number of practical, aesthetic, and educational advantages to multicultural programs.

However, the practice of focusing on holidays, often referred to as the "holiday syndrome," has been criticized on a number of points (Hinderlie, McCollough, Schachter, Simmons, & Wortis, 1978). When holidays are the sole or main focus of a multicultural curriculum, they become token gestures rather than authentic representations of cultural diversity. Without some knowledge of the daily life of a cultural group, children are apt to remember only the exotic differences that were portrayed as part of the holiday celebration, rather than the fact that real individuals with whom they share many similarities celebrate a particular day. Unless children have some information about a people's way of life, the symbols and rituals of their holidays may have no meaning. For example, the symbol of the fish, which is prominent in Japanese Children's Day observances, does not mean very much unless the children have some exposure to the idea of the importance of fish as a source of food. (Children living on the coast of Oregon might have this awareness, but perhaps not children living in the middle of Kansas.) Furthermore, holiday stories usually tell of positive events, such as heroic deeds, the arrival of spring, and the bountiful harvest, leaving a romanticized or "postcard" impression that makes the groups seem even more distant from a child's immediate experience. Finally, by celebrating holidays out of context, we imply that particular groups exist only on their holidays. Imagine for a moment that the only information that a group of children had about the United States was the fact that we celebrate the Fourth of July. How well do the firecrackers, picnics, parades, and long-legged Uncle Sams represent the way people live in this country?

In essence, holidays are a legitimate part of a multicultural perspective. They have the potential to promote positive cultural identity, appreciation of other lifestyles, an awareness of the larger society, and positive social interactions among children. Furthermore, they are high-interest vehicles for teaching skills in all academic areas. They should be presented, however, as part of a comprehensive world view, not as isolated events. Since they tend to embody the unique traditions of a culture, teachers should be sure that children do not simply see them as exotic rituals. This chapter will discuss ways of integrating holidays into children's immediate experiences and an overall multicultural perspective.

CURRENT PRACTICES: ASSUMPTIONS AND ALTERNATIVES

Before considering how to incorporate unfamiliar holidays into the curriculum, we will first analyze some of the biases and values that are reflected in common holiday-related activities in schools. These criticisms are not intended to dissuade teachers from these observances, but to help them to recognize the assumptions that are conveyed in certain classroom traditions and media images and to consider ways of challenging them.

National holidays are by definition ethnocentric. They glorify the past events and future potential of a particular country and in some cases a specific group within that country. This phenomenon is particularly true of Columbus Day and Thanksgiving, which celebrate the

European "discovery" and "settling" of the Americas. Both holidays tend to stress the heroism of the Europeans and ignore or distort the implications for the indigenous peoples of these continents. Teachers can provide a more balanced view of these holidays by focusing on how the indigenous nations felt about the arrival of the Europeans and by providing a more realistic image of the relationships between the Europeans and these groups. Instead of reinforcing the usual European-centered point of view, these occasions can be used to heighten children's appreciation of the diversity and richness of traditional and contemporary Native American life and to dispel negative stereotypes (Califf, 1977; Hirschfelder & Califf, 1979; Ramsey, 1979).

Largely due to commercialization, the elements of competition and materialism have become part of holiday celebrations. This emphasis contradicts the goal of promoting acceptance of self and others. Costume contests at Halloween create pressure for children; parents feel that they must either buy or make elaborate costumes so that their children will not be poorly judged. At Christmastime many activities focus on what children hope to get and what they did receive for Christmas. This attention paid to the acquisition of possessions reinforces the idea that a person is worth what she or he owns. It also exacerbates the disappointment of children who do not receive highly advertised and expensive gifts and draws attention to the disparity of wealth between children in a given group.

Ironically, Valentine's Day, a celebration of friendship, can also be a time of competitive social comparison among children. While preschoolers may be less conscious of their classroom status, by kindergarten children are often heard comparing the number of cards they received. A teacher recently reported that her first graders had decided that only certain cards were acceptable, making children who gave less expensive or less popular cards the brunt of a lot of teasing. In one preschool, whether or not the cards had envelopes was a source of conflict and hurt feelings among four-year-olds.

As teachers approach any of these holidays, they need to consider carefully the social values embodied in any activity and to be mindful of the fact that the children are exposed to a lot of holiday-related products in stores and on the media. Classroom celebrations can challenge this perspective by stressing nonmaterial expressions of giving and by planning cooperative rather than competitive events. While children may initially object to the absence of more tangible expressions (such as valentines), their interest in experiencing new ways of observing holidays will outweigh their disappointment.

Holidays such as Mother's and Father's Days, which are meant to celebrate the family, reflect sex-role stereotypes and the myth that everyone lives in the traditional nuclear family. Teachers often talk about their discomfort with the preparations that surround these days because there are children in their classes who live in single-parent households, blended families, or foster homes. For this group of children these celebrations only highlight their alienation from the idealized image of the American family. As an alternative, teachers might want to have a "Family Day" celebration in which *all* members of children's households are honored, rather than specific members. In one preschool, this event was the culmination of a week of activities during which children brought in photographs of their families, family members visited the class and did special activities with the children, and children enacted the roles of different family members. The final "Family Day" celebration was a picnic with all the members of the children's families who could come.

Clearly one of the major issues around the observance of holidays in schools is the fact that not all children celebrate them. The Easter Bunny may not mean very much to a Buddhist child. Many of my Jewish contemporaries speak poignantly of their discomfort at singing Christmas carols in school. Many schools have responded to the religious and cultural diversity of their students by banning all holiday celebrations. While this effort to avert these alienating experiences is admirable, simply ignoring the holidays does not help the children who feel isolated because most of the families in their neighborhoods are celebrating an unfamiliar holiday. Nor does it help children who do celebrate the Euro-Christian holidays to understand and respect the fact that their holidays are not universally celebrated and to see their own holidays in a broader cultural context. Finally, the elimination of holidays altogether deprives the children and teachers of valuable learning experiences and pleasurable social occasions. In the following sections ways in which schools can respond positively to this issue will be described.

COMMON THEMES

When holidays are compared across many cultures, it is striking how many parallels exist among them. This phenomenon is not surprising, as most holidays celebrate events that are basic to human survival in the natural environment and the maintenance of social cohesion. Many of these themes and their varied expressions are appealing and meaningful to young children.

The majority of holidays are related to the cycle of seasons and the role seasons play in the provision of food and warmth. Spring is a time of planting festivals and celebrations of rebirth, symbolized by eggs, baby animals, and children. Easter, Tan-go-mo-sekku (Japanese Children's Day), Arinanal (Korean Cherry Blossom Festival), and Tu B'Shevat (Israeli Tree Planting Day) are all examples of these festivals. The celebration of the fruits of the summer harvest is observed with events such as strawberry festivals, artichoke festivals, and the Iroquois Green Corn Festival. Water is another theme that is significant in such summer holidays as the Pueblo Corn Dance and the Hopi Snake Dance, which ask for rain, and the Chinese Dragon Boat Festival and the Kandy Perahera in Sri Lanka, which are celebrated on rivers. Autumn has harvest festivals, including the Chinese Harvest Moon Festival, Thanksgiving, and Sukkoth (Jewish). Winter solstice festivals focus on lighting the darkness and warming the cold, as seen in Christmas, Hanukkah, Divali (India), and the Iroquois Midwinter Festival. *Resources for Creative Teaching in Early Childhood Education* (Flemming, Hamilton, & Hicks, 1977) describes many holidays and related traditions by season. Books that have activities organized by cultural groups are also a good resource for information about holidays. Some examples are *Children Are Children Are Children* (Cole, Haas, Heller, & Weinberger, 1978), *A Pumpkin in a Pear Tree* (Cole, Haas, Weinberger, & Heller, 1976), and *Cultural Awareness for Young Children at the Learning Tree* (McNeill, Allen, Schmidt, & McNeill, 1981).

Hunting was, and still is for many groups, an important source of food and also the cause of much celebration. The stories and songs about hunting turkeys that appear around Thanksgiving are probably vestiges of the role of hunting in past centuries. While it may be difficult for some children to grasp the significance of it, rural children might be able to relate to the various traditions and celebrations related to hunting. Books such as Garfield's *The Tuesday Elephant* and Donna's *Boy of the Masai* describe hunting-related rituals in different countries.

Although not necessarily associated with a particular season, most cultures have some way of marking the beginning of the new year. The Chinese people observe it in the late winter, the Jewish people in the fall (Rosh Hashanah), the Iranians in March (Now Ruz), and the Buddhists in mid-April. Aside from the calendar change, these days are celebrated with a common theme of "out with the old, in with the new" and are associated with such rites as bathing in the river, house cleaning, burning old documents, making resolutions, ending feuds, and purchasing or making new clothes. In all its various forms, this holiday seems to meet a human need to feel a sense of closure and renewal by "making a fresh start."

Most countries commemorate significant events in their national history. These holidays usually honor the country's liberation from some recent or historic oppressor, such as the Fourth of July (U.S.), the Cinco de Mayo (Mexico), or Bastille Day (France). Other holidays recognize the contributions of significant people in this liberation, such as George Washington, Abraham Lincoln, or Martin Luther King in this country. For multicultural education, these holidays pose some interesting dilemmas. While there are clear parallels among them, there are also conflicts in how countries regard them. Liberation might be said to be "in the mind of the beholder." For instance, would Great Britain be likely to celebrate the life of George Washington? Or Spain the victories of Simon Bolivar? Or the United States the Russian Revolution or the fall of the Shah of Iran? Changes in the power structure of a country are often met with mixed international and domestic reactions. Still, the common themes of self-determination, freedom from oppression, and the role of heroes in forging a national identity are common in all societies and can be conveyed in classroom activities. Because of the complexity of the issues involved and the potentially frightening image of violence that almost inevitably accompanies such changes, much of the historical material is more appropriate for primary and older children than for preschoolers. For children who do not have a concept of countries and governments, these holidays have very little concrete meaning, and learning only isolated incidents such as Washington chopping the cherry tree tends to trivialize the meaning of the holiday.

By incorporating holidays in terms of their universal themes, teachers provide occasions for children to experience cultural diversity within the context of human commonalities. Another advantage of this approach is that, in most cases, it offers more concrete and understandable experiences. While young children may simply be confused when one half of the class is suddenly dressed as "Indians" and the other half as "Pilgrims," they can participate in the planting and harvesting of the school garden and commemorate their own harvest with a Thanksgiving feast, eating beneath the Sukkoth, or celebrating Kwanzaa (the African and African American Feast of the First Fruits). In one school, the preschool and kindergarten classes worked together to make a Harvest House by covering the arcade climber (a large, arched structure) with corn stalks, squashes, gourds, straw, and flowers. It became the site for snack, group time, and singing. During free play, children used the Harvest House as a base for enacting harvesting and transporting produce. A harvest feast in the house provided an in-triguing and meaningful alternative to celebrating Thanksgiving.

Sometimes teachers find that observing similar holidays from dif-ferent cultures is difficult because the dates do not coincide. With young children, the actual dates are less relevant than the meaningful ways in which information is presented. Thus teachers may decide to observe several spring traditions in the same period, even though they may not fall at the same place in the actual calendar.

The emphasis on fundamental human needs underlying holidays may also help both parents and children deflect the commercial pres-sure and superficiality that accompany many holidays. It often seems that holidays have been reduced to plastic pumpkins and Easter bun-nies, which are bought by the parents and broken by the children. Furthermore, the glamorization of holidays by the media and com-mercial enterprises also tends to excite unrealistic expectations that easily become disappointment. After months of commercial "hype," the post-Christmas letdown is almost inevitable. The prevalence of depression at holiday times has been well documented. By approach-ing holidays as times when we celebrate the simple truths that we are alive, the sun shines, we have food, and another year has passed may help families use holidays to appreciate their growth and shared ex-periences realistically.

Celebrating the winter solstice is a good way of approaching the nearly universal winter holiday season from this perspective of com-mon human themes. It is presented here as one example among many possibilities.

The ancient Druids and Celts observed the winter solstice by light-ing fires to bring back the sun and worshipping the evergreen trees that, unlike the deciduous trees, did not lose their green leaves in the winter. These traditions have been developed in many ways all around the world, making this season an especially rich time of the year. It is a time when children and teachers can think about darkness and light-ness and the importance of having both. Artwork can include painting and collage activities that draw the children's attention to the equal value of dark and light. Children can invent ways of lighting the dark-ness and participate in activities such as making candles, luminarias, and diyas. (Because of safety considerations, any lighting of candles should be done away from the children and in a controlled setting.) Older children can graph the different lengths of day and night, chart-ing the approach and passing of the solstice. Teachers can talk with the children about the relationship between the world and the sun. Younger children will not be able to grasp the full idea but can understand that, while it is getting darker here, for other people it is getting lighter. Perspective-taking activities can be designed using the world and the sun. Older children, who can grasp the idea that people live in other parts of the world, can make a Swedish Peace Tree, a wooden construction on which children hang clay figures that they have made to represent children from all over the world. The variety of ways that people celebrate this time of the year can be introduced with songs, foods, and dances from many cultures.

RITUAL IN CHILDREN'S LIVES

One of the thorniest issues related to holidays is the fact that many of them are associated with religion. Teachers often feel as though they are in a delicate situation when they incorporate songs and ceremonies that refer to specific religions. The line between appreciating a custom and practicing a religion is not always very clear. Teachers and parents should have some discussion and shared understanding about this issue before holidays are introduced into the classroom.

A related dilemma is that some groups, for example Jehovah's Witnesses, forbid all celebrations of holidays. If children from these groups are members of a school class, it would be useful to ask their parents what criteria they use to define celebration and how they distinguish learning about customs of other groups of people from observing a holiday. Teachers often mention their discomfort when they have to remove a child from the room while the class sings "Happy Birthday" and eats cake in honor of someone's birthday. They feel that they have to make the hard choice between eliminating all celebrations or isolating an individual or small group of children. By exploring these issues in some depth with the children and parents involved, teachers may be able to find some acceptable compromises. Perhaps holiday-related activities can be incorporated into the curriculum in a way that will not violate the sanction against celebrations. Sensitivity and acceptance on the part of the teachers are crucial in these discussions, as parents have often had to defend this position against a great deal of social pressure. Care should be taken to insure that the inclusion of holidays in the curriculum does not increase the alienation of one particular group, as that is obviously contradictory to the overall aims of multicultural education.

One way of clarifying the distinction between cultural appreciation and religious practice is to distinguish ritual and religion. Rituals that are separate from religious practice are part of all of our lives. In early childhood settings many rituals mark the passage of the day and the year. At circle or group time there are usually repeated sequences of particular songs, greetings, discussions of the calendar and the weather, sharing, or relaxation exercises. Snack, nap, lunch, cleanup, outside time, end of the day, and many other transitions are usually accompanied by certain rituals. For adults and children, rituals provide some predictability in each day and a sense of continuity over time.

On a larger scale, holidays serve the same purpose for social groups. Because of their cyclical nature, they convey a sense of permanence in the face of many social vicissitudes. Families will often make sure they always take certain items—special candleholders or dishes, for example—that are associated with their rituals as they move from place to place. Given the fast pace of change in our society and the number of transitions that children experience in their lives, the sense of continuity that rituals, both secular and religious, can provide is increasingly important. In fact, many people are reaching back into their ancestry to revive customs that had been forgotten. By stressing the similarities among all people, we can show children that certain holidays recur every year, not only in their lives but also in many places and among many people. In short, holidays can be used to help children develop a sense of belonging to their families, to their school community, to the larger social environment, and to the history of human endeavor.

The common core of most rituals is the articulation and affirmation of our relationships with the natural and social world. As mentioned earlier, many holidays celebrate phases of gathering food. The activities are often social in nature, (e.g., dancing, singing, feasting, and exchanging gifts and cards) and serve to enhance the feeling of social cohesion and common identity. These relationships, while often celebrated by religions, also can be honored and observed without a religious ceremony.

Finally, because religion has been a rationale for discrimination, oppression, and even genocide, children do acquire many misconceptions and suspicions about other religions. It is often difficult for them to articulate their questions and concerns. Children also sometimes become swept up in the competitiveness that characterizes efforts to recruit new members. A teacher recently reported that two of her kindergarteners recently had a fight about whether Pentacostals or Baptists were better. When there is little variation among the children's religions, books such as Goldman's *Turkey: A Week in Samil's World*, Niclas's *The Flower of Vassiliki*, McDermott's *Arrow to the Sun*, or Levitin's *A Sound to Remember* can be used to show how people worship in many ways. A multicultural approach to holidays can help children see the commonalities among many religious responses to basic human concerns and view the differences with interest and respect rather than mistrust.

HALLOWEEN WITH A MULTICULTURAL PERSPECTIVE

This final section of the chapter will offer particular ways to incorporate holidays into the curriculum, using Halloween as an example and following the guidelines that have been discussed. Briefly, these guidelines are:

1. Introduce children to diverse expressions of common themes and experiences.
2. Base holiday-related celebrations on activities that are meaningful to children and involve them in an active way.
3. Present rituals and other customs in the context of how they reflect the physical and social relationships in that specific culture.

Harvest Themes.   Agriculture and harvest themes are imbedded in many Halloween traditions, such as bobbing for apples, making scarecrows, and harvesting pumpkins. Children can be introduced to a variety of other traditions related to these activities with pictures of other ways that people plant, cultivate, and gather food. A lot of these concepts can be experienced very directly if the school has a garden or can provide transportation to a local farm. Even a window garden can demonstrate some of these processes. Children can learn harvest songs from other countries and look at pictures showing all the ways in which people harvest, from highly mechanized fields to manually worked garden plots.

Human Representations.   Making jack-o'-lanterns is similar to other cultures' ways of transforming fruits and vegetables into human figures. In Israel, children make faces on oranges; several groups of Native Americans make cornhusk dolls; in New England, withered apples have been used to depict faces. Children may invent other possibilities and temporarily augment the school doll collection with their own "vegetable people" made from squashes, nuts, corncobs, and beets. To avoid wasting food, these creations can be cooked and eaten after children have had a chance to play with them.

Costumes. One of the major Halloween experiences in this country is costuming. As mentioned previously, this activity has been co-opted by commercial enterprises that pressure children to look like media stars and superheroes. Teachers may be able to counteract this, however, by showing children many different ways in which people disguise themselves throughout the world and by providing unusual materials to stimulate experimentation. This activity also provides younger children with a chance to explore the question of "Who am I?" "Am I the same person if I look different in this costume?" Using polaroid photographs and mirrors, teachers can stimulate a lot of exploration of this boundary between self and costume.

Masks also are associated with costuming and disguise. Here again is a custom that is found in numerous societies and executed with a great array of materials and styles. Using photographs, drawings, and actual masks, teachers can encourage children to make masks in a variety of ways and to identify with the people that they see making and wearing masks. Placing masks and costumes in a familiar context (i.e., Halloween) may help children to appreciate these arts as they are practiced in different places.

The children in one kindergarten were concerned about looking like TV characters for Halloween. The teachers wanted to see if they could interest the children in other possibilities. They took slides of book and magazine photographs of many different masks. As they showed them to the children, they asked them to think about what the masks might be representing. In a subsequent mask-making activity, the children experimented with a lot of different materials and talked about the masks that they had seen and what their masks might be. Television characters had, for the moment, been set aside.

The Trickster. Another theme that is related to Halloween is that of the trickster. Young children often go around saying "trick or treat" without really knowing what it means. Halloween is a good time to introduce children to some of the folktales about tricksters, who are common to many folk traditions. They provide good examples of being clever and fooling people without being destructive and may help children distinguish between tricks and vandalism. Several trickster stories have been rewritten for young children. McDermott's *Anansi the Spider*, Martin's *Raven-Who-Sets-Things-Right*, the Mantis Tales of the Kalahari Desert people in the Perkinses' *I Saw You from Afar*, and Zimmerman's *Yetta the Trickster* are just a few of the many possibilities.

Fooling people requires some understanding of what they are thinking. As discussed in chapter 2, this capability is also necessary for seeing perspectives of other groups of people. Having children plan and perhaps try some tricks will draw their attention to the existence of multiple points of view. Most preschool children will be able to think only of very concrete situations, such as hiding or donning a disguise; primary-school children, who can more accurately assess others' thoughts, may be able to think of more subtle and complicated tricks.

Scary Things.   While children are not likely to understand the idea of "wandering souls" that is the origin of Halloween, they do become involved in the idea of being scared and scaring others. Unfortunately, common symbols such as cats, witches, and goblins are usually made with black materials, which reinforce the negative associations with that color. Teachers might counteract this custom by making scary faces on other colors and nonscary ones on dark colors. In discussions about being scared, children learn about each other and have a chance to identify with their classmates. Books such as *A Book of Scary Things* (Showers) might be used to stimulate discussion and reassure children about fears. Looking at photographs of unfamiliar people who are scared provides evidence that all people share common feelings. People all over the world have found ways of alleviating their fears through performing rituals, creating social cohesion, and offering explanations. Related dances, songs, and rituals might help children to think of ways of reducing their own fears.

Going from House to House.   Another custom that is associated with Halloween is going from house to house for treats. It is the one time during the year that people open up their houses to neighborhood children. Unfortunately, recent fears of poisoning and other violence have made this tradition less popular. It is a sad statement about our society that this time-honored custom—which is part of many traditions such as "souling," caroling, wassailing, the Mereth Lwyd (Welsh), and Purim (Jewish)—cannot be continued. Even if children are not trick-or-treating in your particular community, the class may be able to visit other classrooms or local businesses, wearing a variety of costumes that reflect the diversity of the tradition. These visits are also a way of making children more aware and appreciative of the different people who live and work in their neighborhood.

Symbols.   Primary-grade children might enjoy tracing the origins of Halloween symbols, which have evolved from numerous cultures as disparate as the Celts, Egyptians, and French. *Witches, Pumpkins and Grinning Ghosts* (Barth, 1972) provides a starting point for these investigations and demonstrates that Halloween is a truly multicultural holiday.

In sum, there are numerous traditions reflected in Halloween that provide ways of extending children's activities beyond the symbols of witches and pumpkins. With the inclusion of less familiar but related traditions, Halloween can enrich the curriculum and present occasions for children to experience human similarities and cultural differences concretely in a meaningful context. Other holidays offer equally rich possibilities for expanding children's and teachers' experiences.

6 Constructing Physical Knowledge in a Multicultural Context

At first glance, children's construction of physical knowledge and logico-mathematical relationships might appear to be misplaced in a book about children's understanding of human diversity. As stated previously, however, a multicultural perspective influences all teaching decisions, and children's interactions with the physical environment are no exception. First, one of the goals of multicultural education is to teach children in ways that are most appropriate for their respective backgrounds. Cultural and class influences on relationships between people and their physical world must be considered when making curriculum adaptations for children. Second, to gain an appreciation of other lifestyles, children need to understand the rationale for why people might do familiar tasks in unfamiliar ways. With a focus on physical knowledge, children can experience cultural and occupational variations in a meaningful and concrete context. Third, experiencing the diverse ways that people make and use common materials enhances children's knowledge of physical properties and relationships.

CHILDREN'S ACQUISITION OF PHYSICAL KNOWLEDGE

According to Piaget, children learn about the nature of physical properties through observing the effects of their actions on different kinds of objects. For instance, they learn about which kinds of objects float and which ones sink by placing numerous objects in water. Also through their own actions on objects, children construct temporal and spatial relationships and logico-mathematical relationships such as same/different, means/ends, more/less. As children walk, run, and hop around a room, they are learning about how time and space relate, how different means can be used to cover a certain distance, and how hopping and running are distinct yet similar motions. As children interact with a variety of materials, they increasingly differentiate physical properties and further elaborate these relationships.

I remember one three-year-old who threw a piece of tissue paper up in the air and gasped with surprise as it fluttered slowly down. For fifteen minutes, he tossed the paper in the air with a variety of motions and speed and watched with fascination as it still floated down. Here the child was focusing on the physical properties of paper, which were violating his expectations of how things fall through the air. Although he was familiar with paper in many ways (through folding, cutting, drawing, and painting), its aerodynamic qualities were new to him. With his actions, he was also expanding his knowledge of relationships. The paper was simultaneously like and unlike other objects that he had tossed. It descended as did balls and other more compact objects, but it floated down very slowly. He kept testing the degree of sameness and difference by experimenting with various tosses to see if any of them would make the paper fall in the way that he expected. His attempts reflected a consciousness of his own actions as he both varied them and observed their results. It is possible that his assumptions about temporal and spatial relationships were also clarified by this event. Previously, he may not have consciously noticed how quickly objects traveled over the space between his toss and the floor. When his actions with the paper did not result in the customary responses, however, he may have become more aware of his previous expectations.

This spontaneous experiment illustrates how unexpected consequences can heighten children's awareness of and interactions with their physical environment. Cognitively oriented curriculum developers (e.g., Forman & Hill, 1983) have suggested many ways of drawing children's attention to physical properties and relationships by "throwing them a curve." For example, children can be given paintbrushes that have handles that are bent at several angles so that the paint does not appear at the point where the child is aiming. This discrepancy forces the child to pay more attention to the spatial relationship between the tip of the brush and his or her own hand. As will be seen in this chapter, objects and actions taken from a variety of cultural origins can provide a similar but more naturally occurring source of novelty and surprise.

LEARNING ABOUT THE PHYSICAL ENVIRONMENT IN A SOCIAL CONTEXT

All of our interactions with the physical world occur in a social context that includes cultural values, occupational interests, and socioeconomic constraints. These differences influence our perceptions of the physical world; our ideas about the relationship of people and nature; and our notions of time, space, and causality. A classic example is the fact that the Innuit (Eskimo) people have fifty different words in their language for the various conditions related to snow. Because we are so car oriented most Americans only want to know "How many inches?" and "When will it stop?" Our main concern is getting rid of the snow so that we can move on cleared roads, whereas the Innuit people traditionally consider how to move on it and through it. We, on the other hand, have at least fifty words to describe models of cars. The two groups need and therefore see different information.

Occupational background also influences perception. For example, when nonpainters have to select colors of house paint, they frequently claim that they cannot see the distinctions among the hues, tones, and colors, differences that must be quite apparent to people who work with paint and colors all the time. Likewise, car mechanics hear subtle changes in motor sounds that are inaudible to most drivers.

Relationships between people and the natural environment also reflect cultural values and socioeconomic and occupational needs. In the United States the "conquering of nature" is generally extolled as a major force in achieving our industrial and economic power. Toys such as dump trucks, earthmovers, and other construction-related objects generally reflect this point of view. Most mainstream American children spend a lot of time in block play and sandboxes designing ways to expedite the rapid transit of all kinds of vehicles and toy "people" across space. In contrast, this "conquering" of the land has disrupted the lifestyles and sources of livelihood for most Native American people, who believe in living in harmony with nature. A European American teacher, who had just started a job in a Navajo school, was chagrined when a child, who was picking flowers under her supervision, was severely reprimanded by an older woman for not respecting the flowers. In a somewhat reversed situation, a teacher who was committed to environmentalist causes found that the parents of her students, many of whom worked at a local nuclear power plant, thought that her ideas were "foolish, radical, and elitist." In rural areas, recent arrivals from middle-class urban life often complain about their working-class "native" neighbors' penchant for "junky old cars" and noisy snowmobiles. One group, with their ample incomes, has the leisure to appreciate the aesthetics of their surroundings and wants the country-side to be pristine and quiet. The other, with less financial security and a more utilitarian perspective, sees engines, spare parts, and tinkering as a way to survive their isolation and lack of resources.

Spatial, temporal, and quantitative relationships also develop in a cultural context. In the United States and most other industrialized countries, time, space, and value are measured by standard units such as hours, feet, and dollars. In traditional societies, they are likely to be measured in a more relative and continuous fashion and within the context of the natural cycle of the day or year and immediate human needs. While young children are not likely to be concerned about whether or not someone is "on time" or if two exchanged toys have the same dollar value, at an unconscious level they are learning these different orientations to time, space, and value (Longstreet, 1978).

Two different views of the relationship between time and value are illustrated in the following examples from children's stories. In *Mike Mulligan's Steam Shovel* (Burton), the protagonists, who are a European American man and a machine, are in a race against time to finish making a cellar within a designated number of hours. If they succeed, they will be rewarded. In the Navajo story of *Annie and the Old One* (Miles), the completion of the blanket means that Annie's grandmother will die. When the granddaughter tries to postpone that time, the grandmother admonishes her for trying to interfere with the natural rhythms of life and death.

All of us see the physical world and integrate that information through lenses that reflect our racial, cultural, class, and individual experiences. As a result, there are some cross-cultural differences in the ways people organize, classify, and assimilate information about their environments (Ramirez, Castenada, & Herold, 1974). As a result, teachers and children may not necessarily see the physical world in the same way and may often make what seem to be inexplicable responses to certain physical phenomena. Teachers should be aware of the types of physical environments that children have known, the objects that are familiar to them, and the ways that they have interacted with them, in order to understand how children might perceive physical phenomena. They also should be aware of how people in the community understand their relationship to time and space and should consider how these perceptions might affect children's reactions to classroom structures and routines. For instance, if children live in an environment where people structure time by the movement of the sun and the length of tasks, teachers might avoid using "clock-time" as a structuring device. For these children memorizing the meaning of different positions of the hands on a clock may be more difficult because they do not have experience with this way of thinking. Eventually it will be important for these children to be able to function according to hours and minutes when they need to, but teachers cannot assume that they enter with a readiness to learn about clocks and unitized time. This kind of awareness will help teachers to structure classrooms and design learning experiences in ways that are most appropriate for their particular groups of children.

EXPANDING CHILDREN'S PHYSICAL KNOWLEDGE WITH DIVERSE EXPERIENCES

There are many interactions with the physical environment that are universal. We all breathe air, drink water, eat food, and protect ourselves from climatic extremes with shelter and clothing. People have worked with environmental assets and constraints to develop numerous ways of meeting human needs. For example, most people cook food; however, they do it on open fires, electric stoves, clay stoves, indoors, outdoors, in pans, on rocks, in steaming pits, on drying racks, and with microwaves. There is a universal end, and many diverse means of achieving it. Likewise, similar resources are used by many groups, but how they are used varies widely. Cloth is found in most societies yet is made, colored, printed, draped, sewn, and used in many different ways. Some variations reflect environmental constraints (e.g., the need to dress for maximum warmth), and some have evolved as aesthetic or customary preferences (e.g., dark business suits as opposed to brightly printed dashikis).

Children's ideas about physical properties and relationships are challenged and expanded by experiencing some of these novel ways of solving familiar problems. For instance, when children use chopsticks to feed themselves they not only learn that people eat in different ways but they also pay close attention to the means/ends relationships of moving food from plate to mouth and making two separate things work as one food lifter. As they try to grasp the food, they differentiate the physical properties of texture, weight, and size of food morsels.

Conversely, exploring physical properties and relationships is an effective context for learning about diversity. As children engage in interactions with the physical environment, they learn about similarities and differences among people in concrete and meaningful ways. Traditions and social conventions that are often assumed to be arbitrary and "wrong" can be seen from a more practical point of view. For instance, in some parts of the world, people eat from large leaves, just as we generally eat from plates (e.g., Bergman, 1959). If children learn about this custom in the context of available materials (i.e., large leaves) and environmental constraints (i.e., little water for washing), they may be able to see it as a sensible means of achieving a familiar end. If, on the other hand, they are simply told that "Some people in India eat from banana leaves," they will probably assume that the people are strange. By experiencing diversity during the course of exploring physical properties and relationships, children are less likely to interpret the differences as wrong and inferior, but rather as practical and intriguing alternatives.

In the remainder of this chapter, a few examples of how teachers can facilitate simultaneously children's construction of physical knowledge and appreciation of cultural diversity will be discussed in more detail. These specific suggestions are not recipes but rather illustrations of how themes that reflect children's physical worlds can be enriched with a multicultural orientation. For the curriculum to be meaningful to children, it should be developed from questions and ideas that they themselves present (Kamii & Devries, 1977). The principles illustrated here can be applied to any topic that children want to explore. The possibilities are limitless, and I hope that the examples here will encourage teachers to create their own themes in ways that are most appropriate to their particular children.

The following descriptions focus primarily on children's interactions with physical materials. Many of the activities also have the potential for fostering social interactions, but specific observations and suggestions about this area of development will be postponed until chapter 7.

CURRICULUM THEMES

Food

The topic of food and the ways that it is grown, gathered, prepared, and eaten provide endless possibilities for children to interact with their physical environment in the context of cultural diversity. The following example uses pasta as a central idea.

Activities with Pasta. Because of its varied properties, its appeal to children, and its place in the cuisine of many cultures, pasta offers many possibilities as a theme for expanding children's ideas about food.

- One of the interesting things about pasta is that it comes in a variety of shapes and sizes. Teachers can have children think about the physical properties and spatial relationships by having them examine different kinds of pasta. Preschoolers could match shapes and lengths and sort by similarities and differences. In the primary grades, these variations could be used to introduce some basic geometric principles related to area, angles, and shapes.
- Cooking the pasta draws attention to temporal relationships and physical change. Related activities also can include some material about different ways that people cook.
- Serving pasta with different sauces highlights similarities and differences in people's tastes. There are many different kinds of sauces found in cookbooks. As children eat, they can talk about how their families prepare pasta dishes and compare the differences within their own group.
- Photographs of many different people making and eating pasta in a variety of ways and the introduction of terms (e.g., vermicelli and lasagna) can further extend children's thinking about similarities and differences.
- If a pasta maker is available, then children might experiment with different dough recipes and shapes and sizes of pasta. As they measure and mix ingredients and put the pasta through the machine, they will be thinking in terms of quantitative, temporal, spatial, and means/ends relationships, as well as focusing on the physical properties and changes of the pasta itself.
- A trip to a local pasta factory would enable children to see and meet workers doing a familiar activity. If there is no pasta factory, then a trip to another place that makes food, such as a bakery, might offer a reasonable substitute.
- The children's ideas about pasta could be further expanded by introducing them to other types of noodles, such as Chinese rice noodles, Japanese ramen, or Hungarian egg noodles. While different nationalities may not be meaningful to children, they can compare texture and taste and concretely experience the diverse ways in which people prepare and eat this common kind of food.

Activities with Other Foods.   The same combination of exploring physical phenomena and cultural diversity can be applied to numerous food items such as rice, vegetables, fruits, milk, breads, and so forth. A student teacher recently implemented a two-month project on beans with her second graders, in which they learned about many varieties of beans, compared different farming practices, and experimented with numerous ways of preparing beans.

If teachers do not want to get involved in a lot of cooking, they might be able to arrange for new foods to be introduced at snack or lunch. For example, serving many kinds of breads—such as tortillas, corn bread, pita bread, and French bread—provides an opportunity to compare shapes, textures, and taste. These direct physical experiences can be enriched with photographs of people making and eating different kinds of bread and the introduction of the words for *bread* in different languages.

Water

Water is attractive to all young children, from preschoolers at the water table to eight-year-olds building dams in a stream. As children experiment with transporting, storing, and distributing water, they are exploring its weight, its force of movement, and the ways it changes as it is poured into different containers.

Activities About the Conservation of Water. Because the relative plenty or scarcity of water affects the ways it is used by different groups of people, the conservation of water is a topic that provides a meaningful context for studying ways that people live.

- Children cannot really understand the basic survival need for water, but teachers might want to ask them what would happen if we had no water. As they consider all the things that they could not do if there were no water, they may begin to see how important it is. If children have a hard time imagining life without water, then they can be asked to think of all the things that they do that involve water.
- When children seem to have some understanding of the importance of water in their daily lives, they can be introduced to the idea that there are many ways of conserving and moving water.
- Teachers might pose physical problems for children, such as creating a water "well" in the sand table and challenging children to figure out how to distribute the water to their various projects. Their solutions can be compared with photographs of different irrigation and transportation systems.
- Teachers can remove the "sink" from the housekeeping corner and have the children think of how they could bring the water from the "well" to the house. Containers (empty!) and photographs showing

the different ways that people carry water on their heads, backs, and shoulders can be introduced to promote children's experimentation as they attempt to solve this logistical problem.

- In warm weather, the outside sandbox and wading pool can be used to invent ways of storing water and using it for irrigation.
- As children experiment with water, photographs of different groups of people doing similar things in a variety of countries and under a number of environmental conditions can be introduced to the children. Books such as Bernheim and Bernheim's *A Week in Ava's World*, Clark's *In My Mother's House*, and Niclas's *The Flower of Vassiliki* show many different ways of carrying, storing, and using water.
- With older children, teachers might pose more hypothetical problems, such as, "If you lived in a place where water is very scarce and you did not want the rainwater to dry up, what are some ways that you could store it?" Children could compare their solutions with those in books, such as Clark's *The Desert People*, that depict life in areas where conservation of water is a major concern.

All of these activities draw children's attention to the physical properties of water, such as its fluidity, its weight, its absorption, and its effect on sand and dirt. The storage and transportation of water by the many ways described involves means/ends, quantitative, temporal, and spatial relationships.

Washing. Another water-related activity that is also universal is washing. Children can understand the labor involved in a job they see being done on a regular basis in their own homes.

- A trip to a laundromat might be of interest, even to children whose parents all own their own washing machines. In addition to watching the operation of the machines, children who do have these kinds of appliances at home can consider the fact that not all people have that convenience. The trip could be preceded by some discussion about how clothes would get clean if your house did not have a washing machine and dryer. Children whose parents regularly patronize a laundromat can describe what their parents do at the laundromat, how they help their parents, and what the different machines do.
- Back at the school, the children can wash doll clothes and in the process try some other "washing machines" such as scrub boards or two stones that can be used to pound the clothes. *Chendru* (Berg-

man) has some photographs of both boys and girls washing clothes by beating them on rocks.

- Washing dishes can be embellished with a variety of "tools" such as sponges, steel wool, sand, and roots. Teachers could challenge children by giving them a very small amount of water to use in their washing, to see what ways they find to use it most efficiently.
- Older children could try "inventing" different machines for using water most efficiently.
- Drying is another process that requires various problem-solving skills. Children can experiment with squeezing, wringing, pounding, and shaking the wet clothes.
- Photographs of people all over the world washing clothes and dishes in many environments and with a variety of machines and tools can be used to support the children's efforts at solving some of the problems that they encounter.
- Older children might be challenged to think of alternatives that would reduce the amount of washing (such as the use of banana leaves for plates, as discussed earlier).

One cautionary note when doing activities related to washing is to be sure not to make disparaging remarks about dirt and dirty things. Often the negative associations with dirt heighten children's aversion to people who live in poverty and water-scarce regions. It is better to draw children's attention to the fact that most people use water to wash, but that not everyone has the available water and machines that many families in this country enjoy. In other words, the states of "dirty" and "clean" should be considered in the context of human similarities and the availability of natural and mechanical resources.

These activities involve physical change, means/ends, and temporal relationships and the notions of quantity and similarities and differences. By having them use and observe a variety of methods, teachers can heighten children's awareness of the physical changes that are involved in the simple task of washing.

Shelter

Construction of shelters—from the tents that the Bedouins still use, to the traditional Innuit igloos, to the steel-girded skyscrapers of international urban life—is another source of interest for young children.

Field Trips to Construction Sites.   Construction sites, from small home additions to major civic projects, are an endless source of fascination for children. They enjoy watching adults work with machines and the physical transformations that occur during the construction. Efforts should be made to find a site with a work force that is integrated by both gender and race, in order to reinforce the notion that all people can do different kinds of jobs and work together successfully.

- Preparation for a trip can include thinking about many ways that people build and some discussion of the type of building that the children will be seeing on the trip. For primary children, teachers can prepare a list of questions and activities on a trip board, to give children a specific focus while on the visit.
- Upon return to the school, children can use blocks, art materials, and woodworking materials to represent some of the sights that they have seen. Polaroid pictures of the trip may further inspire their efforts.
- Teachers and children can talk and write stories about different workers on the site and the nature of their jobs and the tools that they used. Children can experiment with simplified and safe versions of tools to move, construct, and secure building materials.

Activities Involving Unfamiliar Shelters.   Visits to more traditional dwellings, such as pueblos and log cabins that have historical importance to different groups in this country, are harder to arrange. Instead, teachers may be able to devise classroom activities that will accomplish the purpose.

- Photographs, models, and contemporary equivalents (e.g., camping tents) can be used to demonstrate the fact that people construct their homes with many different materials and tools.
- Large pieces of material and various kinds of supports (e.g., room dividers, A-frame climbers) can be provided to stimulate children's attempts to make different kinds of tents. Large, graduated cartons can be used to replicate pueblo dwellings. Lincoln Logs often generate speculation about how people build houses out of "trees."
- Posing problems to children about how to adapt houses for different climatic conditions enables them to focus more on the physical properties of different building materials and the structural needs of the houses. These discussions introduce unfamiliar dwellings in a practical context. Books such as *In My Mother's House* (Clark), *The Drums Speak* (Bernheim & Bernheim), and *Growing Up Masai*

(Shachtman), which show the many ways that people have adapted to different environmental constraints, further stimulate children's thinking about similarities and differences among houses.

• Houses that move, such as houseboats and mobile homes, are also interesting to children. They could attempt to construct dwellings that might be moved in different environments.

All of these construction projects involve elementary principles of physics such as balance, relative weight and size, and various ways of supporting structures. Spatial relations will be more evident to children as they both construct and "live in" dwellings of different sizes and materials. The variety of physical properties of materials, from flexible cloth to rigid cardboard or blocks, will also be evident as children construct and compare their houses.

Weather and Seasons

Weather and seasons have a considerable impact on children's daily lives. In many parts of the country, the advent of winter is heralded by the addition of snowsuits, boots, and mittens to children's daily routines. In other parts of the country, children and teachers have to contend with weeks of rainy weather. In warmer weather, when children and teachers want to keep cool and refreshed, water play offers a new kind of enjoyment and the tree in the yard becomes valued for the shade that it provides. Weather changes are universal phenomena that all people respond to. While the climate varies from place to place, all people have found ways of protecting themselves from the extremes and taking advantage of the possibilities of different weather conditions. The following ideas about incorporating the weather into the curriculum can also be integrated with various holiday observances.

The children's responses to different weather conditions will focus their attention on various physical properties. When concerned about protection from extreme temperatures, children notice which materials are warmer or cooler than others. Seasonal changes are good times to focus on temporal relationships. As children try to find protection from the sun, the means/ends relationship between light and heat and shade and coolness will also be more evident. The weight of different objects and materials and spatial relationships will be prominent when children look at the effect of wind on their kites and clothing. Folktales about the weather further stimulate children's thinking about the possible cause and effects of weather changes.

Activities About Dressing for Different Weather Conditions. Because young children are still mastering the skills of dressing, the change of clothing for different weather conditions is of great interest to them. Umbrellas, boots, raincoats, and mittens are frequent topics of children's conversations. Teachers can use this interest to help children consider the different ways in which people react to certain types of weather.

- On hot days, children can try on many different hats and other head covers to experiment with different ways of keeping the sun off their heads.
- Books such as *Playtime in Africa* (Sutherland), which shows people using umbrellas to keep the sun off their heads, can be read in conjunction with this activity. Since most children in this country think of umbrellas in terms of protection from rain, this novel use might expand their ideas about the properties and functions of umbrellas.
- Children can also experiment with different kinds of loose clothing, to experience the fact that more clothes can sometimes make one feel cooler—an experience that is quite mystifying to most children in this country of shorts and sleeveless shirts.
- Photographs of people in different regions wearing various clothing in response to certain conditions will be more meaningful to children who have experimented with a variety of different coverings. Books such as *Ali and the Camel* (Yahya & Jones), which illustrates how animals and people adapt to desert conditions, provide a more personal view of the ways that people and animals live in different environments.

Activities About Wind. Another aspect of weather that children often notice and react to is the wind. They can feel it and see its concrete effect on many objects. People all over the world use, contend with, or play with the wind; windmills, kites, gliders, and sailboats show up in many different forms.

- Children can blow through straws in trying to move different objects on land and on water, to see which objects and which surfaces offer more or less resistance.
- Kites are a popular activity and can be made in many styles that demonstrate different aerodynamic properties as well as illustrate a variety of cultural symbols. Children can compare their efforts with photographs of wind-propelled objects that show up in different regions and countries.

- In a reverse situation, children can try to find ways of keeping things from blowing away when there is wind coming through a window. Photographs can be used to show ways that people have learned to keep the wind from blowing their homes and belongings away, such as the stones on the roofs of the chalets in the Alps.
- In areas of this country where there are frequent tornadoes or hurricanes, children may have many stories from their own experiences about how their individual families contend with the extreme wind conditions.
- Older children can design and make models of towns and houses or clothing that would be suitable in regions with a lot of wind, where securing objects and harnessing the wind would be the priorities. They can do the same for areas with little wind, where smog and accumulated debris might be problems.

Folktales and Legends About Weather. Another way that a multicultural perspective can be incorporated into the experience of the weather is to introduce the children to the many folktales and legends about weather.

- Since young children generally interpret events from their own perspectives, they often have very animistic explanations for the weather (e.g., the sky is crying when it rains, or the sun sets because it is tired). Stories such as *Arrow to the Sun* (McDermott) and *The Old North Wind* (LaFontaine), where the agents of weather are personified, fit well with the children's ideas about the weather and the seasons. While teachers may have some misgivings about teaching children this "wrong" information and perhaps reinforcing some of their animistic thinking, these tales are more meaningful to the children than complex meteorological explanations. After viewing a demonstration of how rain is made with steam and ice cubes, one child told her mother, "Heavenly Father doesn't make the rain, I learned to make it at school" (Kamii & Devries, 1977, p. 401). Stories that explain the weather in ways that are closer to how children think may be a more appropriate challenge to their animistic assumptions.
- Related to folktales and legends about weather are weather-oriented rituals. From the "no school" anticipation of contemporary American children to ancient rituals designed to influence the deities that controlled the weather, people have many traditional responses to weather changes. One group of preschoolers learned a Wampanoag rain dance and subsequently enjoyed dancing to both bring the rain and make it go away. What seemed to intrigue them the most was

that it was a dance about the rain. They then went on to make up a sun dance and a snow dance. The idea of dancing to the weather was appealing and helped them to express concretely their observations and feelings about different weather conditions.

The Arts

People all over the world adorn themselves, their houses, and their communities. Often these works represent some historical event or personal experience (e.g., a statue of a famous person or a painting of a favorite place). Other times they express a feeling about or aesthetic pleasure in the form and texture of a particular material (e.g., "abstract art"; flower arranging, or driftwood sculpture). Most of the art forms that have evolved are replicated in simplified form in the art curriculum of early childhood education. Like adult artisans, children use these activities to represent their experiences and to express their feelings. Children can be actively involved in crafts that extend over many cultures and many historical periods. Through photographs, examples, and a variety of materials and tools, children can see their own work in this broader context.

Art activities usually involve some physical transformations, such as covering the paper with paint; changing the shape of a ball of clay; attaching several separate materials together by pasting, taping, stapling, nailing, or weaving; or changing the shape or quantity of pieces of paper by cutting. Some of these transformations are reversible, such as shaping the ball of clay and folding the paper; others are irreversible, such as painting, pasting, and cutting. As they experiment with different art media, children differentiate between various physical properties and the ways that they interact. For instance, they become aware that paint will not wash off of paper, although it can be removed from one's hands and the surface of the table. They experience changes in size, weight, and spatial relationships as they enlarge projects by taping and pasting and reduce them by cutting and folding.

Children's awareness of some of these transformations can be sharpened by having them experience the different ways in which people work with similar materials all over the world. The challenge in presenting this information to children is to find ways of replicating highly skilled crafts at a level that enables them to try new things with a minimum of frustration. The simplest way is to let them use tools and materials that are familiar yet not quite the same as ones to which they are accustomed.

Painting Activities. From the early cave paintings to current abstract art, people have invented numerous ways of coloring almost any surface.

- There are many different ways of applying paints. Chinese calligraphy brushes and handmade brushes constructed from grasses, sponges, or twigs will highlight differences in the amount of paint brushes will hold and the kinds of strokes they leave on the paper.
- Painting on varied surfaces such as rice paper, clay, cloth, wood, and one's own skin demonstrates the range of interactions between paints and surfaces.

Weaving Activities. Weaving appears throughout the world. People have developed numerous methods of combining fibers into cloth and baskets, whether it be wool, cotton, burlap, hemp, silk, or flax. As they weave, children notice the flexibility of different materials, the sequence of passing the woof over and under the warp, and the fact that many pieces become one.

- Young children can learn about the basic process of weaving with games like "Bluebird, bluebird through my window" or "over, under" obstacle courses.
- Large-scale weaving is probably most suitable for preschoolers. These activities can include weaving different materials such as cloth, grasses, flowers, and wires in and out of cyclone fences in the yard.
- Slightly older children (kindergarteners and up) can easily handle straw looms, "God's Eyes," small frame looms, inkle looms, and can make simple baskets.
- Samples of different kinds of weaving and photographs of people weaving using all kinds of looms provide children with an opportunity to see their own efforts in a broader context.

Cloth-Dyeing Activities. Dyeing cloth is another common activity that has spawned numerous techniques and types of designs.

- Young children can easily learn how to do tie-dyeing and dip-dyeing. The advantage of these techniques is that the end product is always somewhat unexpected, as the folded or tied material reveals a large symmetrical design that children do not anticipate. Teachers can encourage children to think about spatial relationships by having them predict what they think will happen before they "open" the dyed cloth. Since it does not require the dexterity and time needed to fasten on rubber bands or tie strings, dip-dyeing especially permits a great deal of experimentation with folding and color mixing.

• Older children are able to do simple batiking, which involves not only the color transformation but also the physical change in wax and the interactions among wax, cloth, and dye.

• Samples and photographs that show various methods of dyeing cloth provide both a cultural context for these activities and some encouragement for inventing and trying new techniques.

Jewelry Activities.   Personal adornments of all kinds are made with many materials among different groups of people. Children notice and enjoy jewelry and other decorations. When I have asked children to describe photographs of people, they often comment on jewelry, hair ribbons, and beads, even though they may be only faintly visible in the photograph. The jewelry available in the dress-up props is very popular.

Making and wearing jewelry enhances physical knowledge in several respects. The making process usually involves the challenge of attaching things together, whether it is putting beads and bottle caps on a string or finding ways of holding feathers and ribbons in one's hair. Children often discover the limits of paste in terms of attaching heavy and hanging objects; the process of stringing involves size relationships between hole and string; the difference between stiff and flexible also becomes apparent as children try to feed strings through objects with holes; the spatial relationship between a straight length of string and the circumference of an ankle or wrist also becomes a focus of attention. In short, the process of combining different materials to make products that can then be attached to one's person allows children to work with many different physical properties and to solve problems related to the ways in which materials interact.

• Samples and photographs of different kinds of jewelry made of a variety of materials (e.g., shells, seeds, stones, recycled industrial material, and bones) challenge the usual assumption that jewelry is made of precious metals.

• Photographs of men wearing jewelry (e.g., in Shachtman's *Growing Up Masai,*) as is common in some cultures, may expand children's ideas of who can wear it.

• While it probably is not feasible for children to try on authentic headpieces and jewelry, they can think about what it would feel like to wear certain kinds of adornments by moving as though they were wearing a particular decoration that is shown in a picture.

- One advantage of making adornments that can be worn is that the learning continues long after the object has been made. When children wear jewelry, either their own creations or those provided in the role play collection, they usually "play" with the ways in which they can make the jewelry swing, dangle, and twirl. The sensation of different weights on various parts of their bodies makes them more conscious of their own motions and the separate yet related movements of the jewelry. Teachers can challenge children to find new ways of using their bodies in this respect by suggesting that they do things such as make their necklaces move without using their hands or walk so that their anklets do not make any sound at all.

Music and Movement Activities.   Music offers children the opportunity to explore many physical phenomena, such as pitch, volume, and tempo. By singing and using musical instruments, children learn what vocal and motor actions create different sounds. They also learn sequencing, as songs usually have repeated cycles of verse and chorus, often accompanied with particular motions. As mentioned in chapter 4, music is a common yet varied activity in virtually all cultures. The variety is relatively accessible to teachers and children, as there are numerous recordings and songbooks from many cultures.

- Children can learn songs using unfamiliar intervals, melodies, and words and experiment with different ways of projecting their voices as they imitate all kinds of chants, calls, and songs. Young children also readily learn new words and enjoy the feel and sound of them as they sing in other languages.
- When dancing to different kinds of music, children can experiment with a range of tone sequences and rhythms. Jewelry and long pieces of material can be used by children to accentuate their motions and to experiment with the ways that they can make other objects move.
- Drawing to music enhances children's awareness of different rhythms and tones.
- While preschool children cannot learn very complicated dances, those in kindergarten and primary grades are able to master a variety of folk dances. In one first grade, a teacher had some sixth-grade children teach her class several Portuguese dances.
- With or without music, children experience the feeling of different environments by moving through a variety of imaginary spaces. Us-

ing photographs and verbal descriptions, teachers can challenge children to move as though they are on a sandy desert, a busy street corner, on top of a mountain, or in a small room with lots of people. They can experience with their bodies and actions the ways that space influences movement.

- Throughout the day, teachers can call children's attention to the ways that carrying things and wearing different kinds of clothing affect their gait, balance, and posture. If they are transporting dolls in cradleboards or in slings on their hips or pretending to bear water on their heads, then they are experimenting with the ways that they hold and move their bodies to support the extra bulk and weight. As they physically adjust, they are experiencing interactions among motion, weight, and balance. Likewise, wearing different clothing and shoes (e.g., saris, fishing boots) requires adjustment in their posture and movement.

General Notes on Art and Music Activities.   When engaged in art and music activities, children's sense that they are participating in activities done by children and adults all over the world can be heightened by showing them samples of work and photographs of artisans and performers from many places. When showing these illustrations to the children, teachers want to make sure that the children not see them as "models." If a medium is unfamiliar, it is better if children initially explore it on their own. After children have begun to experiment themselves and seem to be able to express their own ideas, then the samples and photographs can be used to stimulate their ideas and inventions. In order to diminish children's attempts to simply imitate, the samples and photographs can be introduced with comments such as "There are many ways of working with clay. Here are some pictures of people doing different things with clay, just as Judy and Rosy are making different kinds of bowls." Likewise, when introducing unfamiliar music, teachers can encourage children to experiment with many ways of moving before learning specific steps or sequences of movements.

The possibilities for incorporating a diversity of cultural experiences into the arts are virtually limitless. All of these media have the potential to inspire experimentation with the physical properties of pitch, rhythm, volume, form, color, texture, and weight. As children are interacting with these materials and sounds, they are also constructing spatial, temporal, means/ends, and quantitative relationships.

The goals of increasing awareness of diversity and fostering the construction of physical properties and relationships are mutually supportive and enriching. By experiencing many different cultural responses to common physical needs and experiences, children enrich their constructions of physical properties and abstract relationships. Conversely, the emphasis on observing and exploring physical phenomena gives children a more meaningful and concrete context for understanding why people do things differently.

7 Understanding Oneself and Others

The development of children's understanding of themselves and others is a major goal in most preschool programs. In the primary grades, however, most social interactions are relegated to the playground and "free time," when children frequently fend for themselves. While academic skills are broken down and taught in small increments, it is assumed that complex information about social relationships is learned by the time children are beginning to read. Given the current state of human relationships in neighborhoods, cities, countries, and the world, the fallacy of this assumption should be clear.

Intrapersonal and interpersonal dynamics are critical for the achievement of the goals of multicultural education. While knowledge of unfamiliar people and lifestyles may reduce children's fears and avoidance of differences, their motivation for reaching beyond cultural, racial, and class barriers largely rests on their self-confidence, their ability to empathize with others' experiences and feelings, and their anticipation of pleasure and satisfaction to be derived from expanding their social relationships. Moral development, defined by Piaget (1965) as the development of autonomy, is also relevant. Only people who can critically and independently relate to the existing order will be able to withstand the social pressures that support discrimination and to work for social change.

The social goals of multicultural education reflect research that has been done in the areas of identity, self-esteem, social cognition, cooperation, group dynamics, and moral development and include the following:

1. Positive cultural, racial, and class identities
2. High self-esteem and confidence in one's efficacy
3. Awareness of others' emotional, cognitive, and physical states

4. The ability and willingness to interact with diverse groups of people
5. Skills and motivation for cooperative play and work
6. Skills and trust in the process of conflict resolution
7. Autonomy in making moral decisions and the ability to actively analyze and influence the social environment
8. A sense of social responsibility and an active concern for people's welfare

Achievement of these goals occurs over a lifetime, not simply in early childhood. However, as children are gaining their first insights into the nature of the social world and forming their early relationships with others, teachers can support experiences that will create more fertile ground for later development.

RACIAL, CULTURAL, AND CLASS IDENTITIES

Prejudice often serves the purpose of validating certain groups and individuals at the expense of others. We have probably all had the experience of reassuring ourselves that our status, no matter how precarious or unfortunate, was at least better than someone else's. In studies of adult prejudice, it has been found that an increase in self-acceptance is linked to a greater acceptance of others (Rubin, 1967). While this relationship has not been specifically studied in children, it is reasonable to suppose that, at all ages, higher self-esteem mitigates the need to prove one's ascendancy over others. Thus, before considering children's feelings about other groups, our discussion will focus on group-referenced identification and self-esteem.

Looking back at the studies on racial identification described in chapter 2, it appears that African American children in this country have been historically more likely to misidentify themselves racially or to express a desire to be members of another racial group. While analogous studies have not been done with other racial or cultural groups or with class identification, it is likely that children of all groups that are underrepresented in the media and/or negatively stereotyped are vulnerable to the same ambivalence about their group identification. Autobiographies of immigrants contain many poignant accounts of their efforts to hide their "foreign" accents and customs, attesting to the cultural denial that occurs in the face of discrimination. Likewise, in a society where personal worth is often equated with wealth, shame related to one's income is a common experience. People of almost any income group try to "keep up with the Joneses" or hide their lack or loss of income. For example, teachers often mention how the growing gap between their salaries and those of other professionals makes them question their personal and professional worth. Likewise, children's group identification is inevitably influenced by the ways that their cultural, racial, and class groups are viewed by the larger society.

It is encouraging to note that the misidentification pattern evident in early research studies of African American children has appeared to diminish in recent years. Researchers generally believe that this change is a result of the emphasis on positive African American images that have been promoted in some communities and schools. Even in the face of continued economic discrimination, children are more likely to value their group if they see reasons to be proud of their family and community.

Children from middle- and upper-class white families may have identification difficulties that follow another pattern. Often they grow up with unrealistically high opinions of their reference group and grandiose expectations of what they, as members of that group, are destined to accomplish. These children often experience considerable anxiety about how they are measuring up to their high-status-group norms. For them it is helpful to learn about other measures of human worth and to see the achievement expectations of their own group in a broader and more realistic perspective.

The cultural and class analysis of the classroom will provide teachers with some clues as to what identification issues might be most prominent among the children in the class. If a group is underrepresented in the media, then one starting place may be to validate the experience of that particular group. If a group is overrepresented and/or portrayed in an unrealistically positive manner, then material showing other lifestyles and arenas of success may be appropriate.

The self-concept curricula that are commonly found in early childhood education programs can be easily expanded to include this focus on group-referenced identities. Some of the published curricula, such as *Developing Understanding of Self and Others* (Dinkmeyer, 1973), have a multicultural perspective that emphasizes children's families, communities, and physical similarities and differences. Some preschool curricula on self-awareness explicitly include this focus (e.g., Flemming et al., 1977; Kendall, 1983). By knowing how different traits, interests, and activities are regarded by the community, teachers can specifically support the positive group identification of the children in their class. This information can assist teachers in selecting equipment, tools, displays, clothing, props, and materials that both validate children's reference groups and provide opportunities for demonstrating their particular areas of competence.

Knowing the social expectations of the community is also helpful, as this will help teachers to foresee and address potential conflicts between cultural identification and the goals of the program. For instance, if a group feels that it is more important for girls to keep their dresses clean than to learn how to throw a ball, then teacher encouragement for girls to develop various athletic skills may be confusing and disconcerting to children. Teachers can discuss these issues with parents ahead of time and achieve some compromises and mutual understanding before the children are confronted with conflicting expectations.

The physical features of the children are a major focus of self-concept curricula. Children draw self-portraits; do body tracings; and compare hair, eye, and skin colors, and heights, arm lengths, and fingerprints. As children participate in these activities, teachers might listen carefully for feelings and beliefs that children have about their own physical characteristics, as well as ideas that they have about others'. They can then design activities to support positive feelings, to challenge negative ones, or to raise questions about erroneous assumptions. For example, if some girls are wishing they could have long, straight hair, then pictures, puppets, and dolls with short, curly hair can be used to point out its advantages.

Books and photographs should be chosen carefully to support many different physical attributes and lifestyles. One teacher described the distress of an African American child in her class who discovered she could not make herself look like the blonde Cinderella in a storybook. At that moment the teacher realized that she did not have any pictures of comparably attired African American women that she could show to this child to challenge the child's assumptions that beauty could only be associated with white skin and blonde hair.

Disparagement of certain physical features may be reduced if physical attributes are portrayed as continua rather than polarities. One student teacher was in a class where the children were calling each other "old black (child's name)" in a derogatory manner. She made up a skin-color chart using white, black, and various gradations of brown. Each child had a chance to see where she or he matched the chart. At the end of the activity it was clear to the whole class that everyone was a shade of brown. The classroom rabbit alone was black, and only the chalk was white. The name-calling abruptly stopped. Likewise, instead of referring only to physical polarities such as straight and curly hair or long and short hair, comparisons can be made with more intermediate points.

In addressing socioeconomic differences, one might well ask, How can we—and should we—try to help low-income children feel good about the fact that they are poor? As mentioned in chapter 2, young children's aspirations are often formed at an early age by their adult models and their living conditions. Do we want to reinforce these constraints by extolling the virtues of poverty? Ideally, we want children to feel competent, attractive, and unique on a personal level. At the same time, we can help them to become aware that their families' circumstances are not the only way of life and are often the result of social injustice rather than personal failure. While young children cannot distinguish between these social and personal issues, teachers can empower children and help them to expand their ideas about possibilities and aspirations. At the same time, their lifestyles should be validated with photographs, visitors, and field trips. Books such as *Sweet Pea* (Krementz) and many of the Face to Face Series portray families that have few resources but have healthy and happy lives.

Some of the same dilemmas are present when considering the group identities of children from middle-class and wealthy families. While we want to validate their lives, we do not want to support overly positive stereotypes of these lifestyles. Here teachers can emphasize the non-material aspects of the children's family lives, such as time spent together. With photographs and books, they can challenge their assumptions that everyone has access to the same resources that they do.

SELF-ESTEEM AND SENSE OF EFFICACY

As young children are constructing their self-concepts and group identities, an important element is the degree to which they feel that they can influence their environment, that is, the strength of their sense of efficacy. Because they can see the world only from their own point of view, they generally have unrealistic expectations about their own power and control. Confronting the limits of that power is often a frustrating and bewildering experience. As children become more aware of the existence and influence of the external world, they begin to compare themselves with others and with adult expectations. How resilient they are when disappointed or confronted with their short-comings reflects their previous experiences of success and failure and the supportiveness of their environment.

This concern is particularly relevant in high-unemployment areas where children may not have models of adults who feel able to control the circumstances of their lives and to accomplish the basic goal of making a living. Children who feel torn between two cultural systems also may have low self-esteem because they assume that they cannot be successful in either society. In a study of Native American adolescents (Luftig, 1983), those subjects who felt that they had to choose between being part of the Anglo-American culture or their tribal culture had lower self-esteem than their peers who felt that they could belong to both.

Children in the primary years are concerned with mastery and judge themselves by what they can accomplish. This age has been characterized by Erikson (1968) as a time when children are experiencing a conflict between industry and a sense of inferiority and believe "I am what I can make work." For most children in this society, school is the proving ground for whether or not they are competent. The degree to which school fosters children's positive self-esteem reflects, to some extent, the status relationship between themselves and the educational environment.

This point can be illustrated with the following observations. In a low-income inner-city second-grade class, I observed the following responses to the assignment of a relatively short series of phonics exercises. First, several children, with great bravado, said "how easy" the task was. Then they proceeded to roam the classroom and look over the shoulders of their peers who were attempting to do the assignment, chiding them about the slowness and poor quality of their work. Despite continuous admonishments from the teacher, these children avoided any direct focus on the assignment. When it was time to collect the papers, they attempted to copy their peers' work or simply crumpled up their papers and threw them away. In a contrasting observation, middle-class suburban second graders, when confronted with a similar task, tried to outdo each other as they raced to its conclusion. For these two groups of children, academic tasks triggered different levels of efficacy. Many of the children in the first group anxiously avoided the assignment; those in the second plunged in with confidence.

Both observations also illustrate how the nature of a task and children's engagement with it interact with their perceptions of themselves and their peers. In this case the "right-answer" nature of the tasks appeared to stimulate a "cover-up" on the part of some of the urban children and a contest of speed among the suburban ones. In neither case were the children engaged in the actual content of the task.

To foster a sense of efficacy, teachers need to design learning experiences that encourage children to express and explore their own ideas and perceptions of the world, rather than being measured by an external standard. This effort challenges some basic premises about the nature of the teacher-child relationship. Showing genuine interest and respect for children's ideas requires that teachers shift from a subject focus and a right/wrong orientation to trying to "enter" the children's own worlds. From that vantage point they can find areas where children do feel confident and then can construct the environment and expectations in ways that foster those feelings. Children also learn that they do have ideas that are valued and appreciated.

The lesson to be drawn from the observations of the phonics lessons is that it might be better for children to learn to read in their own voice, using the language experience approach. Seeing their own words in print is an empowering experience for all children. Also, the more familiar the content, the easier it is for them to relate to it. Rather than avoiding figuring out the answer, they can create something out of their own experiences. This alternative would also help the suburban children to direct their focus to the actual content of what they are reading and writing, so that learning is not reduced to a contest of speed.

Preschool classrooms have more open-ended activities, and the experience of failing or competing is less common. With the current emphasis on early acquisition of academic skills, however, children at this age may begin to feel these pressures. Teachers should avoid any activities that might undermine children's confidence and delight in learning about the world. At this age children's sense of self is summarized by the statement, "I am what I can imagine I will be" (Erikson, 1968). For these children, teachers can contribute to their sense of efficacy by making every effort to expand their realm of possibilities with books, photographs, sociodramatic play, field trips, and classroom visitors.

Viewed from a multicultural perspective, self-concepts of children relate not only to their racial, cultural, and class identification but also to their feelings of power in the school environment. The task is to help them to build positive perceptions about their reference groups and past experiences and to develop confidence in actively participating in social discussions and change.

AWARENESS OF OTHERS

Children are interested in other people's thoughts and feelings. Even infants have been observed to respond to the sound of another baby crying; young children often show interest in others' mishaps or signs of distress. Still, children cannot separate their own reactions and point of view from those of others. For instance, a child looking at a photograph of someone with a sad expression on his face described in great detail how "The boy is sad because he does not want to go to school and his mother makes him." According to this child's teacher, he himself cried every morning because he did not want to go to school. Children present an interesting paradox in their awareness of others: They resonate to others' feelings and experiences in an empathic way, yet they cannot distinguish between their own feelings and experiences and those of others.

While this fusion is limiting, it also may foster the development of understanding of others. In a recent study (Hill, 1983), groups of kindergarteners attended sessions in which the teacher showed them pictures of people in various emotionally laden situations (e.g., a birthday party or being chased by a dog). The group that was consistently asked to think about how they themselves would feel showed a greater increase in ability to take another's point of view than did the children who were asked to think about how the person in the picture would feel. In other words, self-reflection heightened their awareness of others' feelings. (As children develop the ability to distinguish between their own and others' perspectives, their interpretations of others' feelings and ideas will be more accurate and less limited to their own immediate experiences.)

The ability to see another's point of view clearly requires fairly complex cognitive structures and cannot fully develop until children are in their middle- and late-childhood years. The *willingness* to see another's point of view, however, can be fostered in children from their earliest social experiences (Flavell, 1968). The following guidelines, adapted from Flavell's work, have been developed to help teachers foster children's interest and motivation in learning about others' perceptual, emotional, and cognitive points of view.

Noticing Other Points of View

First, point out the existence of another's point of view whenever the opportunity presents itself. When reading stories, looking at photographs, and watching adults working or children playing a game, teachers can ask questions about how the children would feel if they were engaged in that particular activity. For instance, if the class is watching construction workers carry heavy materials, teachers might ask, "What do you suppose those people are feeling in their arms?" The children can act out the motions and describe how it feels. Facial expressions and gestures, such as wiping one's brow, are another subject of inquiry. As mentioned previously, photographs and stories should include both sexes and be representative of a wide range of ages, lifestyles, and physical appearance, in order to reinforce the notion that, while people may look different and have different words for feelings, they all experience the same basic emotions. Also, since people generally have a harder time distinguishing feelings and individuals when looking at faces of races other than their own, children will benefit from deciphering the feelings or reactions of people who look different from themselves.

Conflicts are an obvious time when children are experiencing (usually unwillingly) the existence of another's point of view. However, they are also the occasions when children are the least able to detach from their own needs to see another's. Trying to persuade an enraged child to feel interest or concern about his antagonist is a frustrating task. Older children in the primary grades might be able to compare their sides of the argument somewhat dispassionately after a few minutes of cooling off time. Preschoolers cannot de-center from their own perceptions enough to engage genuinely in this kind of dialogue. However, they can discuss conflicts and points of view in more hypothetical situations (e.g., skits or puppet shows). For children of both ages, role playing a conflict (hypothetical or actual, depending on the ages and disposition of the children) from both points of view, so that they literally "stand in the other's shoes," is a challenging and broadening experience.

Assisting Others

A second strategy is to arrange for children to assist younger peers and/or people with special needs. This involvement will help children learn how to interpret more accurately others' actions, needs, and requests and thereby become more effective in their efforts to help. In one preschool, a teacher spent a day with both her arms in slings (Forman & Hill, 1983). Throughout the day, the children responded to her expressed and implied needs. They solved various problems, such as how to hold a cup to her mouth and scratch her nose. The teachers all felt that the experience had prompted the children to take more social responsibility and had challenged their assumptions by having a teacher be a recipient of help instead of filling her usual role as a source of assistance.

Our society is somewhat unique in terms of the lack of responsibility that children have for the well-being of others. In many countries and among some ethnic groups here, children take a great deal of responsibility for childcare and domestic chores. Assisting others not only draws children's attention to others' needs but also may foster their sense of efficacy and importance.

Photographs, books, puppet shows, and skits can be used to challenge some of the existing stereotypes about who helps and who receives help. These images could portray African American, Asian American, and female doctors attending European American and male patients, men comforting crying children, girls helping to carry heavy loads, and children assisting adults.

Social Interactions

Increasing the frequency of children's social interactions is a third way of fostering willingness to focus on the needs and perspectives of others. As children experience the pleasures of social interaction, the need and desirability of understanding others' points of view become more evident. Moreover, as children have more social experience, their skills at distinguishing their point of view from others and "reading" others' thoughts and feelings will increase. Studies of children's social interactions suggest that preschool and kindergarten children who are more successful at entering groups are more likely to adapt to the ongoing activity of the group (Corsaro, 1981, 1985; Putallatz & Gottman, 1981). Thus, children are reinforced for being able to recognize others' points of view and for making appropriate adaptations to them.

Another dimension of social behavior is the extent to which groups are inclusive or exclusive. In a comparison of European and Polynesian preschools in New Zealand, Graves (1974) found that children in the former settings tended to show many more exclusionary behaviors (e.g., "John is my friend; you can't play with him") than those in the latter ones. Conversely, the Polynesian children more frequently invited passersby to join their groups and did not seem to be concerned about maintaining exclusive use of the materials or control over peers. The behaviors of the parents in the two groups reflected similar differences. Also, the Polynesian classroom was set up in ways that encouraged more sharing of resources. These findings suggest that the social and physical environments are related to children's social interactional styles.

The design of space and the selection of equipment and materials can influence the type and frequency of social interaction. For instance, in one study of a preschool environment (Ramsey, 1980b), single-entranced spaces such as lofts or small houses tended to be the scenes of more territorial behavior than were more open spaces. While the closed areas were conducive to some intimate contact among the children inside them, these relationships were frequently cemented by the shared exclusion of other children. Blocking the entrance with a cushion, "shooting" from windows, pushing "intruders" away, and making verbal threats were all used to delineate the "in" group from the "out" group. To justify their rejection of their peers, children would disparage some physical or behavioral attribute (real or imagined) of the "intruder." These exchanges reinforced the "common enemy" (Sherif, 1966) basis for relationships and led children to view peers in terms of the grounds that they could construct for rejecting them. This pattern parallels the way that prejudice toward the "out" group is used to maintain "in"-group cohesion and identity.

In the same study, the design of equipment also was related to varied social interactions. A striking difference was apparent between the behaviors on the single swing and on the horizontal tire swing. Whereas the former, which could only accommodate one child at a time, was frequently the scene of disputes or complaints regarding having to wait one's turn, the latter, which was more fun with a group of children, prompted invitations to passersby. The tire swing also required children to take the responsibility for helping each other get on and off and to coordinate their motions in order to make the swing go fast; hence the experience fostered awareness of other people's positions, wishes, and actions. Similar observations have also been made about single versus double slides. Seesaws also require attention to the actions of another, as children use their own weights to move their partner into the desired position.

The arrangement of furniture equipment also influences the kinds of social interactions that occur. For example, if the sand table or water table is placed against a wall, the children will have less eye contact with each other and less direct interaction. Housekeeping equipment is often placed against the wall, which means that children who are working at the stove or sink have their backs to the other children in the area. Just as "islands" in adult kitchens have enabled adult cooks to work together more companionably, experimenting with the placement of the housekeeping furniture may reveal ways of promoting more social interaction. (It is important to make sure that any freestanding furniture is stable enough to prevent accidents and injuries.)

The arrangement of work areas also limits or facilitates social engagement. As an example, in most early-childhood classrooms manipulatives are usually used independently and the work areas provided for them are often small tables or shelves, which limit the engagement to one person at a time. In a comparison of Chinese and American children's social interactions (Navon & Ramsey, 1983), it was observed that in China, the children worked with manipulatives while sitting at tables with at least three other children. There was a great deal of exchange of materials and ideas among the children, with relatively few disputes. The children negotiated with each other and frequently redistributed materials if one child seemed to have too few or too many. While many factors contributed to these differences, it is possible that the physical arrangement did facilitate more interaction and helping behaviors. If teachers provide more socially conducive work spaces, materials that are generally used by single children may become the focus for social interaction.

In primary classrooms, the arrangement of desks influences the extent to which children collaborate and turn to each other for assistance. Here teachers usually need to balance the benefits of cooperation among the children with the disruption caused by distractions. However, seating arrangements and assignments can be designed to promote positive group interactions.

Communication Skills

The development of communication skills further enables children to see and to take an interest in others' points of view. Effective communication rests on being able to understand what others mean and to make oneself understood. Younger children are often oblivious to the conversation around them and frequently speak in "collective monologues" where two or more children continue to speak according to their own trains of thought, without regard to the others' statements. As children experience more verbal and nonverbal communication, they become increasingly interested in and skilled at seeing themselves and their actions as the subjects of someone else's perceptions, thoughts, and feelings.

There are numerous activities that foster children's communication skills; the following are a few suggestions.

- Children can "mirror" each other's gestures or facial expressions, in order to "see" themselves as imitated by another.
- By pantomiming feelings and events, children can learn how clearly they express themselves and practice trying to interpret what another person is conveying.
- In small group discussions, teachers can model and instruct children on how to express themselves more clearly. Older children will slow down and listen if they are challenged to repeat the question or statement that they are responding to before they speak. Younger children will listen more attentively when playing games that involve repeating nonsense words, rhymes, and rhythms.
- When children are asked to "be the teacher" and instruct their peers in some way, they learn to be more precise in their communication.
- One activity that kindergarten and primary children enjoy is to sit in pairs, back to back, and describe things to each other that the other one cannot see. The first one might draw a picture or build a block structure and then have the second one replicate it, based only on the first's verbal instruction. Such activities require that children think about what the other person knows and is imagining.

Through classroom arrangements, curriculum design, and various interventions, teachers can foster children's willingness to see others' perspectives. Drawing children's attention to other points of view, providing occasions when children can assist others, increasing opportunities and support for social interactions, and fostering communication skills can be incorporated into all areas of the curriculum and all aspects of teaching practice.

INTERGROUP CONTACT

The ability and willingness to interact with diverse people is clearly a central goal of multicultural education. The avoidance that often characterizes intergroup contacts becomes increasingly apparent as children get older. Apparently, as people learn the prevailing prejudices against certain groups and become more imbued with the expectations and social styles of their own groups, their disdain or fear of other groups becomes magnified. It is obvious that younger children, who have less to "unlearn," are potentially more receptive to cross-group interactions.

While this section addresses particular issues that might emerge in a classroom with a diverse population, these reactions often occur between individuals and groups in relatively homogeneous classrooms. Although children in these classrooms do not have immediate opportunities to expand their interactional skills beyond their own group, they can learn how to respond to individual differences in a more receptive manner that may predispose them to be more accepting of other groups.

What Makes Intergroup Contacts Difficult?

First we must ask what some of the factors are that make intergroup contacts difficult. At a perceptual level, children may feel some fear and aversion when confronted by differences in appearance, language, clothing, and customs. As mentioned previously, in one classroom the smell of the coconut oil that an Indian child had on his hair caused his American classmates to avoid and scapegoat him. Thus at a sensory, perceptual level, children may feel that it is difficult to approach a particular person. Many of the curriculum ideas that focus on body awareness and the similarities and differences in physical attributes provide opportunities for children to explore these feelings and for teachers to challenge their bases of rejection.

Differences in interactional style and social orientation also contribute to children's discomfort in cross-group interactions. Studies of desegregated junior and senior high schools (e.g., Patchen, 1982; Schofield, 1981) showed how consistently the European American students saw the African Americans as aggressive and threatening, while the black students saw the whites as passive, aloof, and conceited. Friendly overtures were frequently misinterpreted. Playful aggression by the blacks was interpreted as anger by the whites; offers of academic assistance by the whites were seen by the blacks as patronizing claims of superiority. However, intergroup experiences may reduce these mutual antagonisms. Many students, after a year in a desegregated school, remarked that, now that they knew the other group better, they felt that they could find ways of being friends. Furthermore, students who had had experience with other groups in their early childhood years adjusted more quickly (Schofield, 1981). Thus, as groups learn to "read" others' actions they become less disdainful and fearful and adjust their own responses and expectations in order to participate in positive interactions. The advantage of having these experiences at an early age is that young children have less crystallized social expectations and respond more openly to others.

There are numerous ways in which interactional style and content vary among groups and individuals. If teachers sense that individuals from different groups are having a difficult time communicating with each other or with the teachers, they may want to analyze some of their interactions for ways that differences in the following factors (Long-street, 1978) may be disrupting attempts to communicate and to make contact.

1. *Verbal communication*: tempo, voice quality, inflections, pronunciation, function of speech (different levels of reliance on spoken versus nonverbal communication), the connotative qualities of different words (e.g., the various interpretations of "he's bad!"), and word games (e.g., "the dozens"; riddles and puns).
2. *Nonverbal communication*: eye contact, touching, proximity, hand gestures, frequency and meaning of facial expressions.
3. *Orientation modes*: body positions, relationships to space and time (e.g., tempo of movement through space, expansiveness/containment of actions), attention modes (e.g., what kinds of activities attract and maintain different children's attention).
4. *Social-value patterns*: For children this aspect centers on immediate relationships with peers and adults, shared activities and preferences for different kinds of material goods. For adults, these differences emerge around lifestyle decisions and political, social, and economic partisanship.

Expectations in social interactions are all influenced by these factors. Teachers and children alike may find themselves surprised, nonplussed, and irritated by different styles and responses. Although children cannot consciously articulate the sources of their uneasiness, teachers need to be aware of what behaviors they themselves find annoying or confusing. To avoid conveying negative feelings toward particular individuals or groups, teachers should be sure that when they are reprimanding children, they are doing so because of a breach of rules that are equitably applied and not because of violated cultural expectations. For example, wearing a hat means different things across groups. Teachers who insist that hats be removed according to the standards of middle-class Anglo-American etiquette may find themselves embroiled in conflicts of cultural conventions and values.

Teachers can set a tone of cross-cultural respect by modeling social flexibility and receptiveness to the range of social behavior that is presented. It is important to note here, however, that receptiveness and flexibility do not mean permissiveness and anarchy.

Facilitating Intergroup Relationships

To facilitate positive interactions among different groups within the classroom, teachers should look at their observations on children's grouping patterns (see chapter 3) and analyze what factors seem to cause the attraction among children (e.g., similar play styles, shared preference for certain activities, or similar language).

In some cases the physical environment can be arranged to promote cross-group interactions. If it is apparent that some groups—be they defined by race, culture, class, or gender—play exclusively together in particular areas, then rearranging the physical space may be a means of increasing intergroup contact. For example, the gender split that often occurs between housekeeping and blocks might be reduced if these two areas were adapted and combined so that sociodramatic play could span both areas and both populations. If the housekeeping area becomes a store, then the roads and trucks in the block area can be used to deliver the groceries and other goods. In cases where children seem to be isolated because they avoid certain areas, teachers may want to analyze the location, size, accessibility, and attractiveness of the spaces, from those children's points of view. In one classroom, teachers observed that the boisterous play that often occurred in the open area in the middle of the classroom seemed to intimidate some of the quieter children, who did not venture out of the "safer" areas. By creating a gross-motor-play area at one end of the classroom, they contained the rough-and-tumble play and increased the accessibility of the rest of the classroom to other children.

In primary classrooms, a lot of the exclusionary behavior occurs in the cafeteria and during recess, when children are less closely supervised. Assigning lunch groups composed of a variety of children and structuring part of recess with cooperative games may curtail the in-group/out-group dynamic.

Much primary-level teaching occurs in small groups; but, because these divisions commonly reflect academic skills, the class often becomes stratified by skill level. All too often these divisions reflect the social status of the children's parents. If the curriculum requires that specific academic skills be taught in "ability" groups, then teachers should be sure that children are reshuffled frequently and that groups are heterogeneous for projects, sports, music, art, social studies, and science. While children might complain about them, assigned groups are recommended for providing the maximum amount of intergroup contact.

Teachers should be particularly alert to any scapegoating and deliberate exclusion that may occur. Sometimes it is very subtle and may
require some concentrated observation before it is discerned. If a particular child or group seems to be doing a lot of scapegoating or excluding, a teacher might want to have an open-ended discussion with
these children about their reasons for this behavior. Here it is not effective to use platitudes such as "We can all be friends" or "Lawrence
is a very nice boy; you should let him play with you." Instead, children need to express their feelings about the excluded party as honestly as possible and be assisted in finding ways of relating positively
to that child.

If the children point out aspects of a child's or group's behavior that
is disruptive to their play, then the teacher may want to provide the
target of the scapegoating with some support and "coaching" (see
Bierman, 1983; Oden & Asher, 1977) to help change that behavior. Some
studies have shown that unpopular children in elementary schools gain
status and are more integrated into the mainstream if they are given
visible and responsible classroom roles (Asher, Oden, & Gottman,
1977). Sometimes children's assumptions about other groups can cause
exclusionary behavior. One kindergarten teacher reported that, in response to her queries about the fact that the boys always played baseball by themselves, several boys said that girls did not like to play
baseball. As the teacher questioned the boys further, they acknowledged that they did not really know if girls liked to play baseball or not.
When the girls were brought into the discussion, several of them said
that they did want to play baseball. The teacher then set up some game
times where everyone played baseball on mixed-gender teams. To help
children to generalize from their immediate discussion, she also displayed photographs of women and men playing many different sports.

Rejection and scapegoating often require careful scrutiny of the individual and social variables involved. In one preschool classroom,
several children spoke disparagingly about a child, saying, "He is black
and yukky and always bad." In classroom observations, it was evident
that this child spent a disproportionate amount of time in the "time-
out" corner and, as a result, had less opportunity to interact with other
children. This pattern had also taught the children, who were very interested in "bad" behavior, that this child was "bad." After discussing this issue, the teachers decided to emphasize the positive things
that this child did and to try to limit the number of times that he was
in the "time-out" corner. They also planned situations where this child
and a peer could work together under close supervision so that a teacher
could assist if the interaction began to deteriorate. Since other African

American children in the classroom were not referred to as "black and yukky," the teachers felt that this term was more related to the behavior of this specific child than to generalized feelings about blacks. However, because that comment suggested that children readily, although not consistently, associated blackness with negative qualities, they designed materials and activities that would counteract negative associations with darkness.

As this example illustrates, scapegoating and excluding can occur as a result of many complex dynamics among the children and between teachers and children. Likewise, trying to reduce it requires a comprehensive analysis of its causes, as well as multifaceted interventions. The old adage, "It takes two to tango," usually applies to these situations, and teachers should respond to the situation from all points of view.

The Intergroup Contact Hypothesis

Specific factors that influence the quality of intergroup contacts have been studied in integrated camps, schools, housing projects, workplaces, and recreational groups. Much of this work has been based on Allport's (1954) intergroup contact hypothesis. The following discussion is based on reviews of this research written by Yehuda Amir (1969, 1976) and some more recent studies. While most of these studies have had adults and children over the age of eight as subjects, these findings will be discussed in terms of what strategies teachers of young children might employ to facilitate the development of positive intergroup relationships.

Opportunity for Cross-Group Contact. First, opportunity for cross-group contact is clearly a significant variable in promoting better intergroup relationships. Face-to-face contact is the time when people experience their reactions and potentially begin to see other groups as composed of individual people with whom they can identify. For private early childhood programs, providing these experiences has obvious implications for enrollment policies, sliding-fee scales, and recruitment programs. (More will be said about how to maintain a diverse enrollment in chapter 9.) Busing, magnet schools, and community programs are some ways that public schools have attempted to create diverse learning environments. Unfortunately, local resistance to these programs and the persistence of segregated housing patterns frequently undermine these efforts. In many areas, there simply may not be much cultural and racial diversity. However, if income is a differentiating factor in a particular community, then schools can work to be sure that children from all income groups are represented in the program.

In homogeneous communities, teachers need to rely more on creating experiences that provide this contact. Some schools plan outings and visits with centers in other communities, in order to expand their children's range of social experience. Older children often have pen pals from other communities and regions. While short-term contact is far from ideal, these experiences can begin to broaden children's limited social expectations and stimulate interest in other people. The effects of these interactions can be maintained by taking photographs that keep the experience alive in children's minds and by having repeated visits so that children have a chance to begin building relationships.

Equal Status of Groups.   The equal status of members from all groups is a second factor. Group activities should be designed with the abilities and potential contributions of the various individuals in mind. When there is not a shared language among the participants, nonverbal instructions and activities such as drawing and pantomiming can be used. If there are different levels of ability, then activities can be structured so that there is little direct interpersonal comparison. While teachers have little control over the previous experiences of the children and their levels of expertise, they can design activities so that children are able to be equal participants. Research has shown that, in mixed adult groups, external inequalities such as education, income, and occupational prestige become less salient as soon as people are engaged in a task where they enjoy equal status.

Related to the issue of equal status, studies have suggested that contact with prestigious members of low-status groups seems to have a positive effect on people's regard for the whole group. Teachers may want to have the children meet people from diverse groups who have skills and jobs that the children find attractive, such as fire fighters, ambulance drivers, dancers, and heavy equipment operators. A poor or elderly person who does not have a prestigious job may fascinate the children with folk songs or a particular craft. On one field trip, I took four-year-olds to the home of a self-employed weaver. The children (all from middle-class homes) were initially quite wary of her rudimentary living conditions. However, they became awed and enthusiastic as they watched her work and participated in cleaning, spinning, and weaving the wool.

Social Climate.   A third factor is a social climate that is favorable to intergroup contact. Research has shown that, in situations where intergroup contact is actively encouraged and is seen as sanctioned by authority (but not forced), more positive changes in intergroup feelings occur (e.g., Deutsch & Collins, 1951; Aronson, 1972). In early childhood environments, teachers can establish that atmosphere with their own modeling, the assignment of children to mixed groups, and stories and photographic displays of people from all backgrounds working and playing together.

Intimacy of Contact.   A fourth factor is intimacy of contact between group members. Some studies have indicated that casual or superficial contact only serves to reinforce people's negative cross-group stereotypes, whereas more prolonged and personal contact potentially changes them (Amir, 1976; Jordan, 1971). Teachers may want to form intergroup "snack families" or "lunch groups" that meet each day, in order to provide sustained relationships among children who might not spontaneously choose to be together. This sustained contact provides an opportunity for children to get to know each other and to work through some of the differences that might create tension. Too often lunch and snack become "eat-and-run" occasions and their potential for enhancing social skills and relationships is not realized. With young children, teachers should sit with these groups and actively facilitate the flow of conversation. For older children in classrooms with one teacher, such attention is not possible, but teachers can rotate among groups and visit with each one at least once a week. While children may initially object to being grouped with children they do not choose, teachers can encourage group-building activities such as group names, slogans, songs, and jokes that may heighten group allegiance.

The intimacy factor obviously poses a real problem when teachers are relying on occasional visits for children's cross-group contacts. By having children from both groups meet, work, and play in consistent small groups, teachers may be able to create a more intimate atmosphere. Also, activities can be designed to promote group feeling and personal sharing. Children might work with partners in activities such as body tracing, self-portraits, and cooperative creative movement activities so that their attention is focused on each other in a fairly intense and positive way. If the distances are not too great, parents can be encouraged to follow up the school contacts with family visits.

Rewarding and Pleasant Environment.   A fifth variable is insuring that the contacts occur in a rewarding and pleasant environment (Amir, 1976; Jordan, 1971). In a study of children at an integrated camp, the children who generally enjoyed the camp also made the most gains in interracial acceptance (Mussen, 1950). When designing and implementing activities in which intergroup contact will be a focus, teachers should include activities that the children like. That is one argument for using food-related activities such as lunch, snack, and cooking. Other activities could be anything from a quiet storytime to outside games.

Common Goals.   The sixth factor is providing common goals for participants of all groups. Studies have indicated that competition among group members can have a very detrimental effect on group relationships (e.g., Sherif, 1966). Since many people in this society see others and themselves as competitors for jobs, housing, and other resources, it is particularly important that the schools provide activities where children can engage in cooperative activities. We all know from our own experience how working on a joint project often facilitates efforts to communicate, accommodate, and enjoy each other's company. As a community organizer, I remember how cohesive our neighborhood action group became after a sweltering week spent painting and setting up our tiny storefront office.

Some of the most promising work that has been done in the area of facilitating intergroup relationships has been in the formation of cooperative learning teams in desegregated schools (e.g., Aronson & Bridgeman, 1979; DeVries, Edwards, & Slavin, 1978; Johnson & Johnson, 1982; Slavin, 1979). Almost all activities that young children engage in can be done cooperatively. Art projects can include large-group murals; scores for board or ball games can be counted as a group total; and communal structures can be built with blocks and constructed in the sand and water tables. Older children can write stories, present plays, and design treasure hunts in groups. The possibilities are endless. In the next section some specific guidelines will be offered on designing and implementing cooperative activities.

Emphasis on Similarities.   More positive cross-group feelings seem to emerge if participants perceive others as similar to themselves. Many of the suggestions already mentioned fit this goal. In discussions and activities, teachers may want to make particular efforts to emphasize similarities among children who may not have a common background or shared interests. For example, a teacher might say, "Amar said that he was afraid of dogs, just as you said that you were afraid of spiders, Susie. I bet all the children at this table have something that they are afraid of."

Group Entry.   In most of the studies mentioned in this section, the subjects were assigned to mixed group settings. In early childhood

programs, children are often moving from group to group as they begin and complete various activities. Children have different levels of
skill in entering groups and receiving newcomers into groups. Because
children from different backgrounds may vary in the ways in which
they approach others (Longstreet, 1978), the processes of entry and
group reception may be more difficult in cross-group situations. If
teachers notice that children's efforts to make contact seem to be
impeded because of some of these stylistic differences, they can help
children understand the intent of others' actions and to accept a variety of approaches.

Acceptance Versus Friendship.   As mentioned in chapter 2, the rate of
interracial *acceptance* appears to be much higher than the rate of interracial *friendship* (Asher et al., 1982). Given the segregated housing patterns, the lifestyle differences, and the possible resistance on the part
of parents, it is unrealistic for teachers to expect many best-friend relationships to develop across racial, cultural, and class groups. However, classroom environments can contribute to the development of
cross-group acceptance, communication, and cooperation.

Symbolic Representations of Intergroup Relationships.   Teachers can
motivate children to want to form intergroup relationships by sym-
bolically presenting positive outcomes for these experiences. In homogeneous groups, teachers have to rely heavily on these kinds of
activities, because the opportunity for cross-group contact is so limited.

One teacher of three-year-olds wrote a story about two groups of
shapes that were suspicious of each other; when they were blown together by the wind, they discovered that they could make many more
interesting shapes by working together. This story was enacted on the
flannel board, and the children were fascinated by the variety of designs that could be made when the two groups came together. As a
follow-up activity, the teacher set out the flannel board, sometimes with
only one set of identical shapes and sometimes with both sets. The
children were then able to experience tangibly the advantages of integrating both sets of shapes.

Another preschool teacher had the children make "Martin Luther
King Bread," to convey in a way that three- and four-year-old-children
could understand the idea that there are advantages to having dissim-
ilar groups come together. She and the children mixed two different
bread doughs, one light and one dark. The children then made rolls in
which both doughs were entwined in lots of interesting ways. Their
delight in making these designs prompted many comments about the

advantages of having two different colors of dough. This experience provided a concrete analogy for subsequent discussions about the value of different people coming together.

These kinds of activities do not provide children with the reality of cross-group experiences, but they may help them to see the benefits of diversity and to anticipate cross-group contacts in a positive way.

COOPERATION

The value of fostering cooperation among children has been mentioned in several contexts in this book. Cooperative activities promote children's awareness of others, they facilitate positive interactions among children of diverse groups, and they offer an alternative to competition, which often causes intergroup tension. In this section, issues related to cooperation will be discussed and guidelines for early childhood teachers will be described.

The question of the relative value of cooperation versus competition arises frequently. Learning to compete is considered a necessary skill for being successful in this country. Some educators feel that it is particularly important for children from backgrounds that are less competitive to learn how to compete with their Anglo-American peers. While it is true that the lack of a keen competitive edge may be a limiting factor in some cases (women often bemoan their lack of combative skills in the competitive business world), the larger goal of multicultural education is to challenge the assumption that the success of an individual or group has to be gained at the expense of another.

While it would be naive to suggest that multicultural education programs will change the economic system of this country, schools and teachers can provide alternative definitions of success and help children see, in a broader context, the competition that they will inevitably experience. Competition is part of our national culture, but teachers can balance its pervasive influence by engaging children in cooperative alternatives and fostering their ability to collaborate. It is interesting to note that some studies of working environments have suggested that groups who are able to work more collaboratively are more successful (e.g., Bakeman & Helmreich, 1975).

Some authors (e.g., Kamii & Devries, 1980) advocate the use of competitive games as ways of motivating children to focus on others' points of view, since many games involve outwitting one's opponent.

They also provide more impetus for children to learn, abide by, and negotiate the rules of the game. While competition does intensify involvement, it does not necessarily lead to an *empathic* concern about another's point of view or an *objective* understanding of the rules. More precisely, when trying to win, people use their perceptions and understanding of others to manipulate and outwit them, and knowledge of rules is used to find strategies and exceptions that work to one's own advantage.

An important issue related to cooperation in early childhood programs is the question of whether or not children at the preoperational stage, with their egocentric point of view, are able to engage in cooperative activities. True cooperation, which involves the anticipation of others' needs and requests and the deliberate attempt to address them, is not possible with very young children. Even very young children, however, can learn how to coordinate their physical actions with each other. Some successful activities in this respect are described in *Constructive Play* (Forman & Hill, 1983). One example is the "cooperative board," where a board is suspended from ropes and pulleys on each end. Two children raise the board together by each pulling one of the ropes. In order to hold the board level and to keep things from falling from it, children have to pull at the same rate and vigor. Other games, described in Orlick's *Cooperative Sports and Games Book* (1978), also involve physical rather than intellectual coordination among two or more children. For example, "Turtle" is played by having several children lie on the ground under a large blanket or mat. The "turtle" has to move in a coordinated fashion so that the "shell" (blanket) stays on everyone.

Cooperative games also can be done in a physical way with children in the primary grades. Examples include cooperative volleyball games or "Blob," which is like "Tag" except that people *join* "It" when they are tagged, so that eventually everyone is part of a large group moving as one. These children can also participate in cooperative activities such as puppet shows, plays, and group stories, which require a more conscious awareness of others' points of view. Children at this age begin to play a lot of competitive games such as board games and cards. Most of these games can be played with accumulated or group scores, which provides a different kind of challenge. For instance, if children are each trying to complete a turn around the game board, they can see how quickly they can get everyone's pieces "home," or they can try to get them all "home" on the same turn. Not only does that take the focus off of trying to outdo each other, it also means that all participants have a stake in the progress of the other players, which reduces the restlessness that often occurs when people are waiting for "their" turn.

Regardless of whether or not children are responding to others on a physical or intellectual level, they are still learning to "read cues" of other children and to adapt either their motions or their intentions to their co-participants. In other words, they become accustomed to monitoring their own actions or ideas in terms of how they fit with those of others. The pleasure that children (and adults) find in cooperative activities is apparent in the laughter and excitement that accompany them. The challenge of seeing how long teams can keep the ball crossing the net in volleyball is as involving as the challenge of trying to make it impossible for the other team to hit it.

The following are general guidelines that teachers can use in their efforts to incorporate cooperative activities in every phase of their classrooms (Ramsey, 1980a):

1. Organize games so that cumulative group accomplishment rather than individual performance is stressed (e.g., group long jump, cooperative balloon tap, and group scores on board games).
2. Include activities where children focus on one another's actions, characteristics, and statements (e.g., mirroring actions, interviewing peers, and identifying each other by voice sound and verbal clues).
3. Design activities and materials that involve coordinated actions (e.g., using a cooperative board, moving heavy tables and buckets of sand, and making group sculptures).
4. Avoid time pressures in physical and academic tasks, to reduce the "finishing-first" anxiety.
5. Either avoid elimination games or make them more inclusive (e.g., "out" children in "Simon Says" become "Simon"; and musical chairs is played either with enough chairs for everyone or by allowing as many people as want to to sit on the same chair, so that at the end the group is in a pile around one chair and all participants are still part of the game.)
6. Provide physical structures that will accommodate groups of children (e.g., large horizontal tire swings, big sacks, large cartons, and double slides).
7. When dividing children into groups, guard against "popularity contests" or the exclusion of certain children by counting off or drawing numbers or colors.
8. At the conclusion of games and activities, recognize individual and group efforts without naming winners.

CONFLICT RESOLUTION

Conflict and aggression are often associated with intergroup hostility. Although it is impossible to determine a causal relationship, some psychologists (e.g., Weissbach, 1976) have suggested that limiting aggressive cues might help to reduce prejudice. Unfortunately, teachers cannot control some of the most powerful aggressive cues in children's lives: the violence on television. When thinking about responding to children's aggression and conflicts, one must remember that they see numerous adult and cartoon characters resolving conflict through violence. In classrooms, however, children can learn how to prevent and negotiate conflicts effectively by using alternatives to the dominant/ submissive and aggressive solutions that they see on television. This section will discuss ways that teachers can respond to conflict among children.

During the early childhood years, children pass through several stages of social reasoning (Damon, 1980). Children of four and under typically assert their desires rather than try to justify them ("I should get it because I want it"). Around the ages of four and five, children justify their desires with arbitrary but observable reasons ("We get to use it because we are wearing blue today"). From age five to seven, children believe in applying strict equality in distribution ("Everyone should get three"). During the period of six to nine, merit emerges as a criterion ("He did a good job, so he should get the most"). As teachers approach conflicts, these general trends may provide some guidance as to what principles may lie behind conflicts and which ones might be most relevant to efforts at resolving them.

Many teachers try to avoid conflicts altogether by reducing the kinds of situations that potentially induce them. I remember one experienced teacher telling several neophyte staff members always to provide each child with an equal share of the play-dough, clay, paper, paints, or whatever material was to be used, in order to prevent conflicts over the distribution of materials. While it is true that this practice reduces the number of conflicts that may occur, it also limits children's opportunities to resolve conflict and to engage in deliberations about fair distribution.

If teachers are aware that a dispute is beginning to occur, they can try to intervene in a preventive fashion. The point at which a conflict of interests has become apparent, but before the parties have become angry, is an opportune time to have children think about the needs of others and to try to think of some solutions. The potential of children to engage in this kind of discussion has been illustrated in responses of two- and three-year-olds to skits that present dilemmas about distribution and fairness (Edwards, 1983) and in the negotiating skills observed in young Chinese children (Navon & Ramsey, 1983).

When a conflict has blossomed, teachers often try to settle it as expediently as possible. In one study (Ramsey, 1980b), teachers often ended conflicts over materials by giving the parties equivalent objects so that "each of you can have one." With this intervention, they were reinforcing the idea that having absolute control over an object is the only way that children can avoid conflict. Instead, efforts can be made to work out joint solutions where materials will be used by both people. For example, if two children are fighting over the use of a truck, they can both continue to share control by alternating the roles of "driver" and "traffic director."

One question that teachers frequently ask is, At what point and with how much authority should I intervene when children are fighting? Since the action is usually unfolding at a rapid pace, these decisions have to be made in a split second. Often teachers see better solutions in retrospect than they do in the heat of the moment. Unfortunately there are no absolute guidelines, as the type and extent of the intervention depend to a large extent on the temperaments, ages, and relationships of the children involved, the history (both immediate and long term) of the conflict, and the possibilities for resolution. One can keep in mind, however, the need to balance children's needs both to learn how to resolve conflicts on their own and to be safe from being hurt or hurting others.

The experience of resolving conflicts fosters children's sense of autonomy and confidence in their problem-solving skills (Kamii & DeVries, 1977, 1980). By projecting a reassuring presence but not mandating a solution, teachers can encourage the children to articulate the problem and generate solutions. It is of questionable value to use threats such as, "If you can't use the sand together, then you will have to find another activity," or to enforce social amenities such as "Tell Jason that you are sorry." These interventions do not encourage children to take responsibility for their actions but simply reaffirm the teacher's power. Instead, teachers can model listening with respect to all points of view and guide children through a negotiating process. In their book, *Group Games*, Kamii and DeVries (1980) describe in detail particular conflict situations and teachers' responses to them and analyze the consequences of these interventions in terms of whether or not they promoted children's autonomy.

What about situations where an injury to a person or a piece of equipment or material has already occurred? In these events, emotions are high and the opportunities for preventive negotiation are nil. Mutual blaming, the tears of the injured party, and anger often prevail. One way of trying to conciliate the parties is to help children focus on restitution to the victim. As described by Schaffer and Sinicrope (1983), restitution is a positive alternative to retribution. By focusing on ways to aid and compensate the victim, (e.g., helping rebuild the block tower that was knocked down or getting a cold towel to put on the wound), the effects of the aggressive act become a shared problem instead of the object of vociferous blaming. Furthermore, the aggressor, who may be feeling some remorse, is able to reestablish himself or herself in a positive way. The different conclusions that children can draw from consequences of retribution and restitution are seen in the models in Figure 7.1.

One problem, of course, is that the target of the aggressive act does not always want to receive the help of the aggressor. Here teachers can help the victim say what would make her or him feel better so that she or he has some feeling of control. Also, if it appears that direct contact between the two parties is too combustible at that point, the aggressor might perform an indirect but related restitutive act. For example, if one child has torn another's painting, she or he could put fresh paper on the easel and clean the brushes so that the materials are available if the second child wants to paint another picture.

Young children do not distinguish between intention and effect, and this fact often makes it difficult to resolve conflicts that arise from ac-

---

Figure 7.1: Conclusions Children Draw from Retribution and Restitution

Retribution
I got caught $\longrightarrow$ I'm in trouble $\longrightarrow$ I get punished

Possible conclusions:
    I'm a victim.
    I survived the punishment.
    It's worth the risk.

Restitution
I did something wrong $\longrightarrow$ I'm in trouble $\longrightarrow$ I have to make up for it

Possible conclusions:
    I feel bad when I do something wrong.
    I feel better when I make up for my misbehavior.

Adapted from Schaffer & Sinicrope, 1983.

cidents (e.g., knocking over the block tower by mistake). As many studies have shown, young children tend to judge a child who breaks ten cups by mistake as more culpable than one who breaks one cup on purpose. Therefore, telling an injured child that "Sarah did not mean it" has little effect. Here again, focusing on "What can we do to make Rachel feel better?" removes the question of intention and moves the episode to a more positive conclusion.

AUTONOMY

Another aspect of children's social orientation is their moral development, as described by Piaget (1965). He saw the process as the shift from a state of heteronomy, in which children viewed rules and decisions as absolute and immutable, to a more autonomous state in which rules can be changed to meet emerging social needs. In his famous "marble studies," Piaget (1965) observed how children pass through this transition between the ages of five and twelve.

The development of autonomy has several important implications for helping children to develop a multicultural perspective. First, it is people who can speak their own minds (Kamii & DeVries, 1977) who can resist and challenge discriminatory social attitudes and practices. Dependency and fatalism are among the traditional ways of maintaining conformity. The progress that has been made in civil rights has occurred because some individuals and groups were able to see the status quo as unjust and changeable. Second, children who are more autonomous may not as readily absorb and accept negative attitudes about other people. They will be more inclined to question the sweeping assumptions and contradictions of prejudice. Finally, if children learn about rules as responses to emerging social needs, then they will be able to see unfamiliar lifestyles and social conventions in that context. For instance, they might understand more readily that people who do not use silverware might have rules about touching food with their hands that differ from those of the children's own families.

While children do not become truly autonomous until they reach adulthood, the origins of autonomy are evident in young children. The oppositional behavior of toddlers and two-year-olds and the efforts at mastery and independence of preschoolers are necessary stages in children's self-determination. Preschool and primary-level classroom practices and organization can foster this development by involving children in decision making related to their own actions and the functioning of the classroom.

One practice that is fruitful is to have children participate in deciding the classroom rules. Preschool teachers will have to set restrictions that involve safety, since their children are unable to predict consequences of potentially dangerous situations. Primary-school children can be involved with more regulatory decisions. Children at all ages have many ideas about appropriate interpersonal behavior. In the process of deciding on rules, children articulate their own needs; listen to the needs of others; and think about the purpose, fairness, and enforcement of the rules. As rule makers (instead of rule breakers), children experience the reality of different points of view. Often children who are eager to curtail the rights of others realize that, when it applies to them, there are disadvantages in repression. As children debate the merits of different routines and regulations, they are reflecting on a small scale about what it takes for a society to function.

Decision making about rules or any other classroom business is often a cumbersome process with young children. It is hard for them to weigh genuinely the various options. When given the time and guidance, however, they often arrive at very fair and impressive solutions. Ideally decisions about rules are made with a consensus rather than strict majority vote. One problem with "majority rule" is that the emphasis often shifts to peer pressure and winning rather than the purpose and acceptability of a particular rule.

One teacher described how his class deliberated for several months about whether or not there should be a rule not to interrupt the teacher when he was helping another child. In the end, the children arrived at a rule that offered several alternatives, according to the urgency of need. The teacher also agreed to the students' request that he be available for questions at certain periods. The rule was impressive, as it demonstrated that, through their deliberations, the children came to see the problem from both points of view and to recognize the existence and potential for many different contingencies that made an absolute rule unfair and unenforceable. While preschool children are not able to arrive at such complex solutions, they are able to make more simple decisions about level of noise, whether or not children can hit, and uses of various pieces of equipment.

Children can also participate in decisions about other aspects of the classroom. Teachers need to be aware of children's developmental capabilities, in order not to overwhelm them. A group of preschoolers would not be able to reach a group decision about where to go on a field trip, but they could decide what snack to take with them. On the other hand, older children might enjoy investigating field trip options and reporting back to the class, which could then choose on the basis of their peers' information.

Children should be allowed to make meaningful decisions, not just superficial ones. If children are assigned specific pages to do in their workbooks, giving the choice of doing them in crayon or pencil is not very meaningful. However, if they are given the choice among real alternatives, then they can make a decision based on preference. Needless to say, preschool teachers, who designate a large portion of the day as free play, find this guideline considerably easier to follow than elementary school teachers, who usually have certain curriculum materials that they must cover in a given period of time. In the latter case, the range of options is narrower, but there are usually alternative ways of teaching a particular concept.

Children also can make choices about their "self-management." If a child's need and the group's need are in conflict (a typical example is a child who cannot sit still during storytime), then the child has the responsibility of deciding between the option of staying with the group and being quiet or going to another area of the room. Often this choice is presented in a punitive way, where a child is threatened with removal. This response diminishes rather than enhances children's confidence that they can control and manage themselves. As with most discipline issues, if this conflict is handled preventively instead of in the heat of the moment, teachers will be in a position where they can offer a legitimate choice.

Another way in which teachers can engage children in social decision making is to present them with dilemmas, either in story form or with puppets or skits. In a recent study (Edwards, 1983, 1986), children as young as two and a half were able to ponder whether or not the bigger child should get more of the cookies than the smaller one, or whether it was all right to break the rule of not running in order to go get help for a child who was hurt. As children tried to resolve some of these dilemmas, they frequently experienced confusion that was followed (sometimes several days later) by new insights into the nature of the problem. Using this technique, teachers can help children to become more aware of their assumptions and the possibility of questioning them.

Classroom rules embody different values and vary to the extent that they foster or limit children's autonomy. Teachers should be aware of the "messages" conveyed by the rules and how meaningful they are to the children. In general, preschool rules tend to emphasize interpersonal respect and caring for one another, so that their purpose is easy for young children to understand. In contrast, elementary classroom rules tend to focus on classroom order ("no talking," and "get permission before going to the bathroom") (Schaffer & Siniacrope, 1983). Ironically, these latter rules tend to be more physically constraining than preschool ones, even though the older children are able to function more autonomously. Another problem with these rules is that they convey the message that classroom order is more important than human needs.

When children see rules as arbitrary and meaningless, they often try to break them, and the cycle of rebellion and constraint begins. One way that these rules work against social harmony is the prevalence of "tattling" that is seen in many classrooms. The rules become weapons that children use in competing for the teacher's approval. Tattling puts the teacher—the rule maker and enforcer—in the position of either being caught in a squabble between children or having to say that it does not matter if a rule is being broken. While rebelling and tattling will occur in any situation where there are authority and rules, they are greatly reduced if children see rules as reasonable ways of making the classroom a comfortable and safe environment for themselves and their peers.

There is a difference between democratic structures that foster autonomy and total permissiveness that fosters anarchy (Kamii & Devries, 1977, 1980). In order to interact harmoniously, children must feel safe. When the teacher is a strong and reassuring presence in the classroom, children do not worry that they or someone else will lose control. At the same time, teachers can try to engage children at their highest level of moral judgment, rather than assume that they cannot make reasoned choices. All of us live down to expectations, as well as live up to them. If the message of classroom rules and structure is "You have to be controlled," children will usually set out to prove it.

SOCIAL RESPONSIBILITY

The question of what makes people take responsibility for the welfare of others has been a focus for a lot of social science research in the last decade or more. These studies have been in large part prompted by the 1968 slaying of Kitty Genovese in New York City, whose prolonged murder was witnessed by dozens of people who did not respond or even help indirectly by calling the police.

This issue of social responsibility is central to a multicultural perspective. In order for group relationships to change in this country, people must be willing and able to fight not only for their own rights but also for others'. Many of the factors that seem to be related to people's willingness to become involved have been addressed elsewhere in this book: identifying with others, seeing situations from others' points of view, and feeling a sense of efficacy. This section will discuss ways that these findings can be translated into classroom practice.

Assisting others is one way in which children become aware of others' needs and gain confidence in their ability to help. Teachers can encourage children to assist each other in many ways. Younger children can help peers with smocks and snowsuits. Older children can explain assignments or help measure the yarn for another's weaving project. While young children's efforts to help or comfort an injured or frightened peer are often egocentric (e.g., offering the blanket that they themselves go to for comfort) and therefore not always successful, teachers can still encourage this kind of reaction. Older children enjoy learning rudimentary first aid and willingly accompany their injured peers to the school nurse. As children gain confidence and experience in their efforts to assist, they will be more willing to take the risk of getting involved.

A student teacher did a curriculum project with her kindergarteners on caring for living things. It started with a dentist and hospital role play; however, as she and the children discussed and enacted activities involved with caring, the scope expanded to include babies, pets, plants, and grandparents. Her cooperating teacher observed that during and after this project the children were more attentive and responsive to each others' needs in all areas of the classroom.

Classroom pets also provide many opportunities for children to observe another living being's needs and to respond appropriately. When given the responsibility, children will (adamantly!) alert the teacher to the fact that the guinea pig's water jar or food dish is empty and needs to be replenished.

Older children can extend their involvement to people outside of the immediate classroom. Visiting the elderly, raising money to buy a piece of equipment for the classroom, and a bake sale to support a CARE child are a few of the many ways that children can become involved in their larger social environment.

Caring for the physical environment also promotes a sense of social responsibility. Participating in clean-up, picking up the trash outside of the school, rearranging the room, and decorating the walls all involve the group in taking responsibility for their shared environment. One school has a clean-up day once a month where all the children and teachers wash tables, chairs, dolls, and anything else that needs it. This occasion is also an opportunity for children to participate in decisions about rearranging any areas. Low, open shelves, easily cleaned surfaces, and nearby water supplies are a few of many physical adaptations that make it easier for young children to take responsibility for the appearance of their classrooms.

Children may make a lot of mistakes as they attempt to take responsibility, but, with sensitive guidance, these occasions can be used to help children become more effective in assessing others' needs and wishes and responding appropriately.

The development of positive group identities and interpersonal skills are critical components of multicultural education. Because of the complex and pervasive nature of social interactions, these goals affect all areas of curriculum and classroom management. Throughout the classroom, from the arrangement of furniture to the ways that limits are set, social expectations and values are conveyed overtly and covertly. Often very minor modifications in the structure of an activity can make a major difference in the social experience that children have. As teachers plan activities and classroom structures, they should carefully consider the social implications of each decision.

8 **Multilingual Classrooms:
"I'm George, Not Jorge"**

"I'm George, not Jorge!" This quotation from an adamant six-year-old Hispanic child illustrates several of the issues related to children from families who speak a language other than standard English. The repudiation of his Spanish name first reflects the frequency with which children's names are mispronounced or Anglicized by teachers and peers. Second, it is indicative of the higher social status that is generally accorded Anglicized names. Third, it illustrates how, at the most basic level of linguistic learning, one's name, some children distance themselves from their home language in order to belong to the larger social group.

For many generations of immigrants, speaking English was considered a major ingredient for success; as a result, one's language of origin and vestiges of it were regarded with embarrassment. A college student whose family came from Italy described how her father always refused to answer the telephone because he was ashamed of his accent and did not want it to reflect badly on the rest of the family. This concern was reinforced by the host community, which derided accents and "poor English." Schools traditionally forbade the use of any languages other than English, in their efforts to Americanize children. Similarly, dialects that differed from standard English were seen as evidence of linguistic deficits. In the 1960s and 1970s many early childhood programs specifically targeted African American children, in an effort to eradicate their dialects and instill standard English.

Today there is more tolerance of different languages and dialects and even some recognition that monolingual English-speaking Americans are at a disadvantage in international and regional communication. However, perceptions of language are still biased; not all variances are equally valued. A Hispanic American child may be described as having a "language handicap" and an African American child as speaking "substandard English," whereas a child visiting from France may be admired for having "a charming French accent." Likewise, Anglophone children are applauded for their attempts to speak a few words in Spanish, whereas Hispanic children are criticized for not speaking better English. It is ironic that educational efforts are expended both to eliminate other languages from some children's repertoire and to teach these same languages (often with little success) to monolingual English-speaking college and high school students.

A major goal of multicultural education is to prepare children from all language backgrounds to participate fully in every aspect of our society. Skills in speaking, reading, and writing English fluently are cornerstones of this effort. A common language is also crucial for the attainment of the goal of promoting cross-group relationships. At the same time, ethnic identities and distinctions, which include home languages, are also highly valued. Not surprisingly, many teachers feel confused about the appropriate role of home languages in the classroom. There is a lot of debate as to the degree to which standard English should be used, the value of maintaining the home language, and the implications for literacy and social relationships that might result from any of these decisions. The following sections address some of these issues and provide guidelines for teachers confronting these choices.

WHEN ENGLISH IS A SECOND LANGUAGE

There has been considerable controversy about the role of home languages and English in classrooms. As the following descriptions illustrate, existing programs reflect a variety of social goals and theories of learning.

Programs Using English Exclusively

SUBMERSION PROGRAMS

As mentioned earlier, public schools have traditionally tried to teach all children to be fluent in English and to eliminate or eradicate their home languages. To achieve these goals, a method referred to as *submersion* or *sink or swim* has been widely used. Children are placed in settings where all classroom business is conducted in English. In some schools children are actively discouraged and sometimes forbidden to speak their own languages, even at lunch and on the playground. The theory behind this approach is that, the more children use English, the more fluent they will become.

In recent years some of these submersion programs have been augmented with English as a Second Language (ESL) programs. Varying in the level of intensity, this instruction consists of anywhere from a few hours a week to a few hours a day of individual or small-group lessons in English vocabulary and grammar. The intent of these sessions is to accelerate children's progress in English and to provide a formal context for their conversational skills. In cases where the ESL class is taught by someone fluent in the children's home language, the children can use the sessions to clarify directions and concepts that they are trying to follow and learn in their regular classroom. However, the instructors are often working with children from several language backgrounds and so frequently cannot serve as interpretors.

Both with and without ESL tutoring, submersion programs emphasize the value of the second language and make no attempt to validate or retain the home language. Under these conditions, children quickly learn that it is most advantageous to switch to English as quickly as possible, as without this fluency they cannot participate fully in the formal and informal activities of the classroom. It is not surprising that children in these programs start denying their home language in favor of English. Furthermore, as children learn all their new information and skills in English, their home language becomes more obsolete because it does not keep pace with their knowledge.

These programs have been criticized, as they force children to "play a dangerous game of catch-up" (Krashen, 1981). As a result, many are soon behind in their work and often never become full participants in their schooling. Another deleterious result has been limited bilingualism, where some children do not gain true proficiency in either their first or second language. They stop speaking their home language and do not really master their second one (Saville-Troike, 1982). Furthermore, critics have suggested that attempting to eliminate children's home languages, rather than being a pedagogically sound practice, reflects disparaging views of different languages and teachers' discomfort with not understanding children's communication among themselves.

IMMERSION APPROACH

A second form of intensive language teaching is called *immersion*. In these programs, all classroom business and subjects are conducted in the second language, but, in contrast to the submersion programs, none of the children are fluent in the second language. Thus, the second language is used and spoken in ways that are appropriate to the comprehension and fluency levels of the learners. This kind of program has had widely acclaimed success in teaching French to Canadian Anglophone children. Some American educators have urged that these immersion programs be used with language-minority children in the United States (Daley, 1983). However, in considering this proposal, the different contexts in the two countries should be compared. In Canada, English is the most commonly used language and generally the one spoken by people in power, so that Anglophone children retain and develop their English fluency as well as learning French. In other words, for children in high-status language groups, this intensive form of exposure is successful in developing true proficiency in both languages. However, for children of low-status language groups, whose home languages are not supported in the larger social environment, immersion programs function more like the submersion ones and are likely to lead to a reduction of home-language skills (Krashen, 1981).

The Bilingual Approach

In the 1960s and 1970s, many ethnic groups resisted the notion that English should be taught at the expense of the home languages. This movement, along with the widely acknowledged failure of the submersion programs to achieve the goal of true second-language fluency and literacy, created some momentum for programs that simultaneously maintained the children's home languages and taught them English. These programs, generally referred to as *bilingual education*, have been federally supported since 1968 with the passage of Chapter 7 of the Elementary and Secondary Education Act. In addition, the *Lau* v. *Nichols* Supreme Court decision in 1974 stipulated that special language programs were necessary if schools were to provide equal educational opportunities to all students. If a district has more than 25 language-minority students, then a special language program must be provided in all subject areas. Since the court decision, several states have mandated that schools provide bilingual programs; in many districts, schools have voluntarily established bilingual programs. In some communities, however, the parents have had to sue the district before getting these programs into the schools.

The intent, form, and content of bilingual programs vary widely, and they have been hailed and assailed by supporters and critics alike. Their common characteristics include instruction of subject matter and reading in the home language and either rapid or gradual introduction of the English language through direct instruction and in less abstract activities. As students gain skills in English, they are increasingly integrated into classes where all instruction occurs in English. Many programs are also bicultural, which means that they incorporate the traditions, foods, arts, and values of the home culture, as well as the language.

The ways that these programs are organized vary widely, but one form that has been deemed successful (Legarreta-Marcaida, 1981) is one in which the two languages are consistently used for certain portions of the day and for specific subjects. For instance, math, science, reading, and social studies are taught in, say, Vietnamese in the morning; and art, music, physical education, and drama are conducted in English in the afternoon. Students learn how to read and begin to work with abstract concepts in their home languages. After they have a solid grounding in these skills and a high level of fluency in English, the percentage of instruction in English increases, until students exit into all-English classes (usually after three to four years).

Although the goal of learning to function in English is paramount, these programs also emphasize the development of the child's home-language skills. Some of these maintenance bilingual programs enroll native English-speaking students in order to reduce the segregation of the bilingual students from the other groups in the school and to provide opportunities for English-speaking students to learn a second language. For these students, these programs are somewhat analogous to the French immersion programs for the Anglophone Canadians.

Other bilingual programs are more transitional; both the home language and English are used in all activities, the goal being children's learning how to function in English as quickly as possible. The children are transferred into all–English programs as soon as they achieve a certain level of fluency, and there is little effort to maintain and develop home-language skills.

Preschool bilingual programs have a different structure, since the days are not divided by subject matter. Sometimes the different languages will be used on alternate days. Other programs may split the day, with, say, Chinese in the morning and English in the afternoon. In cases where some of the teachers are monolingual, they each speak to the children in their own language so that children learn to shift languages according to teacher. One disadvantage of this latter arrangement is that children might avoid their cross-language teachers and depend more on their home-language teachers.

RATIONALE FOR BILINGUAL PROGRAMS

Bilingual programs have been the center of political, financial, and philosophical controversies, which will be discussed later. Many studies have suggested, however, that they are the most effective way of helping economically disadvantaged, low-status, language-minority children to gain true proficiency in English and to maintain academic progress (e.g., Egan & Goldsmith, 1981; Legarreta-Marcaida, 1979; Rosier & Farella, 1976). Many educators find it difficult to believe these results, as common sense suggests that proficiency in English is directly related to the amount of exposure and use. Also, they assume that learning in two languages is confusing and cumbersome and retards rather than accelerates academic progress.

These arguments rest on the assumption that proficiency in each language is learned independently and stored separately in the brain; therefore, the two languages are competing for a limited amount of time and mental capacity. An alternative view of this process is that there is a common underlying capacity for the development of linguistic skills, which is interdependent across languages (Cummins, 1981). For instance, if children learn how to associate printed words with spoken ones in their home language, they do not have to completely relearn that process when they switch to another language. Evidence for this theory is found in the high correlation between the reading skills in both languages of bilinguals. As further support, older arrivals to this country who have already learned to read in their primary language achieve grade-level proficiency in reading in English more quickly than their younger counterparts who learn to read in their second language (Izzo, 1981).

This last observation appears to contradict the conventional wisdom that young children learn languages more easily than do older persons. First, it is possible that this observed facility may really reflect the lower level of competency expected of younger children or their lack of self-consciousness in using their rudimentary knowledge, more than it describes any innate ability (Saville-Troike, 1982). Second, even if young children do quickly acquire conversational skills, it takes considerably longer for them to be able to use the second language in more cognitively demanding and abstract tasks (Cummins, 1981). Educators often assume that children who have mastered enough English to participate in classroom routines and peer interactions are ready to learn to read, write, and master abstract material in English. The often puzzling failure of children to manage these tasks in their second language supports the notion that there is another level of proficiency that is required for them.

It is not hard to understand this difference if we think about our own experiences with "foreign" languages. People traveling in foreign countries often report, with chagrin, that their rudimentary French or Italian, which was sufficient for ordering food and getting directions, was embarrassingly inadequate for conversing about more abstract topics. In short, academic tasks require more fluency and structural understanding of a language than conversations and routines do. In order for children to progress in these subjects, they need to learn them in their familiar language until they have achieved true fluency in their second one.

Further pedagogical support for bilingual programs comes from evidence that children who are truly proficient in two languages are more cognitively flexible (Cummins, 1979) and have more advanced linguistic skills and metalinguistic understanding (Albert & Obler, 1978; Lambert & Tucker, 1972). Thus, truly bilingual children may enjoy a more enriching educational environment than their monolingual peers. This phenomenon appears to be true, however, only in cases where children have fully developed linguistic skills in both languages; the opposite tends to be the case when children have a low level of development in both languages.

CRITICISMS OF BILINGUAL PROGRAMS

Very strong objections have been raised about bilingual education because in effect it isolates language-minority children from the mainstream (e.g., Rodriguez, 1981). Critics point out that, if children spend all of their early schooling only with peers from the same background, they will not learn the social styles, values, and childhood rituals that facilitate successful entry into the mainstream when they enter English-instructed classrooms.

This criticism is legitimate and needs to be addressed by schools in which there are bilingual programs. There are some ways of reducing the isolation. The most obvious one is to integrate native English-speaking children into the bilingual classrooms so that many children, not just members of one particular ethnic group, participate in the bilingual program. Also, increasing the number of children who speak more than one language improves the likelihood of both languages being used on the playground and during informal activities. Another way of integrating the groups is to combine bilingual and English-speaking students for certain activities such as art, gym, music, and language arts. In these circumstances teachers need to be careful that the activities are structured to prevent the situation from becoming a "sink-or-swim" one for the children who do not speak the dominant language in the class. Here, teachers can also apply some of the guidelines for promoting cross-group interactions that were discussed in chapter 7. By making a commitment to becoming bilingual as a whole, schools and centers can reduce the gap between nonbilingual and bilingual children; the expectation that a second language will be learned would apply to all children and teachers.

A lot of vehement protesting about bilingual education has come from immigrants of older generations, who feel that they were able to "make it" in the American society without the aid of bilingual programs. That people should resent the expenditure of their tax moneys for services that were not available to them is understandable. Many of these people paid a high price for their assimilation, in terms of cultural isolation and alienation. Community-supported bilingual education is not new, however. German-English schools were established in Ohio in the mid-nineteenth century; in 1837 the Pennsylvania legislature ordered that German-language schools be established on an equal basis with English-language schools (Grosjean, 1982). In some cases, other language schools were not tax supported but communities formed schools on their own that taught in home languages such as German, Dutch, and Swedish (Fishman, 1966). Thus, the claim that bilingual educational alternatives were unavailable to earlier groups is not completely accurate.

Whether earlier groups of immigrants had schooling in their own languages or not, today's world is different, and changes in the nature of the technological and social demands of contemporary society support the current need for more comprehensive schooling of bilingual children. In the nineteenth and early twentieth centuries, many immigrant children worked in factories and did not attend school at all. Those who did go to school usually left at an early age to work as manual laborers. A rudimentary knowledge of conversational English was sufficient for obtaining and performing most jobs. Today, however, students need to acquire a much more advanced level of academic skill in order to meet most job requirements. Thus, the greater proficiency in language skills that seems to be fostered by bilingual programs is required (Ortheguy, 1982).

Much criticism of bilingual programs is premised on the assumption that they do not teach children English, but keep students isolated from the English-speaking environment. This argument rests on a misperception of the goals and practice of bilingual programs. James

Fallows (1983) described his initial skepticism about bilingual education. After visiting a number of bilingual classrooms, he was convinced that the students were, in fact, learning English. Teachers faced with similar resistance from their community or parents may be able to reassure them in a similar way by inviting them to visit the classrooms and see for themselves that the children are, in fact, learning English.

Despite the controversy, research suggests that bilingual programs are most effective with language-minority children in this country (Egan & Goldsmith, 1981; Rosier & Farella, 1976). The higher academic proficiency and the more positive self-esteem associated with bilingual programs are predictive of fuller participation and greater success in both academic and occupational settings. Furthermore, bilingual skills are valuable in terms of future employment.

Finally, there are the language needs of the nation as a whole. Many leaders have expressed concern about the poor preparation that Americans have for working in linguistically diverse environments, both at home and abroad. Not taking advantage of students who already have a capacity for dual languages is, as one school principal said, "a terrible waste of our human resources" (*Bilateral Conflict*, 1983, p. 39).

ALTERNATIVES TO BILINGUAL PROGRAMS

Many schools and programs do not have the distribution of children or the teaching staff needed to develop and maintain a bilingual program that can provide the consistent maintenance of a home language. In addition, some communities and parents might strongly prefer that their children be more fully integrated into English-speaking classes. The opinions of parents may vary according to their length of residency in this country, their status in the immediate community, and their plans for permanent or temporary residence in this country (Rist, 1982). Thus, for a number of reasons, a town, school, or center may not implement a fully bilingual program. Even so, there are many aspects that can be incorporated into any classroom, some of which I will describe.

One of the reasons bilingual education has been successful is that it has increased children's positive regard for their language and culture. While English-speaking teachers may be far from fluent in another language, they can respect children's use of it and learn enough to incorporate it into some classroom routines and resources. Children can hear and learn from records of songs and stories in many languages. Labels in the classroom can be written in several languages,

with the help of parents and community people. Entertaining classroom guests and going on field trips are good ways of bringing other
languages into the school. Books in different languages are generally
available, although a cautionary note is due here: Some authors (e.g.,
Thonis, 1981) have noted that the non–English books are often old and
unattractive compared to those in English, so books need to be selected with care to avoid conveying the message that other languages
are less valued. Teachers also should scrutinize books to see whether
they present the language in its cultural context or if they are merely
translations of English texts. Although the latter types can be used to
show English-speaking children how familiar stories can be conveyed
in different languages, they are less useful for fostering children's appreciation of the cultural context of the language.

At a very basic level, educators should avoid thinking of children
or describing them as "not speaking English." Rather, they should be
described positively as "speaking Thai" (or Hebrew . . . or Farsi). While
it is a small and perhaps semantic point, simply describing children in
terms of a language they do *not* speak implies a lack of interest and respect for the home language. Furthermore, thinking of children in terms
of their inabilities fosters the deficit orientation that has traditionally
characterized approaches to children from diverse language backgrounds. Whether or not a child speaks English will have an inevitable
impact on planning and implementing activities, but a lack of English
skills can be seen alternatively as a potential source of language enrichment for all children in the classroom.

Respect for children's home lives is easily conveyed by incorporating aspects of their cultures into the classroom. As discussed in chapters 4, 5, and 6, there are many possible ways of broadening the cultural
base of the curriculum through props, books, photographs, tools, holidays, activities, parent participation, and field trips. Encouraging
children to bring in objects, songs, recipes, and clothing from home
also lets parents know that the teacher is interested and respectful of
their experience and knowledge. Projects such as art or cooking are
good vehicles for involving parents in the classroom. While it often
happens that the parent and the teacher can only carry on a rudimentary conversation, other children who speak the parent's language enjoy having an adult that they can talk to in the classroom.

Although the children in a class may not share a common language, they can learn how to communicate their ideas without words.
Pantomime, "silent circles" (where teachers conduct group times with
miming and no talking), interpretive gestures, and other nonverbal activities pose some interesting problem-solving situations to the chil-

dren and foster their abilities to both convey and interpret nonverbal information. Increasing these skills will help children be more adept at interacting with their peers when there is not a shared language.

Approaches to Teaching English as a Second Language

Regardless of one's opinion about whether or not the home language should be maintained, attaining fluency and literacy in English is of critical importance to children from different linguistic backgrounds. While there is overwhelming agreement on this goal, the method of achieving it has been the subject of much debate.

Some linguists differentiate between "learning a second language" and "acquiring a second language" (Krashen, 1981; Stevick, 1980). In the first process, students consciously attempt to learn the grammatical rules of the language. Second-language acquisition, in contrast, is a more subconscious process in which effectively communicating with others is the major focus.

Traditionally, instruction in a new language has emphasized language learning, a sequenced teaching of grammatical structure and vocabulary. Current research suggests, however, that the communicative approach of second-language acquisition is a more effective and efficient method (Krashen, 1981; Saville-Troike, 1982). In other words, rather than being drilled on vocabulary and grammar, children can practice speaking and hearing English while participating in games and other social activities. Stevick (1980) suggests that stimulating their imagination and interaction with other peers is a way of engaging children in conversations. Weininger (1982) maintains that there is a relationship between "the close, continuous, and subtle interaction between the child's physical and mental experience and his achievement of a functioning verbal repertoire" (p. 26). If children are engrossed in an activity that they find intrinsically interesting (e.g., playing with blocks or doing a science experiment), then they will more freely participate in the related conversations than they will in artificial dialogues that focus on specific rules of their new language (e.g., "What is your name?" "My name is . . . "). In his criticisms of the formal language instruction of the French immersion programs for Anglophone Canadians, Weininger (1982) suggests that children will learn a second language most readily in "the rough and ready . . . urgent world of play and action with other children who speak [the second language]" (p. 31). These opinions support the plans to enroll English-speaking children in bilingual classes and/or combined bilingual and English-speaking classes for the more social activities such as gym, art, music, lunch, and recess.

Many activities in both preschool and primary grades are ideal for promoting this kind of language acquisition. Dramatic play, group block play, cooperative games, and art activities generate a lot of conversation among children. To organize these activities, children must name and describe objects, people, and situations. There also are many gestural, material, and visual clues that they can use, so that the progress of the conversation will not be unduly stalled for want of a common vocabulary. Sensory experiences also provide opportunities for children to hear and say a lot of descriptive words in a memorable context. Sliding down the slide or fire pole, feeling concealed objects, looking at pictures of familiar and unfamiliar objects, smelling different substances, and moving one's body in unusual ways often prompt children to use descriptive and creative language. Children also have a lot of motivation to learn directions when engaged in activities and games such as "Simon Says."

Emotional factors, sometimes referred to as the "affective filter" (Dulay & Burt, 1977), also impede or facilitate the acquisition of a second language. Not surprisingly, low anxiety, high self-confidence, and positive motivation are associated with effective language acquisition (Gardner & Lambert, 1972; Krashen, 1981; Wong-Fillmore, 1979). Providing high-interest activities in a nonevaluative and encouraging environment is more effective than drilling and testing children on specific rules and vocabulary.

STAGES OF SECOND-LANGUAGE ACQUISITION

To reduce anxiety and to provide an optimal balance of familiarity and challenge, it is useful to keep in mind the stages of second-language acquisition. In games and tasks and in casual conversations, teachers can modify their expectations and questions according to the following stages and suggestions, which are adapted from "The Natural Approach in Bilingual Education" by Terrell (1981).

Preproduction Stage. The first stage is called the preproduction or silent stage. A child's initial response to a new language is to concentrate on understanding what is being said, rather than try to reproduce it. For this period, games and activities designed to elicit only physical responses, such as directed group creative movement exercises, are most appropriate. Children will be most comfortable answering questions about objects, pictures, or people that require only gestural responses or one-word answers. For children with no previous familiarity with English, this stage may last from three to six months. Children should be allowed to stay at this receptive stage until they are comfortable and confident enough to start speaking the second language.

Transition to Production.   The second stage is a transition to production. Teachers may assess whether or not children are ready to begin to give verbal responses by occasionally asking questions that elicit yes/no or here/there answers. If children seem to be comfortable with these minimum production demands, then their speech can be further encouraged with questions that ask for single-word answers, such as either/or questions or requests to label familiar objects ("What is this?") and finish statements ("We are eating . . . "). It is important that these activities not be done in a drill or testing context, but simply integrated into conversations or group discussions.

Early Production.   The third stage is that of early production, in which children can respond to questions and activities that require single-word or short-phrase responses (e.g., "Tell me what Susie is doing"). Children are able to engage in simple conversations, classroom games, and structured activities such as guided interviews.

Expansion of Production.   In the fourth stage, children are ready to expand their speech production in as many ways as possible. Here teachers can ask more open-ended questions, pose problems, and ask children to describe events, objects, and people. To personalize the new language, students can be encouraged to talk about their feelings, families, and friends. At this time word games such as guessing an object from verbal clues or inventing rhymes are enjoyable and effective ways of having children use their new language.

Introduction to Written Forms.   For children in the primary grades, there is one more stage before they are ready to begin to read and write in their new language. As children begin to express interest in the written form of their new language, teachers may help them make rudimentary associations between the written and spoken forms of familiar words. More formal and systematic reading and writing instruction should not begin until students show good comprehension skills and spoken fluency in their second language.

WORKING WITH PARENTS

Although conversations and conferences between monolingual English-speaking teachers and parents who speak a language other than English are often difficult, all efforts should be made to maintain personal contact. Some local service agencies offer free translation and interpretation services that may help teachers in their written and verbal communication with parents. A bilingual parent may be willing to serve as the school interpreter in return for a reduction in fees or a small honorarium. A lot of visual material can be used to show parents what a child is doing in school.

A common concern of parents of children from other language backgrounds is how to promote their child's skills in English. Parents often feel that they should be speaking English in the home and drilling their children in English, in order to accelerate their progress. Traditionally, teachers have urged parents to follow this course of action, even though it hindered the communication between parents and children (Rodriguez, 1981). However, current research suggests that it is better for parents to continue to speak to their children in their home language, especially if the school is unable to provide home-language maintenance programs (Cummins, 1981). The more skilled children are in their home languages, the more able they are to learn a second language. Furthermore, if parents speak only rudimentary English, then the home linguistic environment becomes limited and sparse. Since the English-speaking school environment is often restricted for a child who has only beginning skills in English, it is especially important that the home be linguistically rich. Teachers can encourage parents to read to their children in their own language and, if the children express interest, show them some of the printed words of that language. Because many parents are concerned about their children's English skills, teachers may want to enlist the aid of professionals from the parents' own backgrounds, who can explain the value of maintaining children's home language in terms of their future educational and occupational prospects.

One task that English-speaking teachers and children need to learn is how to speak understandably with children and parents from other linguistic backgrounds. When speaking in their native tongue, people often talk too fast, slur words, and use idiomatic expressions that are hard to translate. Teachers have an enormous number of interactions each day and may therefore have a hard time slowing and simplifying their speech. At the same time, if teachers can speak more understandably, they will save themselves some repetition and misinterpretation. Another problem is the tendency to talk more loudly when addressing someone who speaks a different language, as though we are assuming that the listener is hard of hearing. A loud tone also sounds harsh and impatient and may aggravate the listener's anxiety. Teachers in team situations may be able to monitor each other and use nonverbal cues to remind their colleagues to slow down, to lower their voices, or to speak more distinctly. Alternatively, they can use tape recordings of their conversations with children and parents to obtain feedback on how well they are being understood.

The fact that most Americans speak only English is an embarrassing reflection of our own chauvinism. I remember with chagrin the utter amazement of a French colleague when she learned that I could speak only one language. At the same time, we commonly criticize others for not speaking *our* language, or even worse, *the* language, as though English were the only language in the world. Children who speak other languages are often described as having "no language skills." While it is obviously imperative that there be a common national language, all Americans, including English-speaking children, need to see English in a more international and multilingual perspective.

One way of promoting this orientation is for teachers to model a linguistic reciprocity by trying to learn other languages. For example, one preschool was attended by many children of foreign students, and these children represented a total of fifteen different languages. At the request of the staff, the parents made a book with simple sentences that teachers often needed, such as "Your mother will be here soon" or "Do you need to go to the bathroom?" This project was done for all fifteen languages. The parents and their children then enjoyed "coaching" the teachers. This activity also gave the foreign families, who were having to experience daily their lack of expertise in English, the opportunity to be the experts. The teachers, in turn, gained a better sense of how it feels not to speak the common language and, of course, learned many phrases useful for responding to the children in their classrooms.

DIVERSE SPEECH PATTERNS IN ENGLISH

Aside from the many languages that are spoken in this country, there are also numerous ways of speaking English. These variations range from regional differences in pronunciation, such as the dropping of r's in a Boston accent, to distinct dialects such as Cajun, Ebonics, or Appalachian English, which have different grammatical structures. In between there are distinctions in tempo, word usage, imagery, inflection, and conversational conventions. In fact, the phrase *standard English* is really a misnomer when applied to the spoken form. Many people consider their own particular style to be standard English and readily label other patterns as "accents," "poor English," and examples of regional aberrations. Speakers are often surprised to hear someone say, "You sound so Eastern" or "You talk just like our friend Anna, who is also from Minnesota."

This diversity is a frequent source of confusion and misunderstanding. When two people speak different languages, they do not expect to understand each other, so they compensate with nonverbal communication and accept the limits of the verbal conversation. When both people think that they are speaking the same language, however, they are not as likely to make these allowances. Thus, strong regional accents, different connotations of words, and unfamiliar imagery or references may be mutually irritating to the participants, who each wonder why the other cannot speak "good English." Factors such as tempo; conventions for entering, exiting, initiating, and ending conversations; pitch of voice; and relative use of spoken versus silent language also can disrupt cross-group communications (Longstreet, 1978). One particular problem with these variations is that they often evoke irritation and avoidance, without the participants being consciously aware of the reasons.

Besides being a source of miscommunication, speech patterns are often the basis of judgments about the speaker's intelligence, character, and occupational status. In 1966, Labov had adults listen to different speakers who had a range of accents and dialects and asked his subjects to predict the speakers' occupations. He found that people very readily assigned occupational and SES categories but had a hard time identifying what characteristics of the speech gave them that information. If you monitor your own reactions to unfamiliar speakers, you will probably find that you tend to form mental images of people on the basis of their speech. As Henry Higgins assures us in *My Fair Lady*, "It's words . . . that keep her in her place, not her wretched clothes and dirty face!" (Lerner, 1956). There are many practical consequences of these judgments, as applicants for jobs, housing, and educational programs are often screened on the basis of short telephone conversations.

Dialects are often considered corruptions or degenerated forms of English; for example, certain variations such as deleted sounds or auxiliary verbs are attributed to the laziness of the speaker. Contrary to these perceptions, dialects are language patterns that have existed for generations and are learned from parents and peers, as in any language (Stewart, 1972). The linguistic analyses done in the 1960s and 1970s (Baratz & Baratz, 1970; Labov, 1969, 1975) revealed that the dialects comprising Ebonics, the currently preferred term for Black English Vernacular (BEV) (Scales, 1981), are fully developed languages and are not intrinsically inferior to standard English. In fact, these dialects often have very complex structures and are rich in sound, imagery, and variety, as can be seen in art forms such as African American poetry and rap music. In terms of the pragmatics of communication, they are efficient. In one comparison of Ebonics and standard English speech, Labov (1975) points out that the former is more direct and is clear in conveying the central thought, whereas the latter is verbose and opaque. The particular form of English that is considered "standard" reflects historical power relationships rather than any inherent superiority of that particular dialect.

As educators who are trying to reduce the discrimination based on speech patterns, we are faced with two somewhat contradictory goals. First, in order to prevent children from being summarily judged and possibly rejected on the basis of their speech patterns, we must insure that they are fluent and literate in "standard English." Second, to reduce the prejudicial responses to different speech patterns and to foster children's pride in their linguistic backgrounds, we need to validate and support the various dialects, accents, and styles of English that are spoken in this country. Individual teachers, programs, and schools will have to consider their options and decisions in the context of the prevailing sentiment of the community, parents' wishes, and their own values and goals. The following discussion will help teachers review the possibilities and develop practices that are appropriate to their particular children.

As an initial step, teachers should become familiar with the ways in which the speech patterns of the community differ from standard English (Longstreet, 1978). By understanding the distinctions and learning the structure and logic of the less familiar speech, teachers who are new to the community can move beyond a global assumption that it is "bad English." Furthermore, articulating the ways in which local speech patterns are distinguished from standard English can provide useful guidance in how to introduce "school English" most effectively to young children. Several linguists (e.g., Fasold & Wolfram, 1972; Labov, 1969, 1975) have analyzed Ebonics, but most dialects have not been systematically studied. By tape recording and analyzing children's speech, teachers will gain some insights into the most prevalent patterns.

Another way of gaining more appreciation of these variations is to listen to the poetry, songs, folktales, and children's chants in various dialects. Informal contacts and local gatherings may provide a more realistic picture of how adults and children use their language, as many of them may seem to be very reticent and "nonverbal" at the school. Assessment of children's language and competency should include some study of their home and neighborhood speech patterns, as well as their early efforts in "school English."

The meaning of the dialect to an individual or family is also a significant dimension. Teachers should learn the extent to which a particular dialect is used and its role in group values and alliances in specific families and neighborhoods.

Social scientists have often said that the biggest problem with dialects is the negative ways that others hear them (Entwisle, 1975). This observation has clear implications for educators. While teachers may not speak a particular dialect, they can actively recognize and validate it by incorporating recordings of songs, storytelling, and humor that reflect local speech patterns. These efforts will enable the children to keep enriching their home dialect and to see its potential and past contributions. There are increasing numbers of children's books that are written in dialects, which teachers can make available for children. Often teachers feel self-conscious when reading stories in unfamiliar dialects. They feel that they are mimicking the dialect instead of speaking it with ease. As teachers get more of an "ear" for the dialect, they may find that reading it becomes easier. Alternatively, they could record parents reading these stories and then play the recordings while showing the pictures to the children.

These active efforts to incorporate various dialects into the classroom may be met with some resistance by local school people or parents who may feel that they want only "good English" to be included. Here the issues are similar to those raised in conjunction with the maintenance of the home language in bilingual education. At issue is whether or not schools should help children maintain and further develop the language they already have or if they should attempt to bypass it and focus only on "school English." As discussed previously, the opinions on these issues reflect differences in social goals, views of learning, and assumptions about the home language.

Regardless of the extent to which teachers incorporate the home dialect into the classroom, it is crucial that children also become fluent and literate in standard English. Not only will children be entering a world where they will be judged on the basis of their speech patterns, but as writers and readers they will find that most written transactions and the vast majority of books in this country are in standard English.

Teaching children how to distinguish dialects from standard English poses an intriguing problem. Whereas a separate language with a clearly differentiated written base can be taught as a separate entity, the relationship between dialects is less clear. Furthermore, there is a continuum of variance that sometimes makes it difficult to distinguish specific dialects. While teachers can easily ask, "What is the Spanish word for . . . ?" it is harder to explain to young children more subtle differences such as "pahk" versus "park," the way that negatives are constructed, or the conjugation of the verb *to be*. Thus, while there are distinct ways of speaking, it is a challenge to make the differences explicit and understandable to children so that they can consciously shift dialects, as appropriate.

Some language programs (e.g., Bereiter & Englemann, 1966) have used a direct instruction approach in which children are drilled, corrected, and rewarded until they master school English. These programs have claimed considerable success in raising scores on verbal tests, but these results were not evident in two-year follow-up testing. They have also been criticized for trying to eradicate the home language, rather than building on it. Furthermore, as seen in the comparison between language learning and language acquisition earlier in this chapter, there is some question as to how well children actually learn to communicate with these learned speech patterns.

A more communicative and validating approach might involve activities where children listen closely to the differences between the home and standard dialects and identify which is being used. After the children have become accustomed to school English and seem to understand it well, the teacher could start asking them about how it is different from the way they speak. Standard English could be given a name such as "school-talk" or "Linda-talk," after the teacher; the home dialect might be designated "family-talk" or "child-talk." Then the teacher can design activities such as "Simon Says" in which the children only move when they hear "Linda-talk" or "child-talk." Children can listen to stories read in both dialects and be encouraged to listen for the differences. After they have learned to hear the distinctions, they can begin to produce the different patterns. They can be asked to describe pantomimes, pictures, and objects in both ways. Older children could make "TV programs" where they try to use "TV talk." In order for teachers to support and validate children's home dialects, it is important that these activities not convey the notion of "right" and "wrong" but rather "two different ways of saying the same thing."

Reading readiness and early reading skills are a major concern for teachers of children whose dialect is different from the one that is found in most beginning reading books. As mentioned in the section on bilingual education, it is difficult for children to work on more abstract tasks in a less familiar language. While children who speak different dialects usually comprehend standard English, they cannot see a close match between their own spoken language and what they see on the printed page. The extent to which this disparity affects early reading is the subject of some debate. It is hard to answer this question, as the variable of dialect is usually confounded with ethnic and/or class variables that also are linked to levels of school performance. In some analyses of children's reading, it has been found that black dialect phonology does not hamper children in their reading of a standard English (Jenkins, 1982). Piestrup (1973) conducted a study of different approaches to teaching reading to African American children. In one classroom, the teacher accepted and used Ebonics as well as standard English. In this classroom the children learned more standard English and made more progress in their reading than did their peers in classrooms where Ebonics were either discouraged or ignored.

Some efforts have been made to design reading materials that do introduce children to reading in their own dialects. Given the research findings supporting the use of home languages for the beginning reading of bilingual children, this approach is promising; however, these materials have generated a lot of controversy as families, teachers, and community people perceive that children are being taught to read "bad English." Also, the great number of dialects, with their regional as well as cultural variations, makes it unlikely that representative materials will be produced.

The lack of materials that reflect various dialects can be circumvented in part by using the language-experience approach to reading instruction, which enables children to see the relationship between spoken and written language, in their most familiar dialect. This method, in which children either dictate or write their own stories and then read them, also enables them to expand and appreciate their expressive skills in their home language.

Research and theory in this area do not offer any absolute guidelines for teaching children who speak dialects other than standard English. Decisions about the use of dialects will be influenced by the opinions of the local community, teachers' familiarity with the dialects, and the available materials. There is one point of agreement, however, among most people in this field: the greatest influence of dialects on children's learning is the role they play in forming teachers' expectations of the children. As educators, we need to monitor our reactions to children's speech, to insure that our evaluations about individuals' intelligence, potential, and work habits are not influenced by our reactions to specific speech patterns.

ENGLISH-SPEAKING CHILDREN

The primary intent of this chapter has been to discuss some of the dilemmas and possibilities that teachers of children from diverse language backgrounds need to consider. However, the question of language is not irrelevant to children who are native English speakers. The majority of children grow up in this country with little exposure to the rich variety of languages and dialects that exist here, as their classrooms and schools have only English-speaking children and teachers.

For these monolinguistic children, teachers can adapt many of the resources and activities already discussed in this chapter. Many simple songs can be adapted to include phrases from unfamiliar languages and dialects. Children love counting in different languages. Folk songs and tales are rich in dialectical variations. Parents and teachers who do speak other languages can be prevailed upon to come and sing or talk to the children in that language. The French-speaking mother of a child in one preschool taught the children several French songs and phrases that became a favorite part of the children's repertoire.

When one or two children speak another language, they can be encouraged to share new words with their American peers. In one second grade, with the teacher's encouragement, a girl who had recently arrived from China instructed several children on how to write and speak a few words in Chinese. She also taught the whole class several songs. Far from focusing on the problems of having a "non–English-speaking" child in the classroom, the teacher and other students were eagerly learning as much as they could in Chinese. One word of caution should be mentioned here: If children are very shy or self-conscious about their language, teachers must wait until they feel safe and accepted before expecting them to share it with their peers.

GENERAL GUIDELINES

There is an increasingly wide range of dialects and languages spoken and written in this country and a renewed interest in maintaining home languages. At the same time it is imperative that all children become fluent in written and spoken standard English so that they will not be excluded from higher levels of education and good jobs. While dialects and languages pose somewhat different issues and potential solutions for teachers, there are some common guidelines.

First, given the controversies that have arisen about bilingual and bidialectical education, teachers should be aware of prevailing attitudes and be prepared to explain their approaches to concerned parents and community people. With the disparity between future job prospects of white English-speaking, middle-class children and the offspring of other ethnic groups, many parents justifiably want tangible evidence that their children are receiving the most productive and beneficial education. Any delay in their children's learning to speak, read, and write standard English may be viewed with alarm. Presenting some of the theoretical and research data in an understandable form may help to reassure parents that maintaining home languages or dialects can contribute to their children's fluency and literacy in English, rather than relegating them to being second-class speakers. By responding to parents' concerns and inviting them to participate in the program, teachers might alleviate some of their fears. In short, any approaches with bilingual or bidialectical children should be carefully introduced to parents and the community, with supporting evidence and a balance of steadfastness and flexibility.

Second, regardless of the role of the home language in the classroom, it must be viewed with respect and interest. As teachers shift away from the deficit orientation that has characterized most thinking about language-minority children, they can begin to see children positively as speakers of another language or dialect. Teachers should avoid "correcting" home languages or conveying either overtly or covertly that they are inferior to standard English.

Third, knowledge about the local social conventions of conversation is helpful for a teacher who is a newcomer to a particular community. Conversational behavior that is sometimes interpreted as rudeness or resistance often reflects differences in social convention. The talkativeness of many Anglo-Americans is viewed with dismay by some Native Americans who rely more on silent language. A Japanese American colleague said that as a child she was instructed to speak only if she had something very important to say. This reticence may frustrate a teacher who wants the children to "express their feelings." How people enter and exit conversations varies a great deal by culture (Longstreet, 1978). What might appear to be rude interruptions or intrusive questions in one culture may be an acceptable way of conversing in another. With this information, teachers can help children communicate more effectively across groups and can more articulately assist children in learning what conventions are needed for educational and occupational success in this country.

Fourth, while monolingualism is well entrenched in English-speaking American society, teachers can begin to move beyond this limitation by extending their own language base. By learning a few phrases from parent tutors, taking a course in another language, or simply listening to poetry or songs in other languages and dialects, teachers can model the desirability and feasibility of going beyond the confines of one language. English-speaking children can be encouraged to learn from their peers from other language backgrounds. While this chapter has been directed primarily to teachers who have children from different language and dialect backgrounds in their classrooms, English-speaking children benefit from learning other languages and speech patterns from peers, books, records, and songs.

Fifth, children appear to acquire a second language or dialect most easily in a communicative context where they are encouraged to use their second language in conversations about shared activities, experiences, and important events in their own lives. While drills and sequenced lessons in a new language may provide a more systematic way of teaching the proper grammar, they do not offer children as much of a "feel" for the new language. Furthermore, as anyone who has tried to learn a new language with repeated drills can attest, these methods often evoke a strong aversion to the language.

Sixth, as children are beginning to master a new language, they go through different levels of comprehension. It is easy to assume that, because children have a certain amount of surface fluency, they are ready to learn to read and write in the new language. Monitoring children's use of the new language in a variety of circumstances will provide more accurate information about the relationship between their receptive and productive language and their readiness for more challenging activities. Teachers may feel a great deal of pressure to push children to speak or read and write in the new language, but they should avoid abbreviating the necessary stages of preproduction and prereading skills.

Finally, the possibilities for enriching the language environment are endless. Having more than one language or dialect spoken in the class provides many opportunities for shared learning, experimenting in communication skills, increasing everyone's language skills, and expanding children's understanding about the nature of language and communication.

9 When Parents and Teachers Do Not Agree

Teachers and parents share a common interest in children's welfare, but they do not always agree on educational goals and practices. Given the widely divergent views on teaching and child rearing that prevail in this country, these disputes are not surprising. They are often exacerbated by both groups' frustration about the lack of services and resources for children, families, and schools. Also, the logistics and stress of juggling child rearing and work for the parents, and the multiple demands made on teachers, often limit opportunities for contact and communication.

While an in-depth discussion of parent-teacher relationships is beyond the scope of this book, there are some issues that are particularly relevant to the implementation of a multicultural perspective. They are most likely to center around three areas: recruiting and enrolling children, communicating with parents about the curriculum, and defining behavioral expectations for children.

First, many programs find that it is difficult to attract and maintain a diversified population. Since contact with different groups provides the most fruitful experiences through which children can learn about similarities and differences, enrolling children from many backgrounds is a high priority for any school seriously interested in multicultural education. Changes in publicizing, funding, and organizing programs so that they are both feasible and appealing to a wider range of families will be discussed in the first section of this chapter.

Second, a multiculturally oriented curriculum in itself may be a source of controversy. Because it challenges many prevailing attitudes and assumptions, its implementation may create some discomfort and concern for parents. Since many activities involve parent participation and closer school and home relationships, alleviating parents' fears is critical to the success of the program. Some of the reasons for these concerns and ways to present the program to parents will be covered in the second part of this chapter.

Third, when there is not a shared cultural background between parents and teachers, there is an increased likelihood for mutual misinterpretation of each others' intentions and actions with regard to social values in child rearing. The resulting cycle of withdrawal, blame, and distrust can quickly polarize the two groups. Since a primary goal for multicultural education is the development of mutually supportive relationships between schools and families, this kind of alienation is antithetical to the goals of multicultural education. How some of these misunderstandings and tensions can be anticipated, reconciled, and prevented is the topic of the final section of the chapter.

ACHIEVING AND MAINTAINING DIVERSITY IN THE CLASSROOM

Recruiting and Enrolling Children

The degree of control that teachers and administrators have over the recruitment and enrollment process varies considerably between privately operated centers and public schools. The strategies available to staff for increasing diversity differ accordingly.

Public school teachers have relatively little influence on enrollment decisions. Assignments are made by a central office, with little or no advice from the teachers. In many communities, there is only one public school, so distribution of students among the schools is a moot question. However, teachers and principals may want to consider the following five questions:

1. Who does *not* attend our school?
2. Are there some groups who fairly consistently choose the local private or parochial schools?
3. How many eligible families do not participate in a voluntary desegregation program linking suburban and inner-city schools?
4. In desegregated schools, how prevalent is "white flight" and "middle-class flight"?
5. Are there ways to rezone school districts in order to draw from a variety of communities?

In discussing their responses to these questions, teachers and administrators may think of some changes that could be made to attract a broader range of students to their schools. Some modifications such as redistricting may involve the local government; others such as encouraging parents to choose the public school over the private alternatives may involve publicizing school programs and making personal contacts with families.

In private or community programs, the staff and parents have more control over the recruiting and enrolling process. Since they do much of the advertising and interviewing of prospective families, they are in a good position to know who applies and who does not. While the center or school may be officially open to anyone in the vicinity, access may be limited in some subtle ways. Staff and parents may want to consider these questions:

1. Are we only attracting a certain segment in the community?
2. What are the reasons people give who do not complete applications or do not enroll, once they are accepted?
3. How accessible is the school to people who do not have cars?
4. Is there a sliding-scale fee? Is the range feasible for low-income families?
5. What messages do we convey about diversity, as reflected by our staff, our school description, and the photographs of our program in the brochure?
6. If we are not attracting a diverse group, how can we use local agencies, churches, and social groups to broaden our contacts?

For both public and private schools, achievement and maintenance of a diverse population require a conscious choice and deliberate actions. Given the discriminatory practices in the larger society, the comfort that people find within their own groups, and the difficulties in meeting diverse needs, it is easy for programs and schools to remain segregated. Often this phenomenon is accepted as regrettable but inevitable, proof that "you just can't force people to mix." However, there are many subtle ways in which diversity is discouraged by schools. By being actively involved in the organization of schools and then in the recruitment and selection of families for centers, teachers can identify and mitigate the effects of these discriminatory practices and actively promote diverse enrollment.

One program that had served mainly European American middle-class families developed the following steps to achieve their goal of becoming a racially and economically mixed program (Hinderlie et al., 1978):

1. Recruit families from outside their immediate community.
2. Keep a certain number of slots for people of color and low-in-

come students regardless of the pressures from waiting-list parents and the financial needs of the center.

3. Integrate the staff.
4. Hold ongoing parent meetings to talk about racism and classism.
5. Implement a sliding-scale fee, starting at a minimum cost.
6. Develop a multicultural curriculum that would reflect the backgrounds of all the children in the center.

Each item on this list involved a great deal of work and some potential financial and personal hardship for the center, the staff, and the parents. However, the potential learning and enrichment from providing a more diverse center outweighed the costs. Observers have pointed out (Hinderlie et al., 1978) how easy it is for these kinds of plans to fail. The successful integration of a center or school takes a great deal of commitment and flexibility.

To increase the accessibility of a program or school to diverse groups, some of the logistics of scheduling, transportation, and fees should be scrutinized from the point of view of the populations that currently are not using it.

Scheduling is often an issue for private or public programs that provide daycare. Are the hours long enough for workers at the local factory or parents who commute into the city? Are vacations compatible only with the schedules of teachers and other professionals? If longer hours and more year-round services would make a difference, staff members might want to explore possibilities for increasing coverage by using foster grandparents, parent volunteers, work-study students from local colleges, and high-school child development students. Parents might be interested in working a few hours for reduced tuition. Working under the supervision of a regular staff member, these additional people would also enrich the center with new ideas, perspectives, and experiences.

Transportation is another feasibility factor for programs that do not have any bus service. If the school is not accessible by public transportation, car pooling with other parents is a potential solution. Parents without cars might barter services such as providing some weekend childcare. At one center in a rural area, a parent exchanged rides for fresh produce.

For private centers, costs are another consideration. Sliding-scale fees often provide a means for enrolling children from a wider range of income. If a school cannot afford to reduce tuition, then local business and service agencies might be willing to fund some scholarships.

Again, parents could barter services for reduced tuition. At one school there was a family that came in every Saturday to clean the school for a reduction in fees.

Possible logistical problems and solutions can be discussed with members of the groups that are not currently attending the school. By approaching possible barriers with imagination and flexibility, staff members can find ways to extend resources and exchange services.

In addition to the logistics, the nature of the program is a significant factor in attracting new groups to the school. The goals and content of the curriculum and the teaching practices need to be scrutinized from outsiders' perspectives. Teachers can consider whether the lifestyles and socioeconomic, racial, and cultural groups represented in the current curriculum reflect the experiences of groups they hope to enroll. As described in several previous chapters, there are many ways of incorporating a broad range of lifestyles into the curriculum.

One sensitive area is the structure of the program and the teaching practices. The structure and content of curriculum vary across socioeconomic groups (Bowles & Gintis, 1976; Grannis, 1967). Lower-income children usually are taught in schools that more closely resemble factories, with high values on conformity, products, and speed. In contrast, schools serving affluent communities are more like the executive layer of corporations. Creativity, collaboration, and individuality are encouraged more than they are in schools in low-income communities. Parents who have grown up in a particular type of school are often reluctant to send their children to ones that appear to be radically different.

Across all groups there are often misconceptions about early childhood education activities. Because many activities do not "look like school," parents worry that their children "aren't learning anything." Aside from the goals of broadening enrollment, teachers in any situation have an obligation to educate the public about how children learn and to counteract misperceptions such as the assumption that play and learning are mutually exclusive. By talking to members of the community, teachers become familiar with the local attitudes about education. With this information, they can find ways of relating the program to the goals that parents have for their children. For instance, if parents want their children to read in preschool, teachers can talk about prereading skills and demonstrate the many activities in the school that support them.

Middle-class parents may express reluctance to send their children to schools that serve low-income families because they assume that the school will not have adequate materials to support a full curriculum.

Teachers can point to the variety of activities that do not rely on expensive materials and equipment and the children's inventiveness with recycled materials.

Fear of the unknown is another reason why parents resist sending their children to school in an unfamiliar place with different people. Underlying many concerns are worries that "These strangers won't treat my child well." "The children might be too rough." "The teachers will be biased." "My child will be teased for being poor." Such thoughts are often in the minds of parents when their children are leaving the immediate neighborhood or community. Listening to these concerns and contrasting them with what is actually happening at the school will in some measure reassure parents. For some parents it might also be helpful to point out gently that they might not have these fears if they themselves had grown up in a more diverse setting. They might want to consider if they want their own children to acquire these same fears.

Attracting families from higher-income groups to low-income neighborhoods often fails because of people's reluctance to enter areas that are perceived as unsafe. Teachers can reassure parents by accompanying them the first few times. The initial interview and tour of the school might include a walk around the neighborhood so that familiarity might begin to displace fears. Often perceptions about certain areas are based on sensational crime stories and surface signs of poverty. If parents have the opportunity to express their fears openly, teachers can help them distinguish fact from fiction and overcome some of the unnecessary barriers. One inner-city parent whose children attended a suburban school insisted that her children's friends at school come to visit them in the city. She frequently "shepherded" nervous suburban parents into her neighborhood. Once they arrived, they were surprised and relieved to see that the families, stores, and houses were much like the ones they knew.

Supporting Diversity Through Communication with Parents

Once children are enrolled, careful monitoring of parents' questions, impressions, and criticisms may help to avert later problems. Most parents see only glimpses of classrooms (if anything at all), and, when they ask their children about what they are doing in school, they often hear only the typical "nothing." Newsletters and brief comments about school activities can keep parents informed about the nature of the program. In cases where parents do not transport their children, teachers might want to call each family every few weeks to see if they do have any concerns or questions. If teachers know in advance that a particular activity might be viewed with suspicion by some parents, they might avert a misunderstanding by letting parents know in advance about the activity and its educational purpose. Since many teachers often do not have the time to maintain continuous contact with parents, a parent coordinator is a great help in building and maintaining lines of communication. If there is no funding for this kind of position, a few parents might be willing to volunteer as coordinators.

Staff members can facilitate the social integration of the parents into the school by carefully planning parent meetings and open houses to promote as much cross-group interaction as possible. Informal potluck dinners are a more relaxed and conducive environment than formal meetings. Teachers can subtly arrange groups to be as mixed as possible. If there is a small group of new parents who are in some way a minority, pairing them with "older" parents may make it easier for them to attend meetings and also to ask their questions in a one-to-one relationship. The guidelines for facilitating intergroup relationships discussed in chapter 7 are useful for planning these events.

Parents who are unfamiliar or uncomfortable with school settings may find it difficult to come and participate in these events. In a study of migrant-worker parents (Hughes, Leifeste, & Guzman, 1981), most of the parents indicated that they had never attended a parent-teacher meeting at the local school. Few had any idea what the meetings were about, and many did not realize that the teachers came to them as well as parents. Thus, teachers may need to make a particular effort to encourage some parents to attend. If parents' first language is not English, notices about meetings should be written in the parents' language whenever possible. Personal contacts, such as phone calls from teachers and veteran parents, also may provide the support that these parents need to come to the meetings.

Some centers have found that when they enroll parents from different backgrounds, the disparity between the educational goals of the original parents and those of the newcomers often leads to conflict instead of dialogue. Often the new group feels that their involvement in the school is a one-way adaptation to the status quo (Hinderlie et al., 1978). Teachers and administrators may need to work with the "older" parents to help them see the school in a more flexible manner and to prepare them to listen to the ideas and criticisms of the incoming group. In discussions about policies and curriculum, the person running the meeting should be sure that it is a "safe" environment for parents to present minority and possibly unpopular opinions. Issues can be further explored in small, mixed groups, to insure that everyone has a chance to speak and be heard.

When parents have become comfortable with each other, the school might consider having meetings and discussions that focus explicitly on issues related to class, cultural, and racial differences. These activities are an excellent opportunity for parents to share, explore, and challenge their feelings and assumptions about social differences. Some of the activities and guidelines discussed in chapter 3 can be used to facilitate these discussions.

CONTROVERSY ABOUT MULTICULTURAL EDUCATION

It is ironic that a multicultural focus, with its goal of creating a more collaborative and reciprocal relationship between home and school, is sometimes a source of misunderstanding between schools and parents. Often this tension results from a failure in communication more than any real objection to the program. The words *culture, race,* and *class* are all loaded terms with multiple interpretations. To some people they connote accusations of prejudice; to others they trigger fears of job and housing discrimination; and to many they symbolize isolation and alienation from the larger society. Like all people, parents react in ways that reflect their personal histories and environment. The community analysis described in chapter 3 should prepare teachers for the range of possible reactions and assist them in planning ways of alleviating some of these concerns.

One Head Start teacher talked about the resistance of her low-income white parents whenever she said the word *multicultural*. It appeared from the parents' comments that the term meant glorifying "those people who get all the jobs and services." Because the teacher knew the community and was aware of the controversies and cutbacks related to jobs and welfare, she understood that, before the parents could hear anything positive about other groups of people, they had to explore and share their own feelings of economic and social threat. After some of their anger was dissipated, she tried to help them feel more personally powerful and optimistic, through activities designed to foster their feelings of self-appreciation and confidence. After several sessions, the parents were more receptive to the idea of multicultural education.

A concern that is frequently expressed by relative newcomers to this country, who want to overcome the barriers to American success as soon as possible, is, "I want my child to become a real American so she (or he) can get a good job." Often these parents have experienced discrimination on the basis of their nationality and/or race and hope that their lot will improve if they assimilate as completely and as quickly as possible. While they may actually prefer that their children maintain their ethnic ties and identity, they may assume that, in order to "learn to be an American," the children have to "unlearn" being Haitian or Cambodian. One way of reassuring these parents is to help them see American society as containing diverse groups of people, rather than as a homogeneous monolith. Showing films about the different ethnic groups that live here and inviting guest speakers who have been successful yet have retained their ethnic identity might challenge the assumption that success must be at the expense of one's home culture. Teachers can also point out the practical advantages of being bilingual and bicultural. Using parents as resources for learning and teaching about other cultures might help them to view their membership in a particular group as a potential advantage, rather than as a liability.

Conversely, parents who identify with the mainstream of society but feel threatened by the arrival of new groups, either to this country or to their own community, may bitterly resent any effort to have their children think positively about these "intruders." If both groups are represented in the school, then parent meetings and projects can be planned to mitigate this divisiveness and to help both groups see the other as potential allies. If the school or center is homogeneous, then teachers may want to see whether they can arrange some joint parent nights with another program that serves people from the other groups. When parents have a safe and responsive environment where they can articulate their concerns, they may recognize that their problems extend beyond their immediate group and that, by working together, they can have a more powerful voice in the community. Rather than explicitly focusing on cross-group relationships, teachers can engage both groups of parents in collaborative efforts to raise money for programs, to pressure the school board for better resources, or to lobby community leaders for better housing or fire protection. As mentioned in chapter 7, mixed groups become more cohesive if all members equally contribute to a shared goal. Projects such as putting on a bake sale, stuffing envelopes for a mailing, and refinishing the furniture at the school also provide relatively nonthreatening ways for people to make contact.

In relatively homogeneous communities, parents may be bewildered at the mention of cultural, racial, and economic diversity. They may assure teachers that "we are all the same and all Americans" and question the relevance of materials and photographs from other cultures. Many people feel that the melting pot has worked and that there is an amalgamated American who is the same throughout the country. They often feel strongly that, as new immigrants arrive, they, too, should "melt in" and not try to remain distinct. As frequently reiterated in this book, these are the families that are most in need of a multicultural focus. Teachers might initially ask these parents about activities and ideas that are special about their family and background, without even mentioning the word *culture*. For instance, different families could share information about how they observe holidays such as birthdays and the Fourth of July; the ways they cook particular foods; and their ideas about setting limits with their children. As parents describe their experiences, there will be many opportunities for teachers to point out the diversities and similarities that exist among the families. It is a relatively easy transition from these discussions to teachers' requests that children bring in something special from home that might stimulate the children's thinking about similarities and differences. As parents share information about their own lives, they may also become more aware and appreciative of the diversity within their own community and the influence of culture on their own lives. At this point teachers can introduce parents to the even wider diversity evident in the country as a whole, using films, guest speakers, and participation on field trips, as well as the curriculum in the school.

Although parents may initially resist the idea of a multicultural focus, they often become enthusiastic supporters of this concept. In one homogeneous European American middle-class school that has been incorporating a multicultural focus, parents frequently describe how they feel enriched by the new information that they are learning about other ways of life. They especially enjoy borrowing tapes of the new songs, learning about books and folktales, and participating in various holiday celebrations. Several have commented that they feel that the broader cultural base of the curriculum is, in some ways, compensating for the cultural isolation of the community.

SOCIAL VALUES IN CHILD REARING

Social values related to child-rearing practices are another potential source of misunderstanding and conflict between parents and teachers. This dynamic is not unique to teacher-parent relationships, as is evident in the disputes about child rearing that often occur between spouses, grandparents and parents, and among friends and "experts." The social values, aspirations, and attitudes that adults want to instill in children reflect their own backgrounds, experiences, and world view.

When there is not a shared cultural background between teachers and parents, disagreements often reflect different social priorities, such as the relative dependence or independence of a child; the importance of school achievement versus familial obligations; traditional versus more contemporary sex-roles; respect for elders versus expression of one's feelings; direct versus indirect ways of handling confrontation; and hierarchical versus democratic views of authority.

These value differences emerge in all interactions and are apparent at a very young age. One comparison of Chinese American and European American mother and toddler interactions (Smith & Freedman, 1983) showed that the behavioral expectations of the mothers clearly varied across the two groups. The toddlers' behaviors in terms of independence, control, and attention-seeking already differed in ways that reflected their parents' expectations.

When parents and teachers do not share a common background, they sometimes misunderstand the others' motives and actions. Teachers criticize parents for being too protective; parents may feel uneasy with teachers' efforts to have children be more direct about their feelings; teachers feel frustrated because a child is frequently absent in order to help the family with the English-speaking landlord; some parents are horrified to see their sons dressing up in women's clothing; teachers may criticize parents for not being strict enough with their children; parents might feel that teachers are putting too much academic pressure on their children; parents who value cleanliness and make an effort to dress up their children for school may strenuously object to the "messy" activities that early childhood educators value. In short, social values are reflected in all aspects of child rearing and education, and even minor details, such as the casual dress of teachers and the existence of gender-integrated toilets, can become the sources of some conflict.

With knowledge of the community and insight into the values of the particular groups that attend the school, teachers will be better prepared to both prevent and mediate these kinds of misunderstandings. In addition to reading local newspapers and talking with parents, teachers may also want to read books such as *Ethnic Families in America* (Mindel & Habenstein, 1975) that describe the heterogeneity of family styles and child-rearing patterns. This information can be very helpful, but teachers need to be careful to balance anthropological and sociological generalizations with a recognition of the range of individual differences that exist within every group. For example, in one ethnographic study (Peters & Massey, 1981b), two African American families from similar backgrounds vividly illustrate the divergent and unique ways in which individuals respond to similar environments. It is also important that these studies be read critically, for many are written from a European American middle-class perspective, and the researchers often have a pathological or deficit orientation. Moynihan's (1965) conclusions about the "dysfunctional" African American family are a classic example. Some recent studies (e.g., Peters, 1981) present a more balanced picture and emphasize the strengths of families studied, rather than the weaknesses.

Another step in preventing and resolving these conflicts is for teachers to be aware of the social values and styles that their own teaching practices reflect. When reading about the variety of child-rearing practices, teachers can try to see their own childhoods "from the outside" and to consider how people from another cultural group might interpret the ways that they were raised. It is also helpful to have some awareness about the extent to which our current child-rearing preferences reflect the expectations of our own parents and teachers. When walking around the community and visiting homes, teachers can try to imagine how their outlook would be different if they had grown up in this neighborhood.

Differences in social goals for children pose a dilemma for teachers, who often wonder whether they should continue to teach from their own code of values or try to conform to the parents' expectations. One of the goals of multicultural education is for children to be able to adapt to a variety of social situations. When behavioral expectations differ between home and school, it is an opportunity for children to expand their repertoires of social behaviors. Without disparaging the parents' priorities, teachers can explain to children, "At school, we can play with finger paints, and here's a smock to be sure that you keep your shirt clean," or, "Here at school we do not hit when we are mad; I will help you learn not to hit when you are here." Children learn quite quickly about what behaviors are appropriate for different situations; in fact, within the school program there are already many situationally related behavioral demands. For example, expectations on field trips are different from those in the gym; appropriate snacktime behavior is not acceptable during reading groups or circletime.

Teachers can reassure parents by helping them see the difference between molding children and broadening their range of functioning. At the same time, parents should not be pressured to change their own expectations, because they are teaching their children the behaviors that work in the home environment. A teacher might need to say, "I know that it is important that your children learn to respect their elders and to avoid drawing attention to themselves, but here in school, and in many jobs, children and adults need to be able to speak up and to demonstrate that they are doing a good job." Another explanation might be, "I understand that your children need to be able to defend themselves in order to survive in the neighborhood, but, in schools, that behavior will get them into trouble, so they need to learn other ways of settling arguments." "You have a priority at home that your children should not feel stifled by limits; here at school we have to have some limits in order for children to be able to function as a group." Ultimately, parents have the right to determine, within reason, how their children shall be raised. By respecting that right and by knowing as much as possible about the behaviors that parents value, teachers can work to extend children's social repertoires without disrupting their home relationships.

Even when teachers and parents agree on educational and social goals, differences in style may be the cause of some misunderstanding. The approaches and techniques used in discipline are most frequently misinterpreted. Many parents react negatively to the rigidity of school discipline codes and feel that their children are being repressed. In contrast, the empathic, "humanistic" approaches favored in many early childhood classrooms are often interpreted as "soft" and ineffective by parents who are more directive. In one daycare center there was a detrimental cycle in which teachers withheld from parents their concerns about children's behaviors because they were afraid that the parents would respond too harshly. The parents interpreted this lack of comment to mean that the teachers did not care what the children did and were unable to control them. The children, sensing this lack of mutual trust and support, vigorously tested the classroom limits. In separate conversations with each group, both parties expressed their belief that there should be clear and consistent limits; there was even general agreement about what those limits should be. Both groups, however, misunderstood the other's approach. With a few very carefully planned teacher-parent meetings, the director was able to correct some of these misperceptions and start a dialogue about limits and acceptable punishments.

One way of preventing these kinds of misinterpretations is to have parents and teachers compare their reactions to actual or hypothesized classroom events. Videotapes or photographs of classroom activities provide more concrete examples of teaching practice and may help parents and teachers discuss how their expectations do coincide and to articulate and discuss their differences. For instance, if parents are feeling that "the teachers let the kids play too much," teachers can show a videotape of children playing and accompany it with a discussion about the concepts that children are learning as they play. This demonstration may reassure the parents of the value of that activity. As a secondary effect, it might give parents some ideas for encouraging that type of learning at home. When there are disagreements about discipline, a similar meeting using videotapes or role playing might help parents and teachers see more concretely where their differences and similarities lie. Teachers and parents could "solve" hypothetical situations and discuss how their approaches differ.

In these discussions both groups can explain what certain actions mean. One preschool parent felt that "time out" was extremely punitive, as it was "like putting a child in jail." When teachers role-played it and explained that it was not done punitively but more as a way of helping the child get out of a no-win situation, the parent was relieved and more accepting of the idea. Similarly, teachers are usually relieved to learn that parents' angry threats ("Wait until you get home!") do not result in the harsh punishments that they imagine.

By hearing how parents handle various problems, teachers might learn more effective ways of coordinating their own efforts with those of the parents. Where there are real differences in goals, teachers and parents can use these discussions either to establish some compromises or to discuss how to help children shift between the two sets of expectations. If these discussions occur before any conflicts arise, then they will provide a context and a shared vocabulary for more quickly resolving ones that emerge later.

When children are not responding to the teachers' efforts at setting limits, teachers often wonder if they should change their styles in order to resemble more closely the ways that are common in the children's homes. In considering these dilemmas, teachers need to separate educational values from communicative style. Teachers should never feel that they have to compromise their goals or resort to techniques that they dislike; however, there may be ways they can express themselves that are more comprehensible to the children. Along with the children, teachers, too, can extend their range of communicative styles. If it appears that this kind of adaptation would be helpful, it should be done consciously and frequently reviewed for its effectiveness. The line between communicative adaptations and personal and professional integrity must not be blurred or violated.

In one preschool, teachers customarily handled discipline problems with mild reminders and redirection of behavior. After several frustrating weeks with a new group of children whose parents tended to be quite directive, the teachers realized that the children simply did not "see" their limits. With a great deal of discussion and planning, they instituted a temporary program of much clearer and more predictable

consequences, such as time-outs, loss of access to an area, and repa-
ration of damages. In this case, they were not simply "copying" the
parents' styles but were making their own expectations more explicit
and "readable" for the children. After a month of this program, they
found that the children tested the limits less and seemed to feel safer.
Then the teachers began to work with the children to help them articulate their feelings and find alternative ways of expressing them. During this process, the teachers continuously assessed the children's
reactions and their own feelings about trying a different style. In the
end the teachers felt that, by making themselves understood, they were
more able to meet their educational goals for the children.

In short, by being aware of how their actions are being interpreted
by the children and families, teachers may be able to adapt their communication styles without compromising their long-term professional
goals and personal integrity.

Similar to the misunderstanding that parents have of teachers' styles
and intentions is the disapproval that many teachers feel for the child-
rearing practices of parents. Teachers often feel angry at what they
perceive as neglect, abuse, and disruptions that affect the children in
their classrooms. While teachers should be alert for signs of abuse and
neglect, differences in child-rearing priorities are often misinterpreted
as pathological. Teachers who grew up in relatively unchanging two-
parent families often see frequent changes in family constellations and
location as irresponsible behavior on the part of the parents. Likewise,
the use of sibling caretakers seems careless to adults who were always
carefully "baby-sat." In the eyes of people trained to avoid punitive
approaches, corporal punishment is interpreted as abuse. Teachers who
had strict upbringings sometimes see permissiveness as neglect.

When teachers find themselves reacting negatively to parents' actions, it can be helpful to step back and try to analyze what really is
occurring within the families' contexts. For instance, in a family where
there are frequent changes in household arrangements that seem to be
detrimental to the children, the teacher may find that these changes are
occurring within a neighborhood or an apartment house where there
is an extended family or strong community ties. These arrangements
may provide a thread of continuity that would enable the children to
adjust quickly to changes in the immediate household. The complicated arrangements that are often made in joint custody cases may be
confusing for teachers, but they are the parents' genuine attempts to
maintain relationships with their children that are as satisfactory as
possible. While teachers may feel uneasy about having an eight-year-
old collect a three-year-old brother from daycare, there may be two

cousins, an aunt, and a grandmother who all live in the three blocks between the daycare center and the home. Also the older sibling may have been trained from an early age to assume more responsibility than is customary in many families. The solo traveling of young children between the homes of their divorced parents is often seen as evidence of parental selfishness and irresponsibility. To the parents, however, it may be the only way that they can afford to have the child maintain contact with both parents.

For low-income families, the exhausting and debilitating effects of poverty, unemployment, and underemployment are also a factor. When parents are contending with poor housing conditions, dangerous neighborhoods, and limited financial resources, the resulting parental overload requires a reduction in all but the most essential tasks, with the result that parents may be dominating and controlling in their interactions with children (Longfellow & Weisskopf-Bock, 1980). Also, these parents often need to be more directive in their attempts to protect children from physical and social dangers in their environments (e.g., unprotected stairs or kerosene stoves).

For many ethnic groups the drain of poverty is further exacerbated by the "mundane, extreme environmental stress" of racism (Peters & Massey, 1981a). Regardless of income, families that are targets of discrimination experience this stress, which in turn affects parent-child relationships. Parents have to provide a buffer between their children and the negative views about their group expressed by the larger society. Discrimination adds an extra layer of stress to normally traumatic experiences. For instance, if a family's house burns down, their loss and dislocation are aggravated by concerns about which neighborhoods and landlords will accept them as neighbors and tenants.

All of these examples illustrate why every effort should be made to see parents' behaviors in their own context, as reasonable attempts to cope with their immediate environment and not as reflections of pathology or lack of concern. At the same time, teachers must not become so "accepting" that they fail to recognize when a family is becoming truly dysfunctional and at risk for abuse and neglect. Discussions with people in the community who are familiar with the kinds of stresses and the potential support systems available to the families can help teachers interpret family patterns more accurately. Needless to say, these discussions must be conducted in ways that protect confidentiality, unless teachers feel that the situation must be reported. Abuse and neglect occur in all strata of the society, but often they are the hardest to detect in the more affluent families. Not only do such families have resources for preventing too much public scrutiny (e.g., private family doctors rather than clinics), but they also know how to talk to professionals in a reassuring way and thereby allay any suspicions. When teachers begin to suspect that there may be some extreme problems at home, they should first consider the evidence and sort out how cultural and income factors may be influencing the family and their perceptions of this family. For instance, do suspicions of sexual abuse stem from observed behavior of the child, or are they generated from one's disapproval of the cohabitation of the boyfriend and mother? By the same token, the recurring bruises and accidents of a child from an "all-American" family should not be ignored, regardless of the plausible and articulate explanations of the parents.

It is beyond the scope of this book to discuss how teachers can and should intervene in cases where there are severe problems; however, in general, the better teachers know their community, the more able they will be to help effectively. Their perceptions of problems will be more accurate. They will know about potential resources within the existing relationships in the neighborhood and will predict more accurately how parents might react to various forms of intervention. The next-door neighbor often succeeds where the professionals fail. Conversations at the laundromat are sometimes more instructive than parent education classes at the high school. In short, teachers' knowledge about the informal networks in the community and the child-rearing values of the parents are invaluable when it comes to helping families under stress.

A multicultural perspective includes relationships between families and schools that are characterized by mutual respect and learning as well as by shared efforts to create an optimal environment for children. The commitment to incorporating diverse perspectives, lifestyles, and experiences into programs through enrollment, curriculum, and teaching practices will necessarily involve some conflicts in setting priorities and implementing change. As the facilitators of this process, teachers need to be able to view issues from many perspectives and to see people's behavior as rational responses to the challenges of their own environments. This process requires a remarkable commitment and an ability to see one's own biases, to suspend judgment, and to resist polarization.

10 The Challenge of Teaching with a Multicultural Perspective

A multicultural perspective is a world view, a way of interpreting behavior and events in which diversity among individuals, cultures, genders, lifestyles, and races is valued. Initially conceived as a way of promoting self-respect and understanding among specific ethnic groups, it has expanded to incorporate an appreciation for all differences, an emphasis on interpersonal relationships, and the commitment and confidence to actively create a better society for all people. This way of thinking is a reaction against conformity and apathy; it is the belief that positive relationships among people can have an impact on the world.

The goals of multicultural education are complex, wide-ranging, and relevant to all educational decisions. In some cases, they may appear to be contradictory. For instance, individual backgrounds are valued, yet children are encouraged to reach beyond the constraints of their immediate experiences; teaching is adapted to the needs and interests of each individual yet also aimed at insuring that each person has an equal chance at succeeding in this society. The breadth of the goals reflects the pervasiveness of discriminatory attitudes and practices in contemporary society and the need to understand them in the context of economic, social, and political pressures. The relevance of a multicultural perspective to all educational decisions is indicative of the many overt and subtle ways that learning and teaching are influenced by prevailing social attitudes. All teaching practices reflect a world view; articulating that perspective and broadening it require scrutiny of every decision, from organizing minor routines to setting major programmatic goals. Despite their complexity, breadth and multiple applications, the goals of a multicultural perspective reflect the common belief that, through the strengths and identities of individuals and groups, people can come together to create a more open, fair, and caring society.

CRITICISMS AND RESPONSES

Multicultural education reflects a pluralistic point of view in which the diversity of this country and the world is valued and preserved. An inherent conviction is that people should not be required to abandon their own culture, lifestyle, and language in order to participate fully in the larger society. This perspective is a departure from the earlier tenet of our society that all people should become "Americanized" and conform to Anglo-American ways, at the expense of their home culture. Needless to say, by challenging this assimilationist perspective, multicultural education has attracted a number of critics. Social scientists, educators, and policy makers have all questioned the goals and feasibility of multicultural education. Some of these arguments reflect misunderstanding, while others raise legitimate concerns.

Some criticism focuses on the possible isolating influences of multicultural education. In particular, people have raised concerns that it might cause factionalism between groups and disrupt the shared purpose that is necessary for the nation's survival. This argument rests on the assumption that there is a monolithic "mainstream" of the society where one is either "in" or "out," and that loyalty and access are limited to this one social stream. Multicultural education attempts to join the streams of many groups, to create a common pool of goals, traditions, and languages, but also to make it possible for each stream to thrive and contribute in its own way. Rather than isolate, a multicultural perspective seeks to establish mutual understanding. Instead of forcing conformity through blind allegiance to a mythical "American" way, it attempts to generate a sense of belonging and unity by valuing the unique contributions of each group.

People who are concerned about the fragmentation of this society often point to the tendency for groups to resegregate themselves. In addition to exclusionary practices that may contribute to this trend, there is also the fact that people often need the comfort and ease of the familiar. Anybody functioning in a culturally unfamiliar environment will usually seek opportunities to "just relax" with people who share the same lifestyle, humor, language, and values. However, there is a difference between appreciating one's own background and assuming that it is superior to all others. By fostering children's cross-cultural respect, understanding, and social skills, this type of teaching seeks to help children develop a wider range of accepting and "comfortable" relationships, thereby reducing the need for people to resegregate in order to feel at ease.

Multicultural education also seeks to strengthen social bonds by providing a more realistic view of American life in all of its complexity and variation. One source of alienation is the distance that people feel between their own lives and the image of American life that is portrayed on the television and (all too often) in books for children. Another distancing factor is the tendency for affluent families to ignore low-income or indigent people and/or to blame them for their plight. By representing a more authentic and diversified image of American life, this pluralistic perspective seeks to reduce these sources of alienation and to promote a sense of responsibility for the common welfare.

A second group of criticisms of a multicultural perspective is related to feasibility. For one thing, can educators and children, no matter how well meaning, actually solve such complex problems as racism and discrimination? Furthermore, are we not just training children to be better hypocrites? As one author (Wolcott, 1981) put it, "By the second day of kindergarten I think I had learned to mouth lofty ideas about brotherhood" (p. 4). He continues to say that his real lesson in human relationships had been learned by watching the discriminatory practices of teachers and children toward children from different ethnic and income groups.

Teaching from a multicultural perspective is, in part, a reaction against the hypocritical and grandiose claims often made by educators. It is an attempt to help children authentically explore human relationships in developmentally appropriate ways. For instance, compare these two classroom scenes: In the first one the teacher is exhorting the children to love all other people. He is showing pictures of children from different countries and telling the children that these children are just as nice as they are. This preaching approach does potentially promote children's tendencies to mouth tolerance that they may not understand or feel. In contrast, a teacher is listening to children's reactions to pictures of children from different countries; she is encouraging them to articulate their questions and reactions. Here the children are learning to express honestly their ideas and feelings. With this information, the teacher can design experiences that challenge the children's erroneous assumptions and help them unlearn some of their fears and negative responses and broaden their perceptions of other people. Multicultural education makes no claims to produce perfect human beings devoid of prejudice, but simply to interrupt and challenge the cycle of stereotypical expectations, prejudicial reactions, and discriminatory practices.

Another argument against multicultural education is that it distracts children and teachers from the mastery of basic academic skills. Some critics are particularly concerned that it will prevent children from different cultural backgrounds and low-income homes from learning the essentially middle-class and Anglo-American styles and skills of the classroom.

As explicitly stated in the goals, multicultural education supports the learning of educational skills and the success of all children in the schools. It is not a separate curriculum that is in competition with other subject areas. It does challenge the notion, however, that education is defined as a monolithic, narrow set of skills. With a more pluralistic perspective one sees not only the broad range of skills that people can acquire but also the need to be flexible in order to teach the common skills to children in the ways by which they can most readily learn them. Teachers' awareness of the values and themes that are relevant to the children in their class will enable them to design and adapt materials and experiences to be best suited to children's cultural and individual learning styles.

Finally, teachers often protest against the idea of incorporating a multicultural perspective in early childhood classrooms because the children are too young to understand. They also see it as a burden because it is so hard to find and make nonstereotyped and developmentally appropriate materials to support these efforts.

The concern about the appropriateness of multicultural education for the very young is legitimate. As has been emphasized repeatedly in this volume, teachers must be keenly aware of how their children are interpreting the material and issues related to this perspective. While designing age-appropriate activities and materials is a challenge, the need for this perspective in early education is clear. As we have seen in chapter 2, young children readily see differences and absorb negative assumptions and stereotypes related to racial, cultural, and class distinctions. At the same time, they are socially open, interested in others, and empathic. Preschool and primary-school children are on a psychological boundary between the initial stages of attitude development and more immediate pleasure and interest in others that transcend external values. If they develop their earliest identities and social orientations with a multicultural perspective, they may be able to resist the negative attitudes and social pressures that diminish and isolate groups. Thus, the incorporation of a developmentally appropriate multicultural perspective in the early school years is critically important.

The issue of the extra burden placed on teachers is also valid, particularly given the dearth of good materials commercially available and the endless demands of teaching. However, a multicultural perspective does not entail developing a whole new curriculum; rather, it is a perspective that becomes part of teachers' day-to-day planning and long-range goals. Each activity, theme, area of the room, and educational material is viewed in terms of its potential for conveying the goals of this perspective. While this approach requires imagination and effort, it generates a lot of excitement and enriches the curriculum. Teachers frequently report that the excitement and interest they feel in learning about different groups and sharing this knowledge with the children have been a source of revitalization.

While this book is obviously biased in favor of multicultural education, it is important to listen to the critics of this perspective. As an approach that seeks to educate in a responsive and representative way, it must be constantly scrutinized and adapted to emerging social needs.

GUIDELINES FOR TEACHING

This book was written to encourage teachers in all communities to incorporate a multicultural perspective into their teaching. Because this orientation is particularly crucial for children in ethnically and socioeconomically homogeneous classrooms, a particular effort has been made to include examples and suggestions for these kinds of classrooms. The following comments summarize the major points raised in the chapters of this book.

Since children's responses to human differences are influenced by their experiences and local attitudes, curriculum and teaching practices must be planned with the specific community and group of families in mind. The homogeneity or heterogeneity of the community, the history of local intergroup relationships, the relative assimilation of immigrant or other ethnic groups, and the level of understanding and affective reactions of the particular children must be understood before we can create learning experiences that truly fit their questions, interests, and level of understanding. By exploring these dimensions of children's lives, teachers not only find more appropriate ways of incorporating a multicultural perspective, they also begin to expand their own ideas about how people live, think, and interact.

A multicultural perspective is not a set curriculum but rather a process of validating children's backgrounds and at the same time challenging their assumptions about the world by giving them new information and experiences. It touches all aspects of children's lives. As this book has shown, physical settings, classroom routines, materials, equipment, and holiday celebrations all have the potential for promoting respect for diversity and a more realistic awareness of the world. The visual environment, the display of photographs, and the use of color collectively contribute to children's knowledge and appreciation of diverse lifestyles and physical characteristics. Likewise, holidays provide high-interest occasions for extending children's experiences beyond their immediate social environment.

A multicultural perspective broadens and challenges children's assumptions about not only their social environment but also their physical surroundings. As children explore diverse ways of doing familiar routines and activities such as eating, dancing, and carrying things, their assumptions about physical properties and relationships are expanded. In the most mundane routines as well as exotic experiments, the fact that there are diverse ways of responding to the physical environment and human needs can be amply illustrated.

All aspects of the social environment, including interpersonal contact, friendship patterns, seating arrangements, caretaking routines, and limits and discipline have potential for promoting interpersonal and intergroup awareness, respect, and responsibility. By using every aspect of classroom life to heighten social awareness and competence, teachers foster children's motivation and potential skills for positive intergroup relationships and communication.

Children's language is an important consideration for both the teaching of educational skills and intergroup communication. The extent to which home languages are maintained has been a source of a great deal of controversy. Teachers of children from different language backgrounds must balance the need to respect and foster home languages with the necessity of insuring that children become fluent in both written and spoken English. Bilingual programs are the approach most consistent with the goals of multicultural education and, from various studies, appear to be more successful in promoting fluency and literacy in English as well as in the home language. Children who speak diverse patterns of English should likewise be supported and encouraged to appreciate the richness of their own verbal tradition. It is also crucial, however, that they learn to read, write, and speak standard English, to insure that language is not a barrier to their success. The question of language is also relevant for English-speaking children.

Their functioning in a multilingual society and world will be more effective if they learn the other language(s) spoken by children in the school. In monolingual English-language schools, other languages can be introduced in the many ways that have been described in this book.

Finally, a multicultural perspective challenges some of the traditional assumptions about parent-teacher relationships. Instead of the teacher being viewed as the sole expert, there is a reciprocal exchange where parents are valued as resources. When there are disagreements between the two groups, teachers need to look beyond their personal preferences and professional assumptions and try to understand the parents' opinions and practices in terms of local conditions, aspirations, and values. To meet these disparate needs, teachers need to find creative ways of integrating a number of priorities and perspectives into the program. Group discussions, role playing, and shared problem solving can often help teachers and parents articulate their goals, styles, and intentions more clearly to each other.

EVALUATION

The goals of multicultural education affect all aspects of teaching, from the allocation of classroom tasks to the selection of books and colors of paper. Thus the evaluation of its implementation covers a wide area of activities.

There are two levels of evaluation: formative and summative. At the formative level, teachers continuously use a multicultural perspective to examine their day-to-day decisions about activities, materials, and classroom structures and their minute-by-minute reactions to children and parents. They also use these guidelines when setting long-range goals for the children in the course of developing the curriculum. To assess the impact of this teaching, teachers should continuously monitor children's reactions to specific materials and activities. For summative evaluations, teachers need to set specific goals relevant to the needs of the particular children in their classrooms. At regular intervals throughout the year, teachers can assess how children's ideas and reactions have changed over the past few weeks or months and the extent to which their own teaching has reflected their high-priority goals.

Formative Evaluation

As teachers organize programs, design classrooms, choose materials, review pictures and books, plan activities and events, and arrange parent contracts, they might reflect upon the following goals of a multicultural perspective, described in the first chapter, and ask themselves the following questions.

1. *The development of positive gender, racial, class, cultural, and individual identities.* How does this activity, book, material, event, or routine contribute to the development of positive group identities and sense of efficacy? Does it reflect children's backgrounds in a positive yet realistic way? Are children engaged in a way that is conducive to the development of confidence? Does it help children see themselves as unique individuals, yet members of various groups? How are similarities and differences among individuals and groups conveyed?

2. *The ability to identify, empathize, and relate with individuals from other groups.* What messages are conveyed in this activity or materials, regarding (a) groups represented in the classroom and (b) groups not represented in the classroom? What values are conveyed in the choice of colors? Words? Languages? Illustrations? Is the activity structured in a way that promotes cross-group acceptance and interaction? Are unfamiliar people portrayed in recognizable situations and activities? Are different groups represented by a range of individuals?

3. *Respect and appreciation for the ways in which other people live.* What explicit or implicit assumptions are being made about family lifestyles, social values, and affluence? (For example, does the class field trip cost too much money for some children's parents?) Are cultural conventions portrayed as universals or as simply some of many ways that people do certain common activities? How could the cultural base of this activity or event be broadened? Where can other languages, traditions, foods, art forms, clothing, and houses be incorporated into the activity?

4. *A concern and interest in others, a willingness to include others, and a desire to cooperate.* What opportunities does this event, activity, piece of equipment, or furniture arrangement provide for children to increase their interpersonal skills, awareness of others, and range of contacts? What groups are likely to form spontaneously around this activity? How can they be more mixed? In what ways does this activity or routine build a sense of group and foster cooperation? Are there ways that children could take more responsibility for helping each other? What conflicts are likely to occur? How can the children be guided toward resolving them in a positive way?

5. *A realistic awareness of contemporary society, a sense of social respon-*

sibility, and an active concern for people outside of their immediate environment. To what extent does this picture, book, or game represent a realistic view of society in all of its diversity? What assumptions about affluence, materialism, and social conventions are evident? Are materials available that represent other points of view or experiences? Is there a balance between realism and idealism in the portrayal of people's hardships?

6. *The autonomy to become critical analysts and activists in their social environment.* How well does a particular activity or classroom routine encourage children to develop autonomy and skills in decision making? Are they learning that they need to be constrained by others or that they can learn how to control themselves and make independent judgments? How well do the rules, methods of conflict resolution, classroom organization, and physical structure foster autonomy?

7. *The development of educational skills and social knowledge that will enable them to become full participants in all aspects of society.* To what extent do the teaching methods and curriculum content match the children's strengths and backgrounds? If children are not responding, what are some ways that the curriculum could be adapted to fit their interests and skills? For children with home languages other than English, how are their languages reflected in the classroom? Are songs and stories using the children's dialects included in the collection of books and records? Are children who are learning to read learning the initial association between the spoken and printed word in their most familiar tongue? What opportunities are there for monolingual, English-speaking children to learn other languages and dialects? Are the languages and dialects presented in an authentic cultural context?

8. *Effective and reciprocal relationships between homes and schools.* What do parents see when they enter the school? Read the newsletter? Scan the school brochure? Observe in the classroom? What efforts are made to help parents to feel comfortable? How flexible is the school in response to parent needs and priorities? In what ways are parents involved? Are they just seen as extra bodies on field trips, or are their unique skills and backgrounds genuinely appreciated by the children and the staff? Are all parents equally involved? What are the ways that parents might be involved in each activity and event? Are conferences structured to be as mutual an exchange as possible?

While these questions may seem overwhelming at first, they soon become part of teachers' intuitive thinking and planning. Teachers automatically consider individual children, the season of the year, local events, and available materials when planning activities. Likewise, their ideas can be filtered through the foregoing questions. At every decision point, teachers can ask themselves, "What is the potential in this activity, material, routine, or event for enhancing children's understanding and appreciation for themselves, other people, and human diversity?" These questions also enable teachers to assess continually the impact that their efforts are having on children's learning.

Summative Evaluation

Every program will develop its unique priorities, as teachers attempt to meet the most pressing needs of their children. For example, if children have had virtually no contact with groups other than their own, then emphasizing diversity might be the initial priority. If the program is in a neighborhood in which there are many groups but a lot of conflict, then stressing similarities might be the appropriate place to start. Teachers need to set clear priorities so that they are not feeling overwhelmed by the broad goals of this perspective. The activities and the children's responses to them should be reviewed periodically to see how well the priorities are reflected in both teaching and learning.

Using some of the assessments outlined in chapter 3, teachers can, from time to time, measure children's understanding of and affective reactions to various aspects of diversity. By recording their children's initial responses and comparing them to the later responses, teachers can see more concretely how children's thinking and affective reactions are changing.

A CHALLENGE FOR TEACHERS

This book has been written with the hope that it will stimulate questions, ideas, discussion, and action. As teachers expand their ideas about children, families, and teaching, they will find that there are periods of disorientation and uncertainty. At the same time, there will be curiosity and excitement. Likewise, the frustrations that they may experience in trying to achieve these goals will also spawn creative and imaginative solutions and collaborations. While teachers may feel dis-

heartened as they learn more about the prevalence and effects of discrimination, they will also be inspired to work for change. In short,
learning and teaching from a multicultural perspective is a disconcerting, exhilarating, challenging, and empowering process for children,
parents, teachers, and communities.

References

Aboud, F. E. The development of ethnic identity and attitudes. In J. Phinney & M. Rotheram (Eds.), *Children's ethnic socialization: Pluralism and development.* Beverly Hills, CA: Sage, 1986.

Adorno, T. W., Frenkel-Brunswik, E., Levinson, D. J., & Sanford, R. N. *The authoritarian personality.* New York: Harper, 1950.

Albert, M. L., & Olber, L. K. *The bilingual brain.* New York: Academic Press, 1978.

Allport, G. W. *The nature of prejudice.* Reading, MA: Addison-Wesley, 1954.

Amir, Y. Contact hypothesis in ethnic relations. *Psychological Bulletin,* 1969, 71, 319–42.

Amir, Y. The role of intergroup contact in change of prejudice and ethnic relations. In P. A. Katz (Ed.), *Towards the elimination of racism.* New York: Pergamon Press, 1976.

Aronson, E. *The social climate.* San Francisco: Freeman, 1972.

Aronson, E., & Bridgeman, D. Jigsaw groups and the desegregated classroom: In pursuit of common goals. *Personality and Social Psychology Bulletin,* 1979, 5, 438–66.

Asher, S. R., & Allen, V. L. Racial preference and social comparison processes. *Journal of Social Issues,* 1969, 25, 157–65.

Asher, S. R., Oden, S. L., & Gottman, J. M. Children's friendships in school settings. In L. G. Katz (Ed.), *Current topics in early childhood education.* Norwood, NJ: Ablex, 1977.

Asher, S. R., Singleton, L. C., & Taylor, A. R. *Acceptance versus friendship: A longitudinal study of racial integration.* Paper presented at the meeting of the American Educational Research Association, New York, April 1982.

Bakeman, R., & Helmreich, R. Cohesiveness and performance: Covariation and causality in an undersea environment. *Journal of Experimental Social Psychology,* 1975, 11, 478–89.

Baratz, S. S., & Baratz, J. C. Early childhood intervention: The social science base of institutional racism. *Harvard Educational Review,* 1970, 40, 29–50.

Barth, E. *Witches, pumpkins and grinning ghosts: The story of the Halloween symbols.* Boston: Houghton-Mifflin, 1972.

Bereiter, C., & Englemann, S. *Teaching disadvantaged children in the preschool.* Englewood Cliffs, NJ: Prentice-Hall, 1966.

Bergman, A. *Chendru: The boy and the tiger.* New York: Harcourt, 1959.

Berkowitz, L. Anti-Semitism and the displacement of aggression. *Journal of Abnormal and Social Psychology,* 1959, 59, 182–88.

Bierman, K. L. *The effects of social skills training on the interactions of unpopular and popular peers engaged in cooperative tasks.* Paper presented at the biennial meeting of The Society for Research in Child Development, Detroit, 1983.

A bilateral conflict. *New York Times Summer Education Survey,* August 21, 1983, p. 39.

Bird, C., Monachesi, E. D., & Burdick, H. Infiltration and the attitudes of white and Negro parents and children. *Journal of Abnormal and Social Psychology,* 1952, *47,* 688–99.

Borke, H. Interpersonal perception of young children: Egocentrism or empathy? *Developmental Psychology,* 1971, *5,* 263–69.

Bowles, S., & Gintis, H. *Schooling in capitalist America.* New York: Basic Books, 1976.

Brand, E. S., Ruiz, R. A., & Padilla, A. M. Ethnic identification and preference: A review. *Psychological Bulletin,* 1974, *81,* 860–90.

Califf, J. What one teacher has done. In *Unlearning "Indian" stereotypes.* New York: Council on Interracial Books for Children, 1977.

Carter, D. B., & Patterson, C. J. Sex roles as social conventions: The development of children's conceptions of sex-role stereotypes. *Developmental Psychology,* 1982, *18,* 812–24.

Christie, E. T. *The racial attitudes, preferences, and self-preferences of Chinese-American children in Boston's Chinatown: A questionnaire and curriculum study.* Unpublished CAGS Thesis, Wheelock College, 1982.

Clark, A., Hocevar, D., & Dembo, M. H. The role of cognitive development in children's explanations and preferences for skin color. *Developmental Psychology,* 1980, *16,* 332–39.

Clark, K. B., & Clark, M. P. Racial identification and preference in Negro children. In T. M. Newcomb & E. L. Hartley (Eds.), *Readings in social psychology.* New York: Holt, Rinehart & Winston, 1947.

Coates, B. White adult behavior toward black and white children. *Child Development,* 1972, *43,* 143–54.

Cole, A., Haas, C., Heller, E., & Weinberger, B. *Children are children are children.* Boston: Little, Brown, 1978.

Cole, A., Haas, C., Weinberger, B., & Heller, E. *A pumpkin in a pear tree: Creative ideas for twelve months of holiday fun.* Boston: Little, Brown, 1976.

Coles, R. *Privileged ones: The well-off and the rich in America.* Boston: Little, Brown, 1977.

Cordes, C. Immigration: Mix of culture stirs new fears. *APA Monitor,* 1984, *15,* 12–13.

Corsaro, W. Friendship in the nursery school: Social organization in a peer environment. In S. R. Asher & J. M. Gottman (Eds.), *The development of children's friendships.* New York: Cambridge University Press, 1981.

Corsaro, W. *Friendship and peer culture in the early years.* Norwood, NJ: Ablex, 1985.

Cortés, C. E. Multiethnic and global education: Partners for the eighties? *Phi Delta Kappan,* 1983, *64,* 568–71.

Cottle, T. J. *Black children, white dreams.* New York: Dell, 1974.

Criswell, J. H. Racial cleavage in Negro-white groups. *Sociometry*, 1937, *1*, 81–89.

Cross, W. E. *Black identity: Rediscovering the distinction between personal identity and reference group orientations.* Paper presented at the meeting of the Society for Research in Child Development, Boston, 1981.

Cummins, J. Linguistic interdependence and the educational development of bilingual children. *Review of Educational Research*, 1979, *49*, 222–52.

Cummins, J. The role of primary language development in promoting educational success for language minority students. In *Schooling and language minority students: A theoretical framework.* Los Angeles: Evaluation, Dissemination and Assessment Center, 1981.

Daley, S. Panel asks stress on English studies. *New York Times*, June, 1983.

Damon, W. Patterns of change in children's social reasoning: A two-year longitudinal study. *Child Development*, 1980, *51*, 1010–17.

DeLone, R. H. *Small futures.* New York: Harcourt Brace & Jovanovich, 1979.

Derman-Sparks, L., Higa, C. T., & Sparks, B. Children, race and racism: How race awareness develops. *Interracial Books for Children Bulletin*, 1980, *11*, 3–9.

Deutsch, M., & Collins, M. E. *Interracial housing: A psychological evaluation of a social experiment.* Minneapolis: University of Minnesota Press, 1951.

DeVries, D., Edwards, K., & Slavin, R. Biracial learning teams and race relations in the classroom: Four field experiments on teams-games-tournaments. *Journal of Educational Psychology*, 1978, *70*, 356–62.

Dinkmeyer, D. *Developing understanding of self and others.* Circle Pines, MN: American Guidance Service, 1973.

Doke, L. A., & Risley, T. R. Some discriminative properties of race and sex for children from an all-Negro neighborhood. *Child Development*, *1972*, *43*, 677–81.

Doyle, A. Friends, acquaintances, and strangers. In K. H. Rubin and H. S. Ross, *Peer relationships and social skills in childhood.* New York: Springer-Verlag, 1982.

Dulay, H., & Burt, M. Remarks on creativity in second language acquisition. In M. Burt, H. Dulay, & M. Finnochiaro (Eds.), *Viewpoints on English as a Second Language.* New York: Regents, 1977.

Edwards, C. Talking with children about social ideas. *Young Children*, November 1983, pp. 12–20.

Edwards, C. *Promoting social and moral development in young children: Creative approaches for the classroom.* New York: Teachers College Press, 1986.

Egan, L. A., & Goldsmith, R. Bilingual bicultural education: The Colorado success story. *Monographs of the Center for Bilingual Education Research and Service*, *2*, (1), 1981.

Entwisle, D. R. Socialization of language behavior and educability. In M. L. Maehr & W. M. Stallings (Eds.), *Culture, child and school.* Monterey, CA: Brooks/Cole, 1975.

Erikson, E. H. *Identity: Youth and crisis.* New York: Norton, 1968.

Fallows, J. Immigration: How it's affecting us. *The Atlantic Monthly*, November 1983, 45–68, 85–106.

Farrell, W. C., & Olson, J. *Kenneth Clark revisited: Racial identification in light-skinned and dark-skinned black children.* Paper presented at the meeting of the American Educational Research Association, New York, 1982.

Fasold, R. W., & Wolfram, W. Some linguistic features of Negro dialect. In D. L. Shores (Ed.), *Contemporary English: Change and variation.* Philadelphia: Lippincott, 1972.

Fishman, J. *Language loyalty in the United States.* The Hague, Netherlands: Mouton, 1966.

Flavell, J. H. *The development of role-taking and communication skills in children.* New York: John Wiley, 1968.

Flemming, B. M., Hamilton, D. S., & Hicks, J. D. *Resources for creative teaching in early childhood education.* New York: Harcourt, Brace & Jovanovich, 1977.

Forman, G. E., & Hill, D. F. *Constructive play.* Washington, DC: National Association for the Education of Young Children, 1983.

Furth, H. *The world of grown-ups: Children's conceptions of society.* New York: Elsevier, 1980.

Gardner, P. C., & Lambert, W. E. *Attitudes and motivation in second language learning.* Rowley, MA: Newbury House, 1972.

Gelman, R., & Spelke, E. The development of thoughts about animals and inanimate objects: Implications for research on social cognition. In J. H. Flavell & L. Ross (Eds.), *Social cognitive development.* New York: Cambridge University Press, 1981.

Goodman, M. *Race awareness in young children.* Cambridge, MA: Addison-Wesley, 1952.

Grannis, J. C. The school as a model of society. *Harvard Graduate School of Education Association Bulletin,* 1967.

Graves, N. B. *Inclusive versus exclusive interaction styles in Polynesian and European classrooms.* Paper presented at the meeting of the Society for Research in Child Development, Denver, 1974.

Grosjean, F. *Life with two languages: An introduction to bilingualism.* New York: Harvard University Press, 1982.

Gross, S., & Woodruff, J. *The treatment of workers in preschool children's literature.* Boston: The Children's Center of Brookline and Greater Boston, 1979.

Hall, E. T. *Silent Language.* Garden City, NY: Anchor Books, 1959.

Hall, E. T. *Beyond culture.* Garden City, NY: Anchor Books, 1977.

Harris, D., Gough, H., & Martin, W. E. Children's ethnic attitudes II: Relationships to parental beliefs concerning child training. *Child Development,* 1950, *21,* 169–81.

Hill, T. C. *The effect of self-reflection on preschool children's empathic understanding and prosocial behavior.* Paper presented at the biennial meeting of the Society for Research in Child Development, Detroit, 1983.

Hinderlie, V., McCollough, M., Schachter, M., Simmons, P., & Wortis, S. *Caring for children in a social context: Eliminating racism, sexism and other patterns of discrimination.* Cambridge, MA: Multicultural Project, 1978.

Hirschfelder, A., & Califf, J. A thanksgiving lesson plan: Celebration or mourning. *Council on Interracial Books for Children Bulletin,* 1979, *10,* 6–13.

Hoffman, M. L. Perspectives on the difference between understanding people and understanding things: The role of affect. In J. H. Flavell & L. Ross (Eds.), *Social cognitive development*. New York: Cambridge University Press, 1981.

Hughes, R., Leifeste, G., & Guzman, J. *Assessment of the needs and attitudes of migrant and seasonal farmwork families regarding child-rearing information and resources*. Unpublished manuscript, University of Texas at Austin, 1981.

Izzo, S. *Second language learning: A review of related studies*. Rosslyn, VA: National Clearing House for Bilingual Education, 1981.

Jarrett, O. *Racial attitudes of black and white children in integrated and segregated kindergartens*. Paper presented at the biennial meeting of the Society for Research in Child Development, Boston, 1981.

Jenkins, A. H. *The psychology of the Afro-American: A humanistic approach*. New York: Pergamon Press, 1982.

Johnson, D. W., & Johnson, R. E. Effects of cooperative, competitive and individualistic learning experiences on cross-ethnic interactions and friendship. *Journal of Social Psychology*, 1982, *118*, 47–58.

Jordan, J. E. Attitude behavior research on physical-mental-social disability and racial-ethnic differences. *Psychological Aspects of Disability*, 1971, *18*, 5–26.

Kamii, C., & DeVries, R. Piaget for early education. In M. C. Day & R. K. Parker (Eds.), *The preschool in action: Exploring early childhood programs*. Boston: Allyn & Bacon, 1977.

Kamii, C. & DeVries, R. *Group games in early education*. Washington, DC: National Association for the Education of Young Children, 1980.

Katz, P. A. Perception of racial cues in preschool children. *Developmental Psychology*, 1973, *8*, 295–99.

Katz, P. A. The acquisition of racial attitudes in children. In P. A. Katz (Ed.), *Towards the elimination of racism*. New York: Pergamon Press, 1976.

Katz, P. A. Development of children's racial awareness and intergroup attitudes. In L. G. Katz (Ed.), *Current topics in early childhood education*. Norwood, NJ: Ablex, 1982.

Katz, P. A., & Seavey, C. Labels and children's perceptions of faces. *Child Development*, 1973, *44*, 770–75.

Kendall, F. *Diversity in the classroom: A multicultural approach to the education of young children*. New York: Teachers College Press, 1983.

Kosslyn, S. M., & Kagan, J. "Concrete thinking" and the development of social cognition. In J. H. Flavell & L. Ross (Eds.), *Social cognitive development*. New York: Cambridge University Press, 1981.

Krashen, S. D. Bilingual education and second language acquisition theory. In *Schooling and language minority students: A theoretical framework*. Los Angeles: Evaluation, Dissemination and Assessment Center, 1981.

Labov, W. *The social stratification of English in New York City*. Washington, DC: Center for Applied Linguistics, 1966.

Labov, W. The logic of nonstandard dialect. In J. Alahs (Ed.), *School of language and linguistics monograph series*, 1969, *22*, 1–43.

Labov, W. The logic of nonstandard English. In P. Stoller (Ed.), *Black American English*. New York: Dell, 1975.

Lambert, W. E., & Klineberg, O. *Children's views of foreign peoples.* New York: Appleton-Century-Crofts, 1967.

Lambert, W. E., & Tucker, G. R. *Bilingual education of children: The St. Lambert experiment.* Rowley, MA: Newbury House, 1972.

Leahy, R. The development of the concept of social inequality I: Descriptions and comparisons of rich and poor people. *Child Development,* 1981, *52,* 523–32.

Leahy, R. The development of the conception of social class. In R. Leahy (Ed.), *The child's construction of inequality.* New York: Academic Press, 1983.

Legarreta-Marcaida, D. The effects of program models on language acquisition by Spanish-speaking children. *TESOL Quarterly,* 1979, *13,* 521–34.

Legarreta-Marcaida, D. Effective use of the primary language in the classroom. In *Schooling and the language minority student: A theoretical framework.* Los Angeles: Evaluation, Dissemination and Assessment Center, 1981.

Lerner, A. J. *My fair lady.* New York: Coward McCann, 1956.

Livesley, W. J., & Bromley, D. B. *Person perception in childhood and adolescence.* New York: John Wiley, 1973.

Longfellow, C., & Weisskopf-Bock, S. *Mother-child influences of race and family income.* Unpublished manuscript, Graduate School of Education, Harvard University, 1980.

Longstreet, W. S. *Aspects of ethnicity.* New York: Teachers College Press, 1978.

Luce, T. S. *Political development and attribution of poverty by youth.* Paper presented at the annual meeting of the American Psychological Association, Washington, DC, 1982.

Luftig, R. L. The effect of schooling on the self-concept of Native American students. *School Counselor,* 1983, *30,* 251–60.

Maeroff, G. I. Rising immigration tide strains nation's schools. *New York Times Summer Education Survey,* August 21, 1983, pp. 1, 37, 67.

Mapley, G. E., & Kizer, J. B. *Children's process of sex-role incongruent information: "The nurse's name was Dr. Brown."* Paper presented at the biennial meeting of the Society for Research in Child Development, Detroit, 1983.

McCandless, B. R., & Hoyt, J. M. Sex, ethnicity, and play preferences of preschool children. *Journal of Social Psychology,* 1961, *62,* 683–85.

McNeill, E., Allen, E., Schmidt, V., & McNeill, B. *Cultural awareness for young children at the learning tree.* Dallas: The Learning Tree, 1981.

Mindel, C. H., & Habenstein, R. W. (Eds.) *Ethnic families in America.* New York: Elsevier, 1975.

Morland, J. K. Racial acceptance and preference of nursery school children in a southern city. *Merrill-Palmer Quarterly,* 1962, *8,* 271–80.

Moynihan, D. *The Negro family: The case for national action.* Washington, DC: U.S. Department of Labor, Office of Policy Planning and Research, 1965.

Mussen, P. Some personality and social factors related to changes in children's attitudes towards Negroes. *Journal of Abnormal and Social Psychology,* 1950, *45,* 423–41.

Naimark, H. *Children's understanding of social class differences.* Paper presented at the biennial meeting of The Society for Research in Child Development, Detroit, 1983.

Naimark, H., & Shaver, P. *Development of the understanding of social class.* Paper presented at the annual meeting of the American Psychological Association, Washington, DC, 1982.

Navon, R., & Ramsey, P. *A comparison between Chinese and American preschools.* Paper presented at the annual meeting of the National Association for the Education of Young Children, Atlanta, 1983.

Oden, S. L., & Asher, S. R. Coaching children in social skills for friendship making. *Child Development,* 1977, *48,* 495–506.

Orlick, T. *The cooperative sports and games book: Challenge without competition.* New York: Pantheon Books, 1978.

Ortheguy, R. Thinking about bilingual education: A critical appraisal. *Harvard Educational Review,* 1982, *52,* 301–14.

Patchen, M. *Black-white contact in schools: Its social and academic effects.* West Lafayette, IN: Purdue University Press, 1982.

Peters, M. F. Black beginnings: *Childrearing patterns in a sample of black parents of children ages one to three.* Paper presented at the biennial meeting of the Society for Research in Child Development, Boston, 1981.

Peters, M. F., & Massey, G. C. *Chronic vs. mundane stress in family stress theories: The case of black families in white America.* Oakland, CA: TIES (Toddler and Infant Experiences), 1981a.

Peters, M. F., & Massey, G. C. *Normal stress and coping in contrasting young black families: Two core studies.* Oakland, CA: TIES (Toddler and Infant Experiences), 1981b.

Piaget, J. *The child's conception of the world.* New York: Humanities Press, 1951.

Piaget, J. *The moral development of the child.* New York: The Free Press, 1965. (Originally published in 1932.)

Piaget, J., & Inhelder, B. *The psychology of the child.* New York: Basic Books, 1968.

Piestrup, A. M. *Black dialect interference and accommodation of reading instruction in the first grade.* A Language-Behavior Research Laboratory monograph. Berkeley: University of California, 1973.

Porter, J. D. *Black child, white child: The development of racial attitudes.* Cambridge, MA: Harvard University Press, 1971.

Proshansky, H. M. The development of intergroup attitudes. In I. W. Hoffman & M. L. Hoffman (Eds.), *Review of Child Development Research* (Vol. 2). New York: Russell Sage Foundation, 1966.

Putallaz, M., & Gottman, J. M. Social skills and group acceptance. In S. R. Asher & J. M. Gottman (Eds.), *The development of children's friendships.* New York: Cambridge University Press, 1981.

Radke, M., & Sutherland, J. Children's concepts and attitudes about minority and majority American groups. *Journal of Educational Psychology,* 1949, *40,* 449–68.

Radke, M., Sutherland, J., & Rosenberg, P. Racial attitudes of children. *Sociometry,* 1950, *13,* 154–71.

Radke, M., & Trager, H. G. Children's perceptions of the social roles of Negroes and whites. *Journal of Psychology,* 1950, *29,* 3–33.

Radke-Yarrow, M., Trager, H., & Miller, J. The role of parents in the development of children's ethnic attitudes. *Child Development*, 1952, *23*, 13–53.

Ramirez, M., Castenada, A., & Herold, L. P. The relationship of acculturation to cognitive style among Mexican Americans. *Journal of Cross-Cultural Psychology*, 1974, *5*, 424–33.

Ramsey, P. G. Beyond "Ten Little Indians" and turkeys: Alternative approaches to Thanksgiving. *Young Children*, September 1979, 28–52.

Ramsey, P. G. Beyond winning and losing. *Day Care and Early Education*, 1980a, *8*, 50–54.

Ramsey, P. G. Solving the dilemma of sharing. *Day Care and Early Education*, 1980b, *8*, 6–29.

Ramsey, P. G. *Racial differences in children's contacts and comments about others.* Paper presented at the annual meeting of the American Psychological Association, Washington, DC, 1982.

Ramsey, P. G. *Young children's responses to racial differences: Sociocultural perspectives.* Paper presented at the biennial meeting of the Society for Research in Child Development, Detroit, 1983.

Ramsey, P. G. *Early ethnic socialization in a mono-racial community.* Paper presented at the biennial meeting of the Society for Research in Child Development, Toronto, 1985.

Ramsey, P. G. *Friends and strangers: A comparison of interpersonal and intergroup perceptions and preferences.* Paper presented at the annual meeting of The American Educational Research Association, San Francisco, April, 1986a.

Ramsey, P. G. Racial and cultural categories. In C. P. Edwards, *Promoting social and moral development in young children: Creative approaches for the classroom.* New York: Teachers College Press, 1986b.

Ramsey, P. G. Young children's thinking about ethnic differences. In J. Phinney & M. Rotheram (Eds.), *Children's ethnic socialization: Pluralism and development.* Beverly Hills, CA: Sage, 1986c.

Ramsey, P. G. *Young children's understanding of social class differences.* Paper presented at the annual meeting of The American Educational Research Association, San Francisco, April 1986d.

Rist, R. C. Student social class and teacher expectations: The self-fulfilling prophecy in ghetto education. *Harvard Educational Review*, 1970, *40*, 411–51.

Rist, R. C. Bilingual education: A policy-based research agenda for the 1980's. *The Urban Review*, 1982, *14*, 93–105.

Rodriguez, R. *Hunger of memory: The education of Richard Rodriguez.* Boston: Godine, 1981.

Rohrer, G. K. Racial and ethnic identification and preference in young children. *Young Children*, 1977, *32*, 24–33.

Rosenthal, R., & Jacobson, L. *Pygmalion in the classroom.* New York: Holt, Rinehart and Winston, 1968.

Rosier, R., & Farella, M. Bilingual education at Rock Point—some early results. *TESOL Quarterly*, 1976, *10*, 379–88.

Ross, L. The "intuitive scientist" formulation and its developmental implications. In J. H. Flavell & L. Ross (Eds.), *Social cognitive development.* New York: Cambridge University Press, 1981.

Rotheram, M., & Phinney, J. *Cross-ethnic friends: Variations in four ethnic groups.* Paper presented at the biennial meeting of the Society for Research in Child Development, Detroit, 1983.

Rotheram, M., & Phinney, J. *Ethnic behavior patterns as an aspect of identity.* Paper presented at the biennial meeting of the Society for Research in Child Development, Toronto, April 1985.

Rubin, I. M. Increased self-acceptance: A means of reducing prejudice. *Journal of Personality and Social Psychology,* 1967, *5,* 233–38.

Sagi, A., & Hoffman, M. L. Empathic distress in the newborn. *Developmental Psychology,* 1976, *12,* 175–6.

Saville-Troike, M. The development of bilingual and bicultural competence in young children. In L. G. Katz (Ed.), *Current topics in early childhood education* (Vol. 4). Norwood, NJ: Ablex: 1982.

Scales, A. M., & Brown, B. G. Ebonics: An English language pattern. *The Negro Educational Review,* 1981, *32,* 252–7.

Schaffer, M., & Sinicrope, P. *Promoting the growth of moral judgment: An inservice teacher training model.* Paper presented at the annual meeting of the Jean Piaget Society, Philadelphia, June 1983.

Schofield, J. W. Complementary and conflicting identities: Images and interactions in an interracial school. In S. R. Asher & J. M. Gottman (Eds.), *The development of children's friendships.* New York: Cambridge University Press, 1981.

Sherif, M. *Group conflict and cooperation.* London: Routledge and Kegan Paul, 1966.

Sherwood, J. J., Barron, J. W., & Fitch, H. G. Cognitive dissonance: Theory and research. In W. Gamson & A. Modigliani (Eds.), *Conceptions and social life.* Boston: Little, Brown, 1974.

Simpson, A. W., & Erickson, M. T. Teachers' verbal and nonverbal communication patterns as a function of teacher race, student gender, and student race. *American Educational Research Journal,* 1983, *20,* 183–98.

Sims, R. *Shadow and substance: Afro-American experience in contemporary children's fiction.* Chicago: American Library Association, 1983.

Slavin, R. E. Effects of biracial learning teams on cross-racial friendships. *Journal of Educational Psychology,* 1979, *71,* 381–7.

Smith, S., & Freedman, D. G. *Mother-toddler interaction and maternal perception of child temperament in two ethnic groups: Chinese-American and European-American.* Paper presented at the biennial meeting of the Society for Research in Child Development, Detroit, 1983.

Stabler, J. R., Johnson, E. E., & Jordan, S. E. The measurement of children's self-concepts as related to racial membership. *Child Development,* 1971, *42,* 2094–97.

Stevick, E. W. *Teaching languages: A way and ways.* Rowley, MA: Newbury House, 1980.

Stewart, W. Continuity and change in American Negro dialects. In D. L. Shores (Ed.), *Contemporary English: Change and Variation.* Philadelphia: Lippincott, 1972.

Swisher, K. *Attitudes of parents and teachers of American Indian children toward multicultural education.* Paper presented at the annual meeting of the American Educational Research Association, New York, 1982.

Tajfel, H. The roots of prejudice: Cognitive aspects. In P. Watson (Ed.), *Psychology and race.* Chicago: Aldine, 1973.

Ten quick ways to analyze children's books for racism and sexism. *Council on Interracial Books for Children Bulletin,* 1974, *5* (3), 1–6.

Terrell, T. D. The natural approach in bilingual education. In *Schooling and language minority students: A theoretical framework.* Los Angeles: Evaluation, Dissemination and Assessment Center, 1981.

Thonis, E. W. Reading instruction for language minority students. In *Schooling and language minority students: A theoretical framework.* Los Angeles: Evaluation, Dissemination and Assessment Center, 1981.

Thurman, S. K., & Lewis, M. Children's responses to differences: Some possible implications for mainstreaming. *Exceptional Children,* 1979, *45*, 468–70.

Weininger, O. Learning a second language: The immersion experience and the whole child. *Interchange,* 1982, *13*, 20–40.

Weissbach, T. A. Laboratory controlled studies of change of racial attitudes. In P. A. Katz (Ed.), *Towards the elimination of racism.* New York: Pergamon, 1976.

Williams, J. E., & Edwards, E. D. An exploratory study of the modification of color and racial concept attitudes in preschool children. *Child Development,* 1969, *40*, 737–50.

Williams, J. E., & Morland, J. K. *Race, color and the young child.* Chapel Hill, NC: University of North Carolina Press, 1976.

Wolcott, H. F. Anthropology's "spoiler role" and "new" multi-cultural textbooks. *The Generator,* 1981, *12*, 1–12.

Wong-Fillmore, L. Individual differences in second language acquisition. In C. J. Fillmore, D. Kempler, & W. S. Y. Wang (Eds.), *Individual differences in language ability and language behavior.* New York: Academic Press, 1971.

Suggested Books for Children

The following list offers some examples of books that might be used to support the curriculum described in this book. The specific books included here are ones that I have particularly enjoyed using with children. A more complete annotated bibliography is available from the Council on Interracial Books for Children, 1841 Broadway, New York, NY 10023.

Because there are so few books written for young children that present authentic and contemporary images of life in other countries and in ethnic communities in this country, several books have been included that present more traditional or legendary images. While these stories are limited in terms of their current accuracy, they do introduce young children to the idea that people live in different ways.

In selecting books for this list, particular attention was paid to how easily young children could identify with the themes that were presented in order to help children focus on the similarities that transcend cultural and racial differences. When using this list and other ones, teachers should try to balance traditional images with contemporary ones.

Adoff, A. *Black Is Brown Is Tan*. New York: Harper & Row, 1973.
> In this story about a racially mixed family, a child muses upon the various skin colors of the family members. This book conveys the message that differences are real and enriching and do not separate people.

Baker, O. *Where the Buffaloes Begin*. New York: Frederick Warne, 1981. [Based on the author's text in *St. Nicholas Magazine* XLII, 4. 1915.]
> This story of a traditional Plains Indian boy who dreams of finding the lake where the buffaloes begin captures the wonder and excitement of this legendary search.

Baylor, B. *Before You Came This Way*. New York: Dutton, 1969.
> Using replicas of prehistoric Southwestern Indian pictographs, the author evokes the past lives of Native People. This book challenges the assumption that the Europeans "discovered" this country.

Behrens, J. *Together*. Chicago: Children's Press, 1975.
> The photographs and words in this book illustrate many ways that people

can be best friends. The inclusion of many cross-racial and cross-age dyads illustrates the fact that friendships need not be confined to one's own group.

Bernheim, M., & Bernheim, E. *The Drums Speak*. New York: Harcourt, Brace and Jovanovich, Inc., 1971.

This African story describes a young boy's transition from his home village to school. The traditions of the village, including the importance of the drum as a means of communication, are described in positive but not romanticized terms.

Bond, J. C. *A Is for Africa*. New York: Watts, 1969.

This alphabet book illustrates letters with colored photographs of artifacts and people of Africa. The pictures are appealing to children and offer a rich introduction to the alphabet.

Bond, J. C. *Brown Is a Beautiful Color*. New York: Watts, 1969.

By showing many attractive and varied representations of the color brown, this book can be used to stimulate children's appreciation of the color.

Brenner, B. *Bodies*. New York: Dutton, 1973.

Brenner, B. *Faces*. New York: Dutton, 1970.

These two books use photographs to illustrate physical similarities and differences among people.

Caines, J. *Abby*. New York: Harper & Row, 1973.

This story about an adopted girl coping with her aloof older brother can be used to discuss different family origins and to challenge children's assumptions that black children were originally white.

Cameron, A. *How the Loon Lost Her Voice*. Medeira Park, British Columbia: Harbor, 1985.

This story is one of the Raven tales that were told by the people native to the northwest coast of Canada and the United States. By showing how the animals all cooperate to release the daylight, this book can be used to encourage children to embark on joint projects that would be too difficult to do alone.

Clark, A. N. *In My Mother's House*. New York: Viking Press, 1941.

Written in a poetic form, this book describes the daily life of the traditional Pueblo People. It includes accounts of activities such as getting water and cooking and shows children some unfamiliar ways of doing familiar routines.

Clark, A. N. *The Desert People*. New York: Viking Press, 1962.

This illustrated description of life of the Desert People can be used to stimulate children's experiments with water conservation and distribution.

Clifton, L. *All Us Come Cross the Water*. New York: Holt, Rinehart & Winston, 1973.

In this book, Clifton describes how slaves were brought to this country from Africa. She makes this complex history comprehensible to young children and imbues the slaves with dignity.

Clifton, L. *Everett Anderson's Nine Month Long*. New York: Holt, Rinehart & Winston, 1978.

This story of a black child discovering that a baby is about to be born in his family tangibly illustrates that people of all groups share many common feelings.

Clifton, L. *Some of the Days of Everett Anderson*. New York: Holt, Rinehart & Winston, 1970.

In a series of poems, this book describes the activities of a black child in the city where he lives in a way that is familiar and appealing to young children.

Clymer, T. *The Travels of Atunga*. Boston: Little Brown, 1973.

Based on an old Eskimo legend, this story tells of a man's travels and appeals to different gods in order to find food for his people. It illustrates some of the adaptations that people have made to their physical environment, as well as a system of beliefs different from those familiar to most children in this country.

Coutant, H. *First Snow*. New York: Knopf, 1974.

One of a very few stories written for young children about Vietnamese immigrants, it describes a family's adjustment to the climate and mores of this country. Focusing on the death of the grandmother, it introduces a few Buddhist rituals and illustrates how events familiar to many children in this country might appear magical to a child who has just arrived.

de Grosbois, L., Lacelle, N., LaMothe, R., & Nantel, L. *Mommy Works on Dresses*. Toronto: Women's Press, 1976.

This French Canadian story introduces children to the real-life situation of working in a garment factory.

Feelings, M. *Jambo Means Hello: Swahili Alphabet Book*. New York: Dial Press, 1973.

This book introduces children to simple Swahili words and phrases. The accompanying pictures illustrate some of the ways that Swahili-speaking children and adults live and work.

Feelings, M. *Moja Means One: Swahili Counting Book*. New York: Dial Press, 1971.

This volume teaches children to count in Swahili using pictures that children can easily understand.

Feelings, T., & Greenfield, E. *Daydreamers*. New York: Dutton, 1981.

This poem is illustrated with drawings of Black children with a variety of facial expressions and body postures and beautifully illustrates the richness of individual differences.

Goble, P. *The Gift of the Sacred Dog*. New York: Bradbury Press, 1980.

As a legendary account of how Plains Indians acquired horses, this book explains why horses were important to their way of life. Children may object to calling the horses "sacred dogs," which could lead to a discussion of how and why people call things different names.

Goldman, L. *Turkey: A Week in Samil's World*. New York: Crowell-Collier Press, 1973.

This book, along with others in the same series, describes the daily life of children in other countries. The routines are familiar, but the ways that they are carried out reflect particular cultures and physical environments.

Greenfield, E. *Africa Dream*. New York: John Day, 1977.

Written as a fantasy, this book is the account of a young girl's ideas of what it would be like to live in Africa. It could be used as a way of stimulating children's ideas of how people in other parts of the world live.

Greenfield, E. *Me and Nessie*. New York: Crowell, 1975.

As a description of a child's first day of school, this book shows a black child in a familiar situation.

Hazen, B. S. *Why Are People Different? A Book About Prejudice*. New York: A Golden Book, 1985.

A black child's initial encounter with stereotyping leads to a discussion with his grandmother about the ways that people feel and act when they experience discrimination.

Keats, E. J. *Whistle for Willie*. New York: Viking Press, 1964.

Set in an urban environment, this book describes a young black boy's efforts to master whistling so that he can call his dog. For children who have not had much contact with black peers, this book offers a meaningful way of seeing them as similar to themselves.

Keats, E. J. *Peter's Chair*. New York: Harper & Row, 1967.

This book provides the same opportunity using the theme of the birth of a new sibling.

Krementz, J. *Sweet Pea: A Black Girl Growing Up in the Rural South*. New York: Harcourt, Brace & World, 1969.

With photographs showing the daily life of a family, this book shows how people can have healthy and happy lives with few material resources and challenges negative stereotypes of poor people.

Kurusa. *The Streets Are Free*. Copenhagen: Annick Press, 1985.

This Venezuelan story is based on a true story of how the children of Caracas fought to get a place to play. It emphasizes the need for children and poor people to speak up for their rights and against inequality.

Lewin, H. *Jafta's Father*. Minneapolis: Carolrhoda Books, 1981.

Lewin, H. *Jafta's Mother*. Minneapolis: Carolrhoda Books, 1981.

In these two books, a black South African boy describes his father and mother. While the feelings and routines are familiar, the images and metaphors reflect the culture and environment of the South Africans.

Martin, F. *Raven-Who-Sets-Things-Right*. New York: Harper & Row, 1951.

These tales of the Native People who lived on the northwest coast describe how the raven, a trickster, solves problems with his cleverness. It is a good illustration of tricking that brings good instead of harm.

Maury, I. *My Mother and I Are Growing Strong*. Berkeley: New Seed Press, 1979.
This story of a Hispanic family shows how the mother and daughter learn that they have many abilities when they have to cope alone because the father is sent to prison.

McDermott, G. *Anansi the Spider: A Tale from the Ashanti*. New York: Holt, Rinehart & Winston, 1972.
This traditional folktale can be used as an illustration of a clever trickster. The colorful geometric designs might also inspire some art projects.

Meyers, R. S., & Banfield, B. *Embers: Stories for a Changing World*. New York: Council on Interracial Books for Children, 1983.
This anthology for elementary grades contains stories about friends, families, jobs, and history, all written from a multicultural perspective.

Miles, M. *Annie and the Old One*. Boston: Little Brown, 1971.
A Navaho girl learns from her grandmother that people cannot interfere with the natural processes of aging and dying. This book not only introduces children to some aspects of Navaho life and their concept of time, but it is also a reassuring approach to the topic of death.

Niclas, Y. *The Flower of Vassiliki*. New York, Seabury Press, 1968.
Using photographs, this book describes some of the rituals practiced in a rural area of Greece in a personal and meaningful context.

Nolan, M. S. *My Daddy Don't Go to Work*. Minneapolis: Carolrhoda Books, 1978.
This book about a family facing the unemployment of the father shows a positive image of a resilient black family and provides a way to initiate a discussion about family stress.

Paek, M. *Aekyung's Dream*. San Francisco: Children's Book Press, 1978.
Written in both Korean and English, this book is the story of a Korean child adjusting to life in this country.

Perrine, M. *Nannabah's Friend*. Boston: Houghton-Mifflin, 1970.
A Navaho girl, who is lonely when she is tending her family's sheep, finds another child to be her friend. Set in an unfamiliar setting (for most U.S. children), it deals with the familiar theme of making friends.

Pogrebin, L. C. (Ed.) *Stories for Free Children*. New York: Ms. Foundation for Education and Communication, 1982.
This anthology for elementary school children includes many stories written from a multicultural perspective.

Raynor, D. *This Is My Father and Me*. Chicago: Whitman, 1973.
Reich, H. *Children and Their Fathers*. New York: Hill and Wang, 1960.
Reich, H. *Children and Their Mothers*. New York: Hill and Wang, 1964.
These three photographic essays illustrate how children and their parents enjoy each other all over the world.

Roberts, B., & Roberts, N. *A Week in Robert's World: The South*. New York: Macmillan, 1969.

> Life in the rural South is portrayed through Robert's daily activities. Photographs enable children to see Robert and his family as real individuals.

Schwartz, A. *Mrs. Moskowitz and the Sabbath Candlesticks*. Philadelphia: The Jewish Publication Society of America, 1983.

> When Mrs. Moskowitz moves to her new apartment, she misses her old house until she unpacks her Sabbath candlesticks and then transforms her apartment into a home. This story could be used to illustrate ways that people observe different holidays.

Simon, N. *All Kinds of Families*. Chicago: Whitman, 1975.

> The author shows how members of families with different lifestyles and compositions care for each other and enjoy themselves.

Steichen, F. *Family of Man*. New York: Simon & Schuster, 1955.

> This famous photographic essay illustrates how all of humankind shares many feelings and life experiences despite geographical and cultural differences.

Steptoe, J. *Daddy Is a Monster . . . Sometimes*. New York: Lippincott, 1980.

> A father's changing moods are described from a child's point of view.

Sutherland, E. T. *Playtime in Africa*. New York: Atheneum, 1963.

> With photographs and text, this book shows children in Ghana playing in ways that are appealing and familiar to children in this country.

Tsow, M. *A Day with Ling*. London: Hamish Hamilton, 1982.

> A visit to her Chinese classmate's house enables a child to experience the blend of English and Chinese traditions in various routines.

Wallace, I. *Chin Chiang and the Dragon Dance*. New York: Atheneum, 1984.

> Written about the annual Chinese American New Year celebration, this book describes a young boy's fear of failure and how he is able to overcome it. It also portrays warm relationships between older and younger people.

Yahya, F., & Jones, L. *Ali and the Camel*. Available through Claudia's Caravan, Alameda, CA.

> Written in Arabic and English, this book describes some events in the life of a Bedu boy and is a rare portrayal of this way of life.

Yarborough, C. *Cornrows*. New York: Coward-McCann, 1979.

> While her grandmother braids her hair, a child learns the meaning and history of the different patterns of cornrows.

Yashima, T. *Crow Box*. New York: Viking Press, 1955.

> This book tells the tale of a very small Japanese boy who, in the face of his classmate's scorn, finds his special way of learning.

Yashima, T. *The Village Tree*. New York: Viking Press, 1953.

> This story describes memories of summer fun in Japan.

Yee, S., & Kokin, L. *Got Me a Story To Tell.* San Francisco: St. John's Educational Threshold Center, 1977.

With photographs and excerpts from taped interviews, children describe in their own words their experiences of living in this country. One story is about a child in a black community; the others describe children's adjustments as they have moved from other places including El Salvador, Hong Kong, the Fiji Islands, and the Philippines.

Zimmerman, A. G. *Yetta the Trickster.* New York: Seabury Press, 1978.

This tale, which takes place in a traditional Eastern European village, describes all the tricks that a young girl tries on the adults around her. Set in an unfamiliar time and place, it presents a theme that is appealing to young children.

About the Author

PATRICIA G. RAMSEY is an assistant professor of psychology and education and Director of Gorse Child Study Center at Mount Holyoke College in South Hadley, Massachusetts. Formerly, she taught in the Early Childhood Education Departments at Wheelock College, Indiana University, and the University of Massachusetts. She holds a masters degree from California State University in San Francisco and a doctorate in early childhood education from the University of Massachusetts in Amherst. She is a former preschool and kindergarten teacher.

Index